Preaching
the Parables

Preaching the Parables

From Responsible Interpretation

to Powerful Proclamation

Craig L. Blomberg

Baker Academic
a division of Baker Publishing Group
Grand Rapids, Michigan

Published by Baker Academic
a division of Baker Publishing Group
P.O. Box 6287, Grand Rapids, MI 49516-6287
www.bakeracademic.com

Printed in the United States of America

Library of Congress Cataloging-in-Publication Data
Blomberg, Craig
    Preaching the parables : from responsible interpretation to powerful proclamation / Craig L. Blomberg.
        p.   cm.
    Includes bibliographical references (p.) and index.
    ISBN 10: 0-8010-2749-7 (pbk.)
    ISBN 978-0-8010-2749-9 (pbk.)
    1. Jesus Christ—Parables—Homiletical use. 2. Jesus Christ—Parables—
Sermons—History and criticism. 3. Sermons, American—History and criticism.
4. Jesus Christ—Parables—Sermons. 5. Sermons, American. I. Title.
BT375.3.B57 2004
226.8'06—dc22   2003063698

Contents

Abbreviations

ABR	*Australian Biblical Review*
ASTI	*Annual of the Swedish Theological Institute*
BI	*Biblical Interpretation*
Bib	*Biblica*
BSac	*Bibliotheca Sacra*
BYU	Brigham Young University
CBAA	Catholic Biblical Association of America
CBQ	*Catholic Biblical Quarterly*
CSR	*Christian Scholars' Review*
CT	*Christianity Today*
CTQ	*Concordia Theological Quarterly*
CTR	*Criswell Theological Review*
EQ	*Evangelical Quarterly*
ExpT	*Expository Times*
HBT	*Horizons in Biblical Theology*
Int	*Interpretation*
JBL	*Journal of Biblical Literature*
JETS	*Journal of the Evangelical Theological Society*
JSNT	*Journal for the Study of the New Testament*
JSOT	*Journal for the Study of the Old Testament*
JTS	*Journal of Theological Studies*
LexThQ	*Lexington Theological Quarterly*
Neot	*Neotestamentica*
NovT	*Novum Testamentum*
NTS	*New Testament Studies*
PRS	*Perspectives in Religious Studies*
RB	*Revue Biblique*

RestQ	*Restoration Quarterly*
RevExp	*Review and Expositor*
SBET	*Scottish Bulletin of Evangelical Theology*
SJT	*Scottish Journal of Theology*
ST	*Studia Theologica*
SWJT	*Southwestern Journal of Theology*
TJT	*Toronto Journal of Theology*
TrinJ	*Trinity Journal*
TynB	*Tyndale Bulletin*
USQR	*Union Seminary Quarterly Review*
WTJ	*Westminster Theological Journal*
ZNW	*Zeitschrift für die neutestamentliche Wissenschaft*

Preface

To some readers it might seem presumptuous for a professional New Testament scholar to write a book on preaching. Not only do I not preach week-in and week-out like countless pastors, I have never even held a full-time paid pastoral position! When I compare my sermons with an "all-star lineup" of favorite messages from preachers I highly respect, I am tempted to agree that my meager offerings scarcely merit publication. Most Sundays find me "merely" in an adult Sunday school classroom for my primary weekend ministry.

On the other hand, I have learned from some outstanding teachers—Lloyd Perry, Haddon Robinson, Paul Borden, and Scott Wenig. From my seminary days onward, sitting under excellent exposition has always been a high priority in choosing a church, and I am grateful for all that I have imbibed less formally from Wayne Lehsten, Ray Inkster, Richard Walker, Roy Clements, Frank Tillapaugh, Clyde McDowell, Bill Muir, Jerry Sheveland, Sid Buzzell, and Mike Romberger. Teaching in a Christian college for three years and in a theological seminary for seventeen years has given me the chance to hear many outstanding chapel speakers. While I have not worked as a full-time pastor, I have done interim preaching on more than one occasion, and I usually am invited to give sermons in various churches seven or eight times a year on average. In fact, one advantage of *not* speaking regularly from the same pulpit to the same congregation is that I can revise and reuse some of the sermons that I write within a fairly short period of time, so that hopefully they improve with each successive revision.

Notwithstanding these opportunities, I still would never have imagined writing a book like this except for three additional events. The first was the invitation to co-teach a Doctor of Ministry seminar at Denver

Seminary on "Preaching the Parables," with the man who at that time was my senior pastor, Dr. Jerry Sheveland. Although (or perhaps in part because) we had only four students, we had wonderful interaction with four men who themselves had already established a reputation of being excellent preachers and pastors—Tom Hovestal, Brad Strait, Allan Meyer, and Mike Grechko. I learned much from each of them as well as from Jerry. The second event was an invitation from Allan Meyer to participate in a preacher's conference in Melbourne, Australia, where he pastors. Again we team taught, again on the theme of preaching the parables. It is safe to say that Allan is one of the most gifted preachers in Australian evangelicalism today, and I benefited greatly from his instruction. The third and final catalyst was the suggestion of Jim Kinney, Baker Book House's academic books editor, that I consider producing such a volume and his unflagging support throughout the process.

I am grateful for the less formal input over the years from students at Denver Seminary for whom I have preached and/or outlined a number of these messages in either classes or chapels. I am particularly appreciative of the opportunity to incorporate several of these sermons into courses and church services cross-culturally as well, in conjunction with teaching and ministry in Dublin, Ireland; Melbourne, Australia; Vancouver, Canada; and Guatemala City, Guatemala. This last context, along with a Denver-area Baptist General Conference Hispanic Churches' Families Retreat, allowed me to translate and deliver selected messages in Spanish and get feedback from Latino audiences as well.

Additional thanks go to Jeanette Freitag, assistant to the faculty of Denver Seminary, for typing rough drafts of my sermons from their originally tape-recorded oral format and for other editing work in the final stages of revising the entire manuscript. Also my research assistant for 2002–3, Jeremiah Harrelson, provided helpful literature searches for additional bibliography. I am grateful, too, for the courageous decisions of Zondervan and IBS to continue plans for publishing *Today's New International Version*, despite widespread and unnecessarily polemical criticism, often accompanied by factually inaccurate information about the translation project. I have used the TNIV for all New Testament quotations in this volume, since it is more accurate in rendering generic language for humans into current English idiom and more literal than the NIV in about three-quarters of the other changes it has made.[1]

There is one more person who has influenced me over the years more than he probably suspects. While attending Trinity Evangelical Divinity School, I worshiped at the North Suburban Evangelical Free Church in Deerfield, Illinois. The pastor of young adults in those years was an outgoing, effervescent young man (only four years older than I) named Lee Eclov. It was at that church that I met the woman who would become my wife, Fran Fulling. It was at that church that Lee gave me the opportunity to be part of his leadership team and to fulfill my field education requirements at Trinity at the same time. While I heard him preach only rarely, his teaching on a weekly basis in our young adults fellowship was always creative, challenging, upbeat, true to God's word, and an inspiration for the kind of teacher I wanted to be. When Fran and I got married, Lee performed our wedding—his first as a pastor! A few years later he became the senior pastor of the Beaver Falls Evangelical Free Church in the Pittsburgh metro area; today he is the senior pastor of the Village Church of Lincolnshire, Illinois, on Chicago's north shore. He has mentored seminarians, consulted for *Leadership* and *Preaching Today,* and written for both journals. His commitment to excellence in the pulpit in conjunction with a well-rounded ministry more generally, his faithfulness to God and to his wife, Susan, and son, Andy, and his personal support and warm friendship over the past twenty-five years all combine to lead me to dedicate this modest volume to him. Thanks, Lee, and don't ever stop being the wonderful model that you are!

Introduction

P reaching a parable is a novice preacher's dream but often an experienced preacher's nightmare." So declares Thomas O. Long at the
beginning of his chapter on parables in an excellent book titled *Preaching the Literary Forms of the Bible*.[1] At first glance, the parables appear
familiar and straightforward, but thoughtful students soon realize they
have fallen into a quagmire of interpretive debates.

A Brief History of Interpretation

The history of the interpretation of the parables has been narrated in
detail countless times,[2] so I will sketch its outline very briefly here. The
Jewish backgrounds to the New Testament were quickly lost sight of
as the gospel spread throughout the Roman Empire. By as early as the
mid-second century, Jewish Christianity had become a negligible force
in the church of Jesus Christ at large. Greco-Roman forms of interpretation of biblical narrative came increasingly to the fore; for the parables,
this meant that Jesus' stories were treated as elaborate allegories, with
almost every detail in each expounded as if it had some second level of
spiritual or symbolic significance. Periodic voices protested against this
form of interpretation, including such Christian "giants" as Irenaeus,
Chrysostom, and Aquinas. The Reformers, particularly John Calvin,
took the most substantial steps away from a rampant allegorizing, but
as recently as the late nineteenth century the majority of interpreters
continued to find many lessons and symbols in almost every parable.

All this changed dramatically with the publication, in German, of
the massive two-volume work of Adolf Jülicher in 1899.[3] In his first

volume, Jülicher showed how most of the allegorical approaches to each parable differed substantially from one another, calling into question the very method itself. In his second volume, he defended his own approach to the parables, stressing that the parabolic form is as far from allegory as is conceivable and that each passage makes only one main point. Ironically, he derived this conviction from Aristotle, also clearly within the tradition of Greek philosophy, and not from first-century *Jewish* practice.

Twentieth-century interpreters largely followed Jülicher's lead, while recognizing that one had to allow for exceptions to his principles. Two of Jesus' parables come complete with detailed allegorizing interpretations (the sower—Mark 4:1–9, 13–20 pars.; and the wheat and weeds—Matt. 13:24–30, 36–43). A few others, most notably, the wicked tenants (Mark 12:1–12 pars.), seem unintelligible unless one assumes that the various characters and details are symbolic. But the vast majority were treated as if they taught only one central lesson. Intriguingly, despite the origins of this theory in nineteenth-century German liberalism, almost all interpreters across the entire theological spectrum embraced Jülicher's approach more than they dissented from it. More conservative interpreters simply allowed for the kinds of exceptions just described; more liberal commentators used those exceptions to argue that the process of allegorizing had begun already when Matthew, Mark, and Luke compiled their Gospels, but that those interpretations were not what Jesus originally spoke.

There were, however, nagging problems that led a small minority of scholars in the first half of the twentieth century to demur from accepting the "one-main-point" approach so enthusiastically. Students of the rabbinic parables noted how the several hundred stories the earliest rabbis told regularly developed two, three, or four characters or details in an allegorical direction, even while not finding symbolic significance in the remaining elements of each passage. Others observed that scholars who opted for the "one-main-point" approach continued to disagree about what that one main point in each instance was. Often two or three main points competed for the "honor" of serving as the parable's central lesson, and those points often surrounded the main characters or scenes in the story. Still others pointed out that what seemed most implausible about the history of allegorizing interpretation was the amount of allegorizing and its anachronistic nature. Expositors were reading in all kinds of later New Testament theology that Jesus' original audiences could not have been meant to grasp. But that was a separate point from saying there was no symbolism in the stories at all that they might have been able to understand.

The second half of the twentieth century saw mounting protests against Jülicher. On the more conservative end of the scholarly spectrum, various carefully limited allegorical approaches were proposed. On the more radical end, a new approach to metaphor in general increasingly suggested that it was wrongheaded even to try to sum up the meaning of parables in propositions—whether one or more. A parable, many argued, was like a good joke—if you have to explain it, you have failed already! Rather than summarizing its message with one or more points, preachers were encouraged to "contemporize" the texts—retell the stories in modern garb, implicitly explaining details when the original cultural significance might have been lost and thus hopefully recreating the same kind of dynamic or effect that they had in their original contexts.

An Outline of My Approach

Into this eclectic mix of approaches, I entered my own proposals, beginning with my doctoral thesis under Professor I. Howard Marshall in Aberdeen, Scotland, completed in 1982.[4] Among many other things, I argued that the distinctively Lucan parables (a segment of Jesus' parables that had been recently challenged) were indeed authentic, so that Jesus had spoken them as the Gospel writers present them, and that the interpretive frameworks into which they were placed had not misrepresented his original intention. Following the model of many of the rabbinic parables and of great narrative literature more generally, I argued that Jesus' parables made one main point per main character. I later expanded my study to include all parts of all three Synoptic Gospels (there are no true parables in John), and presented the results in my book *Interpreting the Parables,* published by InterVarsity Press in both the United States and the United Kingdom in 1990. In this way, it was possible to view the evangelists' framing material as often summing up one or two of the parable's main points, even when the story itself made one or two *more* points. One did not have to jettison any of Scripture as inauthentic or relegate it to the category of "the exception to the rule."

Interestingly, the forty or so parables of Jesus exhibited only six different structures when one examined the number of main characters in each and the relationships among those characters. Approximately two-thirds of Jesus' narrative parables presented three main characters or groups of characters in a triangular (or what some have called "monarchic") structure, with a master figure (including kings, fathers, landlords, shepherds, farmers, etc.) interacting with one or more contrasting pairs of subordinates (good and bad servants, sons, tenants, sheep, plants, etc.). One thinks, for example, of the prodigal son (Luke 15:11–32), with its father and two sons; or the talents (Matt. 25:14–30), with its masters, two good servants, and one wicked servant; and many other similarly structured stories. More often than not, there was a surprising reversal between the character a first-century Jewish audience would have expected to be the hero or good example and the one who actually turned out to play that role.

In one instance, a triadic parable did not have a master, but it still had a unifying figure who could judge between good and bad examples. This was the parable of the good Samaritan (Luke 10:25–37). The man left for dead was scarcely in a position of power; he exemplified extreme powerlessness! But he could still recognize that the priest and the Levite, surprisingly, turned out to be the bad models and that the Samaritan, shockingly, became his hero. In two instances, a triadic parable seemed to reflect a straight top-down or vertical-line structure, with a master figure, his subordinate, and the subordinates of that subordinate. These two parables were the unforgiving servant (Matt. 18:23–35) and the unjust steward (Luke 16:1–13).

The remaining one-third of Jesus' parables seemed relatively evenly split between two-point and one-point parables. In the former category were those that presented a master and a single subordinate (e.g., the unjust judge in Luke 18:1–8), as well as those that contrasted a good and a bad example but without an explicit master figure (e.g., the Pharisee and tax collector in Luke 18:9–14). In the latter category were stories that had only one character (e.g., the hidden treasure and the pearl of great price in Matt. 13:44–46).

Much more briefly, I interacted with the so-called new view of metaphor and argued that while it was entirely legitimate, and even important, to stress that the power or force of the narrative form of Jesus' stories was substantially diminished when one tried to summarize their meaning in one or more "points," it was not accurate to claim that they had no lessons to teach at all or that "propositional paraphrase" was itself illegitimate.

My book-length work has led to spin-off articles of various kinds,[5] including updates in light of more recent scholarship.[6] As early as 1984, I published an essay on "Preaching the Parables: Preserving Three Main Points," which showed how one could move naturally from my approach to interpreting the parables to a homiletical theory that proclaimed one, two, or three lessons per sermon based on the parable's structure and number of main characters.[7] Response to my approach has been sufficiently positive, especially within evangelical circles,[8] to encourage me to continue pursuing it and finally, in this work, to develop a book-length treatment of preaching the parables. But before we proceed we need to take stock of what else has been done in the last quarter century or so on our topic.

Other Recent Work

There are many anthologies of inspiring sermons on selected parables of Jesus. A few collect "classic" messages of "all-star" nineteenth- or twentieth-century English-language preachers[9] or present exemplary sermons from one particular famous expositor.[10] Among the works of recent or contemporary preachers, a number implicitly or explicitly adopt the one-main-point approach, though not all their expositions always limit themselves in the way their methodology suggests they might. From this perspective and among evangelical writers, the works of David Hubbard, Earl Palmer, and Stuart Briscoe (the last just on parables in Luke) prove particularly insightful.[11] The expositions of James Boice, Dwight Pentecost, and Robert McQuilkin are frequently used, but they are less consistently helpful because they fairly often revert back to a more extensive and occasionally anachronistic form of allegorizing.[12] With repeated applications for the workplace and reflecting a fairly centrist theological perspective, John Purdy proves very helpful.[13] Within a more explicitly liberal tradition, challenging messages appear in the books by Ellsworth Kalas and Megan McKenna.[14] And there are numerous other works available with sermons of varying quality that do not obviously follow any consistent interpretive principles.[15]

A surprising number of recent books include at least introductory considerations of method before proceeding to illustrate them via parable sermons, yet without ever addressing this most central interpretive debate of all—how many points (if any) can a parable make? Neal Fisher focuses on the historical setting of Jesus' parables, their links with the kingdom of God, Jesus' distinctive use of this genre, complete with form-critical classifications, but the closest he comes to addressing the issue of the number of points is a brief, general approval of Jülicher while at the same time admitting there are exceptions.[16] Robert Capon has produced three very helpful volumes in which he classifies the parables according to the consecutive periods of Jesus' ministry into which they fall, believing them to correspond to the basic topics of "kingdom," "grace," and "judgment," respectively. While it is not clear the divisions are this watertight, many passages do seem to fit the themes assigned to them. But his expositions of individual parables do not produce a predictable number of lessons from any given text.[17]

W. A. Poovey offers fascinating dramas and meditations on the parables but again without any methodological controls.[18] John Killinger has produced wonderful and generally accurate contemporizations of the parables for a modern, Western Christmastime setting. Killinger describes his accounts simply as "a collection of the stories of Jesus retold in the language of Christmas" with "every attempt . . . to preserve the meaning and force of the parables as Jesus told them," including their single points as defended by Joachim Jeremias, the classic mid-twentieth-century German Lutheran parable commentator.[19] But that is the full extent of his explanation of how he composed his work.

John and James Carroll select nine parables among the sixteen passages that they treat in a book on preaching the "hard sayings" of Jesus. Each passage is followed by an interpretation, guidelines for moving from text to sermon, including the major topics or themes, and suggestions for illustrations and applications. Overall the volume is exegetically faithful to the Gospel texts and should prove quite helpful to preachers—on just about everything other than determining how many main points appear in a passage, an issue on which the authors remain silent.[20] In a similar vein, Keith Nickle has penned a volume on preaching the entire Gospel of Luke, complete with a mini-commentary, passage-by-passage, with multiple suggestions for preaching each text. Most of the suggestions relate to one or more central topics, including the themes of the parables. The interpretations overall appear well founded, but one, two, three, or more points per passage (parabolic or otherwise) appear in no discernible pattern.[21]

One might expect treatments of "preaching the Gospels" to give advice on dealing specifically with parables, but here, too, one is often disappointed. D. Moody Smith, in an entire book on that topic, comments on the parables' link with the kingdom and on Jeremias's laws of transformation (a critique of which is found in my earlier book)[22] and provides an illustration via a sermon he preached in the Duke Divinity School chapel on the parable of the sower and its aftermath (Matt. 13:1–23). But he offers the reader no explanation of how many points he decided to make and why.[23] G. R. Beasley-Murray, in a volume of comparable scope, deals with the parables' purpose, theology, and form and then arranges the parables according to major themes, apparently presupposing no more than one theme per passage, but again without ever explicitly introducing the debate that surrounds this issue.[24] An otherwise major evangelical work of extraordinary usefulness on preaching the Bible according to its literary genres, by Sidney Greidanus, devotes a whole chapter to the Gospels, focusing on their numerous figures of speech and other literary devices, yet without including any discrete section on the parables or offering distinctive guidelines for preaching them![25]

The best recent compilation of sermons on the parables, though again without any detailed methodological reflection, is doubtless Roy

Clements's *A Sting in the Tale*.[26] Although the book is not formatted for
footnotes or bibliography, Clements in fact built substantially (though
not slavishly) on my work,[27] so that discrete lessons from main characters or main scenes in the parables may often be discerned. For many
years, Clements was one of the world's finest preachers, no matter what
part of Scripture he was expounding, so his sermons bear studying for
that reason alone.

Another category of recent books and essays on preaching the parables
directly addresses in some detail the issues of whether a parable makes
one point, more than one point, or none. The majority of these works,
understandably, still revert back to the "received wisdom" of the first
half of the twentieth century and look for no more than one central
lesson per passage. David Granskou offers seven additional helpful
principles: treat each parable as a unified passage, watch for critical
turns in the plot toward the end, beware of methods that merely obscure
the meaning, rely on commentators who study historical background,
keep original meaning and contemporary application distinct, study
the form for its literary beauty as well as its historical and existential
meaning, and note the prophetic element that accompanies the text's
"wit and wisdom."[28]

Lloyd Ogilvie argues that each parable teaches one central lesson
that tells us something about God's nature to which we must respond in
specific ways.[29] Richard Eslinger believes that the one point of the parable must correspond to the one point of the sermon, so that the parable
itself is a sermon in brief. He challenges preachers not to "disrupt" the
metaphor's world and "to let the metaphor live and work its power."[30]
Eduard Schweizer concurs, insisting even more strongly that "it is not
our free choice whether we speak in direct or in parabolic language.
There is a kind of truth that we can express only in imagery." Great
preachers, Schweizer believes, can create new parables altogether in
contemporary imagery; otherwise most of us will have to contemporize
and explain Jesus' own stories.[31] Robert Hughes gives some specific
guidelines for how to do precisely this, within broader specifications
for preaching the parables.[32]

Other recent scholars abandon the search for a central proposition
altogether and focus only on the function of metaphor and the process
of contemporization. In fact, though, none of these authors ever avoids
proclaiming propositional truth, however avant-garde, in their actual
expositions, proving our earlier point that it is not a case of *either*
teach lessons *or* contemporize the stories, but a case of needing to do
both. Thus Peter Jones states categorically, "We do well in preaching
the parables to retain rather than jettison the story. We can avoid the
'propositional heresy' of summarizing the simple meaning succinctly

and departing from the story forthwith."[33] But there is an obvious third alternative—keep the story and the summary of its meaning, which is what Jones actually winds up doing with his illustrations of the good Samaritan and the unjust steward. The former parable shows us three kinds of people—those who hurt others, those who are hurt by others, and those who heal others' hurts. The latter parable presents successive scenes involving a desperate plight, an inescapable summons, and a dangerous opportunity.[34] It is a short step from these two lists of three elements to full-fledged sentences describing what we learn, character-by-character or scene-by-scene—an approach that closely matches my own and which reflects no form of heresy, theological or methodological, whatsoever!

Various articles have applied the interpretive and existential insights of recent literary critics. Mark Thomsen draws on the works of Dan Via and Dominic Crossan to produce "a parabolic theology for preaching" that explores the multidimensional possibilities of recreating the power of Jesus' stories in narrative form, expressing entirely new visions of divine reality through which God speaks.[35] Bernard B. Scott's major work on "hearing" the parables[36] has spawned two entire books that have applied his approach to preaching.[37] Scott himself reflected on that task even before he wrote his larger book, enjoining expositors to resist making "a point" but seeking rather to "shatter" old worlds and "create" new ones for their listeners. Yet when he illustrated with the parable of the seed growing secretly (Mark 4:26–29), he admitted that he felt himself "slipping into idolatry" by beginning to say what he thought the parable meant![38] In fact, he makes propositional assertions about the meaning of all the parables in his larger commentary; they just tend to be very unusual or unorthodox propositions. Eric Osborn and Timothy Sensing have likewise inappropriately dismissed "point-making" but otherwise offer very helpful guidance on contemporizing or "imitating the genre of parable in today's pulpit."[39]

All these studies notwithstanding, there are, as of this writing, only two book-length works in print on preaching the parables that offer introductory methodological reflections, several sample sermons, and extended commentary on how those sermons were created and how they were designed to function. The first, by Eugene L. Lowry, although titled *How to Preach a Parable,* is in fact better described by its subtitle: *Designs for Narrative Sermons.* Only one of the four sample sermons discussed actually takes a parable of Jesus for its text; the rest treat other forms of biblical narrative. The real benefit of Lowry's volume is that it illustrates and discusses four ways of relating a text of Scripture to a narrative sermon on it: "running the story" (following the actual narrative flow of the text itself), "delaying the story" (when the text first emerges well into the sermon), "suspending the story" (beginning with part of the text, breaking away for awhile, and then returning to the rest of the text), and "alternating the story" (breaking the text into large sections interspersed throughout the exposition). Lowry stresses that in all four models the preacher's goal is to create "opening disequilibrium," to move through "escalation of conflict," and to arrive at a "surprising reversal" and "closing denouement (in which the table of life gets set for us in a new way by the gospel)."[40] He observes, moreover, that the narrative form of a sermon "is *less authoritarian* in the sense of the preacher being the expert, and *more authoritative* in the sense of the text's dominance in the experience."[41] Thus "issues that are hard to hear often can be heard best when the preacher is 'facing' the text rather than 'facing' the congregation."[42] Retelling a story can powerfully accomplish this because the preacher and the congregation together form the audience in listening to the story.

The second, much lengthier work is by David G. Buttrick. *Speaking Parables: A Homiletic Guide* provides exactly what it promises—detailed treatments of all the major parables of Jesus with sermons on a little over half of them, illustrating numerous structures and themes. Buttrick observes that "parables usually begin rather tritely, depicting our everyday world in an everyday way, but then in most cases there is something surreal that disrupts our world and hints at a wider, more mysterious world—as well as a more astonishing God." "Speaking parables" is therefore "a tricky, exciting craft."[43] Buttrick's theology reflects a consistent "left-leaning" perspective on doctrine, politics, and social ethics. Within his liberal tradition, he candidly observes that previous parable preaching has usually fallen into one of three camps, all of which he believes prove inadequate: "verse-by-verse" commentary, "textual-topical" preaching, and "life-situation" sermons. He prefers preachers to choose one of three different approaches, which he describes as reading and responding to the story section-by-section, staying in the original story but interpreting it by contemporary metaphors, and telling the entire story with contemporary language and imagery.[44] In fact our volume illustrates all of these methods and others, but from within an evangelical theological framework.

Roman Catholic scholar Barbara Reid provides perhaps the most direct and immediate justification for the approach we will take in the body of this book. She affirms my conviction that the parables reflect a kind of sliding scale or spectrum of more or less allegorical texts and that one main point may regularly be discerned when one reads the parable through the eyes, in turn, of each of its main characters. She agrees (as do I) with the new view of metaphor to the extent that ideally one shouldn't have to interpret a parable any more than one wants to have to explain a joke. One simply "gets it," because one understands the punch line. But she also recognizes that in a fallen world, separated by miles and centuries from Jesus' original milieu, we may not always "get it," so we need to be prepared *both* to explain *and* to contemporize the parables. She believes all good sermons present one central proposition, an emphasis well known throughout the evangelical world as "big-idea" preaching thanks to the writings of Haddon W. Robinson.[45] Reid believes the best way this approach can be harmonized with the multiple points in many parables is to "discern which of many possible points is the main one that the assembly needs to hear at this place and time."[46]

We could suggest other harmonizations as well, most notably by looking for a "big idea" that incorporates elements of all of the points of the passage. Most of the sermons included in this volume contain such unifying themes, but they are (intentionally) clearer in some sermons than in others. The danger of limiting a sermon to just one of a passage's two or three main points is, of course, to fail to preach the "whole counsel of God" (Acts 20:27, KJV). Perhaps it is simply due to my lack of creativity or imagination, but I cannot always think of a way to summarize concisely in a simple proposition the three main lessons of a tripartite passage. How does one encapsulate the prodigal son's emphasis on the possibility of repentance no matter how far one has fallen, the need not to begrudge God's generosity in forgiving the most wayward of sinners, and the patient love of the Father for both sons that this parable so poignantly depicts (see my commentary in chap. 1)?

On the other hand, one of my colleagues once suggested to me a remarkably concise big idea that incorporates all three lessons of the similarly structured parable of the two sons in Matthew 21:28–32. In this parable, in which a son who refuses to work in his father's vineyard later changes his mind and goes to the vineyard, in which a son who says he will work in fact doesn't, and in which the father pronounces the former rather than the latter as having done his will, the three prongs of the passage can be neatly summed up with the affirmation, "Performance takes priority over promise."[47] "Performance" points to what the first son did, "promise" reflects the extent of the second son's behavior, and "takes priority over" captures the father's verdict in comparing the two. There really are three points that all merit unpacking embedded in this concise "big idea," so it seems that expositors should not abandon the search for ways to sum up the parables' multiple lessons in succinct formulae. But if nothing comes to mind after a reasonable period of time, better to preach the full message of the text than to curtail one-half to two-thirds of it.

In short, given that no evangelical work has been written in recent decades containing this kind of introduction—a collection of illustrative sermons on each of the kinds of parables of Jesus along with detailed commentary on those sermons—plenty of room still remains for this book to take its place in a world saturated with many books. The rest of this introduction will thus describe the presuppositions, format, and contents of the body of this volume and how I hope it can prove helpful to preachers and teachers of the parables. I will also try to set my approach within the larger world of homiletical theory.

Guiding Presuppositions

There are certain conclusions concerning the interpretation of the parables that have been so thoroughly and convincingly defended elsewhere that I will adopt them simply as presuppositions for my own hermeneutics. Seven in particular merit listing here.

First, Jesus' narrative texts with the six structures identified in the preceding discussion are all formally similar enough to deserve the label "parable," whether that word explicitly appears in the context of the passage or not. The Greek and Hebrew equivalents (*parabolē* and *māsāl*, respectively) in fact referred to an even broader cross section of metaphorical or analogical speech,[48] but we will limit ourselves to those texts that comprise actual narratives.

Second, all of the parables impinge on Jesus' understanding of the "kingdom of God," whether that expression explicitly appears in the context of any given passage or not. For Jesus, the "kingdom" referred more to a power than to a place, more to a rule or reign than to a realm. In short, it referred to God's "kingship," taking on new and greater dimensions on earth, inaugurated with Christ's first coming but to be consummated only at his second.[49] In my previous book on parables I devoted an entire half-chapter to the theology of the kingdom that may be deduced from Jesus' parables.[50]

Third, the parables are authentic in the forms and contexts in which they appear in our canonical Gospels. One does not have to pit Jesus' original meaning against the evangelists' use of the parables in some new setting. One does not have to dissect the parables into more or less authentic parts—what Jesus did or did not likely say. One does not have to remove the parables from the framing material in which they appear in the Gospels in order to understand their true meaning. This, in fact, is one of the major corollaries of our approach that takes one main point from one main character. It was only when commentators felt they could find no more than one point per passage that it seemed that Jesus' (or the evangelists') introductory or closing words often missed that point. In almost every instance commentators in fact debated among two or three possibilities, at least one of which *did* involve the story's introductions or conclusions, in their quest for the "one point." Once we allow for multiple points per parable, we may see this material often as encapsulating *one* of the passage's points but not all of them.[51]

Fourth, the main characters (and often only the main characters) in Jesus' parables do "stand for something." They have symbolic referents in the spiritual realm. This is part of what the term "allegory" has regularly meant. If it seems too misleading to call the parables allegorical, and to safeguard against the overly elaborate and anachronistic allegorizing of other eras, we may label them "symbolic" instead. Either way, it is not wrong to see, for example, in the father of the two sons an image of God, to view the prodigal as symbolic of all wayward sinners in need of repentance (including the tax collectors and prostitutes, most notoriously, in Jesus' world), and to regard the older brother as representing those who think they are God's followers yet who respond with envy when he lavishes grace on the most obviously undeserving (including many Pharisees in Jesus' world). Other elements in a passage should not be given symbolic significance unless clear textual indicators point in that direction and unless the import ascribed to them reinforces rather than distracts from the central lessons identifiable through the behavior of the central characters.[52]

Fifth, Jesus intended his parables both to conceal and to reveal. I explain Mark 4:11–12 and parallels in the context of my sermon on the parable of the sower below and add further explanation in my commentary on the sermon. Suffice it to say that it is today widely agreed that enough opportunity had elapsed in Jesus' ministry by this point for him to see who was increasingly moving toward discipleship and who was increasingly rejecting and even opposing his message. Just as God called Isaiah to pronounce judgment on the Israelites in response to their prolonged disobedience (Mark 4:12 pars. quotes Isa. 6:9–10), Jesus' speaking in parables proves cryptic to outsiders to the kingdom as God's response of judgment to their freely chosen rebellion. And it is not that they fail *cognitively* to understand Jesus' claims; even the Jewish leaders who plotted to kill him can explain his meaning well enough at that level (Mark 12:12 pars.). Rather the "understanding" that outsiders lack is the full-orbed biblical meaning of "understanding"—that which consistently refers to people being willing to *act* on their knowledge. Those who are not Jesus' followers do not understand *volitionally;* they are unwilling to become disciples. From an eternal perspective that is the only kind of understanding that ultimately matters.[53]

Sixth, the process of contemporizing the parables remains crucial. Some portion of a sermon on a parable should remain in narrative form, even if it is only via the reading of that text of Scripture. But in most cases, it will be both easy and helpful to include some modern equivalent to the biblical story in an introduction, in one or more illustrations interspersed within the body, or in a conclusion to the message. These contemporizations should work to recreate the original dynamic, force, or effect of Jesus' original story. It is not true that narratives cannot (or should not) be paraphrased propositionally; it is true that good exposition should not do *just* that.

Seventh and last, especially in series of sermons working their way through large portions of one specific Gospel, messages on parables that are paralleled in other Gospels should stress something of what is unique to the specific version of the parable at hand. Sermons, for example, on the wicked tenants (a parable found in Matthew, Mark, and Luke) should not sound identical irrespective of the Gospel from which the text is chosen. Because all the sermons in this book originated either as "one-off" messages on a specific parable or as part of a longer series *just on parables,* there are not many opportunities to illustrate this principle. But guidance for preaching the theological distinctives of a given Gospel writer may be found elsewhere.[54]

An Outline of This Book

Fifteen parables are treated in the following chapters. First appears my sermon, in its most recently revised form, on each passage. Then I discuss why I did what I did in a short commentary on each sermon. Readers should be able to benefit from the messages and my explanations no matter where they dip into the volume, but there is some logic to the sequence I have provided.

My own thinking on interpreting the parables with one main point per main character began with the prodigal son. The Roman Catholic scholar Pierre Grelot had written an article in which he read and commented on the story three consecutive times, each time from the perspective of a different character. He then tried to create a single "main point" from his readings, but in fact made three points, one apiece from the perspectives of each of the main characters.[55] I was immediately struck by the potential of his analysis (if not his arithmetic!) to apply elsewhere, given the number of Jesus' parables that are structured roughly along the lines of the prodigal. Testing my hypothesis, I found that over and over again the debates among scholars as to the single point of triangularly structured passages amounted to discussing which main character one should attend to the most. When two or three points were permitted, the debates dissolved. But one was still not thrown back into the older era of massive, unjustified allegorization.

So I begin with my sermon on the parable of the prodigal son and illustrate a method of expounding the text according to the three points I believe it makes. I introduce the message with an extended three-part contemporization. The second parable, the rich man and Lazarus, likewise makes three points according to its three main characters, but this time I sandwich my exposition between a shorter introduction and a lengthier conclusion, which includes additional theological reflection and application. The third parable, the good Samaritan, illustrates a different tripartite structure, where the diagram of the relationship among the characters is a straight horizontal line. Here there is no master, only a unifying figure. But again I develop my exposition under the headings of the lessons that one can learn from the three main characters, treating the priest and the Levite together as essentially one character (since their roles in the story are identical).

The fourth and fifth parables presented reflect the two three-point parables of Jesus that yield a vertical-line diagram—a master, his subordinate, and subordinates under the first subordinate. These are the parables of the unforgiving servant and the unjust steward. With this model, we have exhausted all the structures Jesus employed in his tripartite narratives. The unforgiving servant also affords me the opportunity to develop a scene-by-scene exposition, while the unjust steward presents its three points in the three concluding remarks that Jesus appends to the narrative proper. The structures of the sermons thus vary according to these different substructures of the text.

The sixth sermon is my one complete narrative sermon. It expounds the parable of the children in the marketplace, which appears last in the chapter on "simple" three-point parables in my book on interpreting the parables, because it is the one example that fits least well into the model. I discuss two possible ways of diagramming it in triangular fashion, which taken together yield a pair of complementary but not identical sets of three points. But the sermon more self-consciously focuses on a big idea that unites those points, an idea that I believe works equally well with either diagram and with either set of three subpoints.

I turn next to more "complex" triadic models—where one vertex of the triangle represents not merely more than one character but also characters whose roles in some way vary from one another. Thus the parable of the sower contains three inadequate models of responding to the word and one good model. The first three kinds of soil share the characteristic of not producing the fruit desired from the seeds planted in them, but otherwise each teaches slightly different lessons. If there are three points overall in the passage, one point has three subdivisions or constituent elements to it.[56] I also preach an inductive sermon on this parable, rearranging the major parts of the passage to correspond to the climactic sequence I want to generate section-by-section throughout the message.

Because my sermon on the sower was the first in a three-part series on the parables of Matthew 13, I next present the other two sermons on the rest of that chapter. Both of these cover several parables in one message. Also, I don't have to struggle with how to develop an entire message from the short one-point parables (mustard seed and leaven; hidden treasure and pearl of great price; householder). The disadvantage, though, is that I don't have the time to develop all three lessons from the three-pointed parables (the wheat and weeds and the dragnet). Instead, I focus on the one point in each that I believe connects that parable with the surrounding contextual material grouped together for each sermon.

Next appear three messages on two-character parables. The first two represent the horizontal-line model, for they contrast good and bad examples. The straightforward, commonsensical account of the two builders allows me to deal with the parable comparatively briefly and then discuss in some detail the larger context of the Sermon on the Mount, in which Matthew's form of this passage appears. The parable of the Pharisee and the tax collector is equally brief and seems as straightforward, until we realize that first-century Jewish listeners would not have assumed what we "know"—that the Pharisee is the "bad guy" and the tax collector the "good guy." That makes me develop in detail a quite different true-life modern analogy with my story of "the recovering homosexual."

In my earlier book, I point out how several two-point parables could be viewed as implicitly containing a third character (and also how certain one-point parables could be viewed as implicitly containing a second character). As I turn to a two-point parable with a vertical diagram, the parable of the unjust judge, I develop the possible third point associated with the implicit third character, allowing me to offer a classic three-point exposition. The only category of parable remaining, which I have not expounded in an entire sermon devoted only to that particular structure of passage, is the purely one-point parable. Because all the Gospel examples of this form come in pairs, it is natural to do two at a time. Because the tower builder and the warring king are securely nestled into a larger paragraph of "hard sayings of Jesus," it is appropriate to take that entire unit for my text. The form of the message is somewhat unique as well. While each component of the passage makes one point, together the passage presents an introduction, three pairs of sayings, and a conclusion. The six sayings forming the three pairs not only represent some of Jesus' most difficult sayings but also alternate between metaphors whose severity is easy to underestimate, and others whose demands are easy to overestimate. This oscillation forms the skeleton on which the message is then fleshed out.

Finally, I include two sermons that do not fit into the pattern of moving from three- to two- to one-point parables. The message on Matthew 24:43–25:30 shows how one can preach on a sizable chunk of text, in this case containing four parables of varying structures, as one looks for comparisons and contrasts between the big ideas of each and discerns what seems to be the text's intended narrative flow. Again, because of the quantity of material covered, unifying lessons emerge in detail only from the two- and three-point parables that together form our text. The very last message is the only one included in this book that does not treat a true parable. But the sheep and goats is at least "quasi-parabolic" in form, and its message is so often misunderstood that I want to round out the volume by concluding with it. It also immediately follows the parables preached in the previous sermon. This last message is yet again somewhat different from the others presented in that it explicitly compares and contrasts the two most common interpretations of the text throughout church history and explicitly argues for the one that is less well known today even though it has dominated the church's teaching over the centuries. I also include extended application.

Reflections on Homiletical Method

Despite considerable diversity in the form and structure of the messages interspersed throughout this volume (indeed, no two sermons are entirely identical in these respects), the book does not encompass the breadth of homiletical form that one finds in the church of Jesus Christ worldwide today or throughout its history. I remain firmly committed to the tradition of expository preaching as an outstanding way of making sure one's messages are securely grounded in Scripture, without passing judgment on other traditions (as some do) as if they were necessarily illegitimate. Haddon Robinson defines expository preaching as "the communication of a biblical concept, derived from and transmitted through a historical, grammatical, and literary study of a passage in its context, which the Holy Spirit first applies to the personality and experience of the preacher, then through him to his hearers."[57] This definition is both broader and narrower than others. By using the singular expression "a biblical concept," Robinson tips his hand as to what his book will unpack in detail; he believes each sermon should have one unifying, central proposition or "big idea." In an age in which so many media compete for our attention each week, bombarding our brains with so many messages, it makes good rhetorical and psychological sense to adopt this principle. Try to leave your listeners with one thought, repeated, unpacked, illustrated, and applied in various ways; they may not be able to retain any more than this.

On the other hand, as we noted earlier in citing Reid, it is not always possible to claim that a biblical pericope or passage contains only one main lesson. In this instance, one can either select just one of the lessons for a "big idea" sermon, or one can try to create a larger, synthetic idea that explicitly or implicitly contains several parts that the sermon proceeds to explain. This is the option I have chosen more often than not, so as not to lose the richness of the biblical teaching. I tend to resonate more with the approaches of Walter Kaiser and Gordon Fee, who both develop exegetical outlines from grammatical layouts of passages and then incorporate into each preaching outline multiple subpoints that derive from the exegetical outline in addition to the unifying proposition.[58]

While in this sense my preferred form of exposition is a little more narrow (or prescribed in more detail) than Robinson's, in other respects it is broader, since I feel free to include all four of Lowry's forms of narrative preaching under the heading of exposition, including an inductive sermon in which I rearrange the major units of the text. I am not aware of anything in Robinson's philosophy of preaching that would exclude this approach, but his works do not at any point actually endorse it. At this point Buttrick's models provide a helpful precedent (see my earlier discussion of both Lowry and Buttrick).

A second issue of homiletical method involves the larger question of narrative preaching in general. Many in the evangelical tradition, often for no better reason than that they have not been exposed to narrative preaching, look askance at the whole undertaking. However, an excellent evangelical defense and thorough treatment of the method with respect to Old Testament narrative is now available, thanks to Steven Mathewson;[59] additional helpful insights are scattered throughout the more theologically eclectic volume edited by Wayne Robinson.[60] Even very conservative audiences to whom I have preached full-fledged narrative sermons have responded in a uniformly positive way, at times with considerably greater enthusiasm than to my more straightforward section-by-section expositions of a text. On the other hand, narrative sermons are very time-consuming to research, and one needs considerable historical acumen to compose them well; were I to have included more than one I might have been putting a model before my readers that many could not hope to imitate. As it turns out, over the years I have only created one entire narrative sermon on a parable, so the choice was made for me. But it should become very clear that there are elements of narrative preaching in virtually every message included in this volume.

What, then, of other genres of preaching altogether? Some by defi-nition largely exclude themselves from consideration in a volume on preaching parables. Except for the very shortest one-line metaphors that are not full-fledged narratives and thus not normally called parables, the form of "textual preaching" that takes apart a single verse in great detail cannot do justice to an entire multi-verse parable. It would, of course, be possible to glean various legitimate insights and partial understand-ing of a parable by focusing on a central verse or declaration within it. "Topical" preaching likewise usually seeks to discover what a portion of Scripture has to say about a topic or theme that is found in more places than in just one literary form such as parables. Again, though, as I noted previously, one certainly could develop numerous central aspects of Jesus' theology of the kingdom by treating only a collection of references to the parables in some topical sequence.

A more provocative way of categorizing homiletical forms is according to a particular hermeneutical method that is stressed. Raymond Bailey has edited a book that discusses and illustrates, in turn, what are called "historical," "canonical," "literary," "rhetorical," "African-American," "philosophical," and "theological" models.[61] Elements of preaching that could pay rich dividends with the parables appear in every one of these forms. But my training is in expository preaching, and I hardly consider myself a master even of that tradition, so I have not attempted to be all things to all people and illustrate every conceivable homiletical form. I will allow others trained in other traditions to determine what of value they can take from my models and incorporate into their forms.

But enough of prolegomena! It is time to turn to those perennially fascinating narratives, the parables of Jesus, and see what they may teach us, as we seek to apply them first to ourselves as preachers and teachers and then grapple with how best to communicate what we have learned to others. A final introductory comment should make explicit what is too often left implicit in many preaching guides. Nothing written here is intended to bypass or play down the essential role of the Holy Spirit in guiding his human mouthpieces—we who are entrusted with the sacred calling of communicating his word. But the Spirit works through the whole range of human discourse—from carefully thought-out messages to entirely spontaneous discourse. In my experience, I have regularly had the sense of a message "coming together" with a speed and clarity that were not present until a fairly definable moment, after which it seemed that a sermon almost wrote itself. I have no reason not to attribute this consistent experience to the guidance of the Holy Spirit. On the other hand, I have seldom had such an experience until after I had spent a fair amount of time mulling over possible points, structures, sequences, illustrations, and applications, at times following almost a mechanical procedure of identifiable steps in sermon preparation.[62] For me, at least, it seems the Spirit works better when there is already something of value running around in my mind on which to build! And finally, I harbor no illusion that my messages will merit inclusion in any subsequent anthology of "all-star" contributions. I hope, however, that the format of this volume is distinctive and helpful enough that those with more creative juices than I have can take my methods and outlines and do something far more artistically pleasing or spiritually powerful.

1

The Parable of the Prodigal Sons and Their Father

Luke 15:11–32

For several years, Bob was quite active in the Mafia. He had been raised Roman Catholic but turned his back on his upbringing and became a wealthy leader in the world of organized crime in Chicago. He sold drugs, hired prostitutes, and enjoyed many "courtesans" himself, even though he had married Nancy, a woman who claimed to be a believer but who was not very committed. In fact, Nancy had married Bob more for her enjoyment of the jet set, the fast life, the circles in which Bob operated. Then Bob was dramatically converted through the witness of a fellow mobster. You couldn't have imagined a more changed life. Bob did time in prison and even led several prisoners to the Lord. He continued to be a bold, outspoken evangelist after getting out of jail. Even to this day, he regularly shares his faith, on and off the job, at times with entire strangers. Despite an occasional lack of tact, he has been remarkably successful at bringing countless people to Christ.

Bob's marriage, however, is now on the rocks. At first Nancy claimed to be glad of the wonderful change in her husband. But it soon became clear that he had something she didn't. She got tired of hearing all the talk about spiritual things. Today he no longer tells her much of his evangelistic activity because inevitably she interrupts and starts an argument of some kind. She won't go to church with him, and recently she's been talking of divorce. What really gnaws at her is that God never gave her such gifts as he seems to have given Bob. Nancy has always struggled as an introvert in social situations. Some days she's just not sure how much longer she can take all of this religious stuff.

Johnny is a young African-American man. He was raised in Los Angeles's inner city. His father never married his mother and wasn't around for most of Johnny's childhood. When he was, he was often drunk and abusive. There were no Christians in Johnny's family or among his close friends. He got involved in gangs in his early teen years. He committed some minor crimes but was never caught. Finally he heard about a Christian parachurch ministry to teens that integrated black and white kids together. It was run by an African-American man who modeled Christ's love for him for several years as Johnny came and went from the club, straightening out for a while and then falling back into his old ways again. At last Johnny, too, trusted in Christ as his savior. He became part of the student leadership of the club during his high school years. After graduation he went off to become a successful student at a local Bible college. There he met and eventually married a white girl by the name of Debbie, who had a vision for inner-city ministry. Quickly they had one child; now another one is on the way.

Johnny was invited to become a full-time staff person for the organization that brought him to the Lord. But there was a catch—he would have to raise his own support. Several young, white colleagues, roughly his age, do that and get on just fine. All regularly attend primarily white churches in the suburbs where all the money is, but few people or churches have ever pledged to Johnny. In fact, after two years of trying to raise support he has only four hundred dollars a month coming in. His family is still on welfare. He's thought of quitting, of getting a "real job," but he sees his white peers succeeding at this process and feels equally called. It's just that when he presents his ministry to people in their churches, it's clear there's a subtle racism at work. "We're just not sure he's trustworthy," he's overheard some say. "Blacks shouldn't marry whites" has been the reply of others. "We're sending money to Eastern Europe; that's where the real opportunities and needs currently are." Johnny doesn't know how much longer he can tolerate this.

Marla was brought up in a nominally Lutheran home in New York State. Her parents were regular church attenders, and they faithfully took her with them. She believed she was a Christian as a child. She agreed with the concept of trusting in Jesus and being a moral and friendly person. She was married in her late teens to a man who turned out to be severely abusive, and she filed for divorce within months of the wedding. Her husband, too, had claimed to be a Christian, so she soured on church and on spiritual things, until she met some friends at work from a local charismatic congregation. They shared with her their understanding of baptism in the Spirit. She went along to one of their evening services and one night miraculously received the gift of tongues. She was even slain in the Spirit. Life turned around dramatically for Marla. She found a new love for Jesus and began to share her faith. She went overseas on a short-term missions trip and came back thinking about full-time Christian service, eager for more education and training.

That was several years ago. Marla still remains active in the local church, but her zeal today isn't quite what it once was. As she inquired about signing on with different missions organizations in various denominations or parachurch groups, she found most weren't interested in her. For some, she was disqualified because she spoke in tongues. Others did not want to touch her because she was a divorcée, and a divorcée who admitted she was divorced as a Christian who had married a Christian, not because of adultery or abandonment. Marla worked for a while on the staff of a local church as a part-time youth worker. Some thought that a woman shouldn't hold that office; others said nothing but discriminated against her by treating her with less respect than they showed male pastoral leadership. Today she has a well-paying secular job and is not entirely sure what, if anything, she wants to do with the church in the future.

All of these stories are true. Only the names and a few details have been changed to protect the innocent (and the guilty!). The following story, as far as we know, is fictitious, but you should see some striking parallels to the stories already narrated.

Jesus continued: "There was a man who had two sons. The younger one said to his father, 'Father, give me my share of the estate.' So he divided his property between them.

"Not long after that, the younger son got together all he had, set off for a distant country and there squandered his wealth in wild living. After he had spent everything, there was a severe famine in that whole country, and he began to be in need. So he went and hired himself out to a citizen of that country, who sent him to his field to feed pigs. He longed to fill his stomach with the pods that the pigs were eating, but no one gave him anything.

"When he came to his senses, he said, 'How many of my father's hired servants have food to spare, and here I am starving to death! I will set out and go back to my father and say to him: Father, I have sinned against heaven and against you. I am no longer worthy to be called your son; make me like one of your hired servants.' So he got up and went to his father.

"But while he was still a long way off, his father saw him and was filled with compassion for him; he ran to his son, threw his arms around him and kissed him.

"The son said to him, 'Father, I have sinned against heaven and against you. I am no longer worthy to be called your son.'

"But the father said to his servants, 'Quick! Bring the best robe and put it on him. Put a ring on his finger and sandals on his feet. Bring the fattened calf and kill it. Let's have a feast and celebrate. For this son of mine was dead and is alive again; he was lost and is found.' So they began to celebrate.

"Meanwhile the older son was in the field. When he came near the house, he heard music and dancing. So he called one of the servants and asked him what was going on. 'Your brother has come,' he replied, 'and your father has killed the fattened calf because he has him back safe and sound.'

"The older brother became angry and refused to go in. So his father went out and pleaded with him. But he answered his father, 'Look! All these years I've been slaving for you and never disobeyed your orders. Yet you never gave me even a young goat so I could celebrate with my friends. When this son of yours who has squandered your property with prostitutes comes home, you kill the fattened calf for him!'

"'My son,' the father said, 'you were always with me, and everything I have is yours. But we had to celebrate and be glad, because this brother of yours was dead and is alive again; he was lost and is found.'" (Luke 15:11–32)

This parable teaches us three lessons, as we read it with the eyes of each of its three main characters.

The first lesson is that repentance is always possible for those who want to return to God. The traditional title that this parable has come to have is "The Prodigal Son." The prodigal is the character we naturally tend to focus on the most. In the context of Luke 15, he corresponds to the tax collectors and "sinners," who Luke tells us in verse 1 "were all gathering around to hear" Jesus. The plot of the story forms about as dramatic a picture as could have been drawn in Jesus' world of the abandonment of godly living. Family formed one's ultimate human commitment. For the son to request inheritance from his father while his dad was still alive was tantamount to a death wish. The petition of verse 12, recorded so matter-of-factly, amounted in essence to the boy's saying, "Dad, I wish you were dead." We're not told all the details of what happened when he received his portion of the inheritance and went away, but what we are told makes it clear that Jesus is painting a worst-case scenario. The younger son leaves everyone behind, takes all his money with him, and sets off for a distant country. Jews would immediately recognize that this would be unclean Gentile territory made up of unclean Gentile people. There the young man squanders his wealth in wild or riotous living and loses it all. Exacerbating the situation is a severe famine, and so the prodigal needs some kind of job in order to feed himself, but apparently all he can find is a man of that country who sends him to his field to feed pigs, the most unclean of all animals from an orthodox Jewish perspective. These are the depths of degradation. He is so desperate that he wishes he could eat even some of the pig food, the unclean food of unclean animals of an unclean farmer in an unclean land, but even that is forbidden. Of course, his fate is largely his own fault, but circumstances outside his control have overwhelmed him further. In his desperate plight, his only hope is to return home, even though he recognizes that his father may well have performed the standard Jewish ceremony of "cutting off" his wayward son and disowning him, a disowning that might not be revoked. But maybe he could beg to work as a slave; at least he wouldn't be starving to death.

Throughout human history, there have been prodigals like the young man in Jesus' story, including Bob, Johnny, and Marla. You may have been one or had one in your family, and we've probably all known one or more. I've shared three stories of people whom I have known personally and whom I have no reason to suspect that you know. But it wouldn't at all surprise me if several of you said, "I think I know who you're talking about. I know somebody pretty much just like that." The plot recurs again and again. These are people whom God is wooing, calling home, assuring them, "The door is always open." Forgiveness is always possible. The only unforgivable sin in Scripture is the sin of unbelief, committed by those who don't want to repent and be saved and who never change their minds. For those who change, God stands ready to run and hug and welcome. The classic line from the film *The Hiding Place,* placed on the lips of the character playing Corrie ten Boom, the Dutch Christian woman who harbored and protected many Jews during World War II, sums it up well: "No pit is so deep that God is not deeper still."

In another setting we might dwell at more length on the prodigal son. But for a Christian congregation there is a second son and a second lesson to which we must turn. *The second lesson is that God's people ought not to begrudge his generosity for even the most wayward of sinners.*

If all Jesus wanted to teach was the possibility of repentance as long as any human being lived, he could have ended the story with verse 24 and never introduced the second son into the parable at all. The story would have been complete. But there *is* a second son and a second point with which the parable climaxes, providing a second surprise. Instead of rejoicing at the return of the prodigal, as the father did, the older son complains, gets angry, refuses to go in, and whines about how he was the one who had "slaved" all his life, about how his faithfulness had never been rewarded with such a lavish party as the father was throwing for his younger brother. The older son distances himself from his brother, speaking of him merely as "this son of yours" (v. 30). And it seems that he exaggerates or makes up information that he could not have known about the sins of his brother when he accuses him of squandering his father's property "with prostitutes." In short, the brother wants nothing to do with the prodigal.

One of the reasons I chose the three stories of Bob, Johnny, and Marla, which I told at the beginning of this message, out of many more that I could have narrated involving prodigals was because those stories also contained "older brothers"—Nancy, jealous of the gifts and zeal of her converted husband Bob; the white evangelical community, suspicious of the genuineness of Johnny's conversion and his walk with the Lord; and the leadership of churches and parachurch organizations, eager to ban Marla from missionary service because of her past divorce and/or her present spiritual gifts. Bob, Johnny, and Marla all have felt distinctively unloved by a significant sector of the Christian community, precisely where they expected a welcome. In the setting of Jesus' story, the older brother corresponds to the "Pharisees and the teachers of the law," who in verse 2 are muttering and grumbling about Jesus welcoming notorious sinners and sharing the intimacy of table fellowship with them. We need to ask how much of that hard-hearted attitude remains in us. The scribes and Pharisees all had their interpretations of Scripture to justify their attitudes, and so do we. A heart check is in order here. Are we grieving with this mistreatment, or are we, too, mentally trying to justify it? For many, the story should perhaps be titled "The Parable of the Prodigal's Older Brother."

The most important character in the parable, however, is neither son. Although most of us at one time or another can probably identify with one of the two sons, we in fact ought to be focusing more of our attention on identifying with and modeling the love of the father for both sons.

Thus *the third lesson that this parable teaches is that God in his lavish love forgives the sins of both sons and wants us to do likewise.* It's not hard to think of close parallels to the behavior of the two sons in Jesus' story. For all we know, Jesus may have known real-life equivalents in his day who could have provided the impetus for his parable. In my three twenty-first-century stories, however, there is no one corresponding to the father, no one demonstrating his extravagant love. There probably wasn't in Jesus' day either. We often hear of how lifelike parables are, if we just understand the first-century Jewish culture, and in a large measure that's true. But usually each of Jesus' parables contains certain details that turn out to be quite unrealistic, precisely to show how God's ways are radically different, and how his disciples' ways should be radically different, from typical human behavior.

This parable provides several such unrealistic details, all involving the father. The very fact that he simply agreed with his younger son's initially audacious request and divided his property sets this man off from most other fathers in his world. So too does the fact that he apparently never stopped watching for the boy, so that one day as he is looking down the village road that headed into the countryside in the direction the boy had gone—months, perhaps years earlier—he sees him from a distance. Particularly striking is his defiance of the cultural norms that dictated that a well-to-do, male head-of-household, particularly an older man, was not to be seen running in public, for that was most undignified. This man is so overjoyed to see his son return home that he flouts convention, runs down the road, and hugs him tightly. The father continues his unusual behavior in that he interrupts his son's prepared repentance speech and doesn't even allow him to get to the part about coming back simply as a slave or hired hand. It is obvious the father has never performed the common Jewish ceremony of forever disowning the boy; quite the opposite, he throws a party that has been called a "re-investiture," treating him as one would treat an honored guest, killing the fattened calf, celebrating in grand style. Nor is the father any less solicitous with the whining older brother. The older son deserved to be rebuked for his ungrateful attitude. He could enjoy his father's wealth on a daily basis. What if a special party had never been celebrated in his honor? His standard of living day after day was better than the vast majority in his world, and yet the father pleads tenderly with him, going out of the house to the fields to beg him to come in. And Jesus says that the father repeated the same refrain to his older boy that he had applied to his younger one, "This brother of yours was dead and is alive again; he was lost and is found."

I believe I was privileged to have one of the world's great fathers, who is now with the Lord. I remember one night my sophomore year in high school when I came home more than an hour after I said I would without having called to explain where I was, even though I had been doing nothing bad. My father, too, was watching for me, but he did not burst out of the house overjoyed that I had arrived. He and my mother were sitting motionless in the living room. When I came in, I received a calm but quite stern lecture about how worried they had been and what would happen if I ever behaved that way again. And that was an understandable reaction for a human parent, because my father *didn't* know what had happened to me, he *didn't* know what my attitude would be in coming home.

But God *does* know those kinds of things. God *can* act like the father in this parable, precisely because he knows all our hearts. And even at the human level, there are plenty of times when we have more than enough evidence of genuine repentance, particularly when it's been several years since someone's conversion, that our love should be similarly lavish instead of piecemeal, always suspicious of those who come from particularly sinful backgrounds or who are just different from our stereotypes of the all-American, white, evangelical, suburban, middle-class family.

After all, that stereotype corresponds to an increasingly miniscule portion of our society. At least half, and often more than half, of all adults in today's American suburbs are single, many of them divorced or living together with someone out of wedlock. Of those who are married, nearly half will become divorced at some point in their lives. There may not be prostitutes in all our neighborhoods. But there probably are victims of domestic abuse, single moms struggling to get by, divorcées coping with the stigma of broken relationships, those suffering with AIDS or HIV, the increasingly frightened and lonely elderly, people simply of other ethnic groups, and many, many others with whom our suburban churches have a poor track record of dealing. Is there someone near you in one of these situations to whom you can reach out this week? Is there someone near you to whom you should reach out this week?

The parable remains tantalizingly and deliberately open-ended. We don't know how the older son responded. We don't know how long the younger son remained repentant. Neither of those points matters. What matters is how we respond. Are there areas in which we need to repent, in which we may not be convinced that God will even have us back because of all that we have done? Know that he is longing for us to return, wooing and drawing us to himself. Are there those whose dramatic conversions we begrudge, or whose genuineness of change we unnecessarily doubt? God is calling us to break down our barriers and give those people a lavish, Christian welcome. Ultimately, we are called to imitate Christ, who defended his behavior by telling this parable that reflected the love of his and our heavenly Father in forgiving both the overt, rebellious sins against him as well as the covert, more subtle, but equally deadly sins of prejudice and backbiting. Let's take the time to identify with each of the three characters in this story and learn the lessons that emerge from reading the story through their eyes.

Commentary on "The Parable of the Prodigal Sons and Their Father"[1]

As indicated in the introduction, this passage was the one in which my hypothesis that parables make one main point per main character first emerged. So it seems appropriate to begin our series of sermons with a message on this text. The title is designed to highlight that *both* sons display rebellious behavior as well as to set the stage for my focus on each of the two sons in turn, followed by the unifying perspective of the father.

This parable may be the best known of all of Jesus' stories, though perhaps the good Samaritan is as familiar. Centuries of domestication make the need for contemporization acute. As a result, instead of just one, brief modern equivalent to the passage included somewhere in the sermon, I decided to begin with three largely parallel contemporizations. Each reflected the real situations of real people that I knew. Unlike some of the sermons in this book, this is one that I have preached, with slight modification, to congregations of several different cultures on several continents. So I consciously chose stories that would exhibit ethnic, denominational, and gender diversity, along with differences in the characters' individual personalities, with the hope that at least one of the accounts would really hit home with each person in my audiences. I deliberately changed the names and enough of the minor details to conceal the true identities of the people in the stories, but I preserved the important details that create dynamics similar to those in Jesus' parable.

Each of my three contemporizations also, by design, has two parts or paragraphs to it. The first reflects the "success story"—how each person came to faith and ministry despite a difficult background. The second reflects the growing difficulties each faced as time went on, particularly because of others' reactions. The two parts to each story thus roughly correspond to the two main divisions of Luke 15:11–32—verses 11–24 (the departure and return of the prodigal) and verses 25–32 (the resentment of the older brother).[2] Each story intentionally contains two characters (or groups of characters) who correspond to the prodigal and his older brother, respectively, in each instance in at least two ways. Like the prodigal, Bob, Johnny, and Marla all had periods when they were far from the Lord in dramatic ways, and all had dramatic turnarounds in their lives. Like the older brother, Nancy, the white suburban donors, and the administrators of the missions agencies all appeared to reflect a mature reliance on God until one investigated their attitudes in more detail. I did not choose single individuals to correspond to the older brother in the second two stories, so that the application to the typically white middle-class congregations I address would prove more incisive. The remaining details in each story simply reflect what actually happened; they were not intentionally included to parallel subordinate details in the biblical parable. This reflects my conviction, along with the vast majority of contemporary interpreters, that the subordinate details of Jesus' parables were not intended to be allegorized.

As in most of my sermons, I withheld the reading of the Scripture until after my introduction, in this case comprising three somewhat lengthy illustrations. The title of the sermon would have alerted listeners to my text, so that they could think about possible parallels in advance of hearing the passage read. But the three accounts contained just enough distinctive twists so that, I hoped, people would deeply engage the modern stories before jumping too quickly to Jesus' narrative. I first preached this sermon as part of a longer series on the parables that I preached over several weeks. Only in the first of those messages did I go into any detail as to my theory of parable interpretation. Here I transitioned from text to body of sermon simply by means of the brief announcement that we would be looking for three points from the three characters. Even in contexts where I have preached this as a single message by itself, I have not always taken the time to explain my approach. Audiences are so accustomed to hearing three points in a sermon that they are not surprised. A detailed discourse on hermeneutics may actually distract from the power of the stories themselves.

The parable may also be divided into three parts, almost as naturally as the two-part division noted earlier. Thus verses 11–19 narrate the departure of the younger son from the father, with the focus on the prodigal's profligacy; verses 20–24 present the prodigal's return to his father, with the focus on the father's welcome; and verses 25–32 depict the older brother's reaction to his father, with the focus on the older brother's resentment.[3] So a somewhat more traditionally structured exposition could still make the same three points but follow the text sequentially throughout the whole message. It seemed to me, however, that the climactic point that unifies the entire parable (and reflects the most central point for those who insist on identifying one) was the father's magnanimous love for both sons,[4] so I chose a thematic sequence in order to end with that point.

The comparatively brief body of my sermon thus begins with the best known of the parable's lessons: the model of the prodigal's repentance that should be imitated by all who may need to repent. I point out the original symbolism of the prodigal according to its larger context in Luke 15. Relying particularly on the research of Kenneth Bailey, I stress that many facets of the prodigal's behavior would have been viewed as extreme in Jesus' world. Jesus is deliberately painting a portrait designed to shock.[5] We don't necessarily recognize that fact in our Western culture, so it is important to highlight it. From a quick survey of the details of the parable, I turn to reinforcing the lesson for today. I stress this point the least of the three, because I have preached this message to largely if not exclusively Christian audiences. I do not want to neglect it altogether, however, for I hope that some in my audiences may be visiting as unbelievers and that God will use my message to bring them closer to him.[6] For those who may think that they are too far from God ever to return, I want to insist that they are not.

My transition to the second point, the lesson to be learned from the older brother, explains why I haven't lingered longer on the first point. While I did not take the time to explain my theory of parable interpretation earlier, I pause long enough here to explain why I think at least *this* parable makes more than one point. Here most commentators agree, even those who think this is an exceptional passage because of its additional lesson(s).[7] Again I take roughly one paragraph to explain the details in the parable about the older brother and another one to identify the "older brothers" in my three contemporizations. Because I suspect that more people in my congregations will have attitudes similar to those of the older brother than to those of the prodigal, I also include a diagnostic tool for listeners to apply to themselves—are they likewise trying to justify the behavior of the modern-day equivalents to the older brother in my three stories?[8]

Finally, I transition to the third and climactic point, state the lesson that stems from the father in the parable, and point out that there was no father figure in my three contemporizations. Indeed, the very uniqueness of the father in Jesus' parable makes it difficult to find current real-life equivalents, which is precisely part of what I want to stress and why I think this lesson is the one most contemporary Christian audiences need most.[9] I also "sneak in" another hermeneutical principle that is central to my approach: looking for the most *unrealistic* elements of the story—given that parables are usually more lifelike than not—as a key to the symbolic or spiritual meaning of the narrative.[10] I spend the most time unpacking the details of the father's distinctive behavior, again largely following Bailey, because it is here that I see the parable's most difficult and important challenge.

I like to disclose something of my own life in most of my messages. In this one, the disclosure comes as I transition to the conclusion, reflecting on what a wonderful model I had in my earthly father and yet observing how differently he responded (and understandably so) at one key moment in my life when I had disobeyed him. I hope listeners will reflect on their own parents at this point as well and relive a broad cross-section of positive and negative memories. In a world in which many people do not have even generally good experiences with their biological fathers, it is important to stress how God as father is *different* from even the best earthly fathers.[11] The typical Jewish father would have forever "cut off" his son with a formal ceremony—recall Tevye with his youngest daughter in "Fiddler on the Roof." This father does the exact opposite with his "re-investiture."[12]

The conclusion of the sermon recaps all three lessons, inviting listeners
to put themselves, in turn, in the place of each of the three characters
of the parable, even as I think Jesus intended his original audience to
do. Some people will relate more naturally to one character than to
another, but everyone should try on all three roles for size. In a culture
that has spawned a widespread "victim mentality," I want to move people
beyond the issue of how others have treated them to the question of
how they are treating others, whether those "others" are more like the
prodigal, more like the older brother, or anywhere in between. I give
specific examples of what many such people might look like and then
end with the great, unanswered question designed to deflect attention
from Jesus' story back to the real world of his listeners. It doesn't matter
at all how Jesus might have imagined his characters responding later
on; they were fictitious people in the first place. It matters more what
happened to Bob, Johnny, and Marla. (In case the reader *is* interested,
they are all doing very well today; the situations have all resolved for
the better.) But what matters the most is how those hearing or reading
my sermon are responding to others in their lives.[13] That is the thought
with which I conclude.

2

Can I Be Saved without Stewardship?

Luke 16:19–31

I magine a home in which steak or various kinds of seafood are eaten almost every night for dinner. The family serves vintage drinks from its wine cellar whenever it likes. The house has ten rooms for a family consisting of two parents with three children. There are also ten televisions and ten telephones, one of each per room, with a master switchboard controlling the telephone network in the kitchen. Three late-model luxury cars adorn a large garage. A live-in nanny looks after the children when the parents are away for a short time, and a gardener comes to care for the one-acre lot that includes a built-in Olympic-sized swimming pool in the backyard. Believe it or not, I once lived in precisely such a home in 1978 for two weeks in the suburban Chicago area. It was owned by a wealthy lawyer and his family whom I'd come to know through tutoring their children in junior high and high school math. Now they were off to Europe for a more extended vacation, a longer time away than that for which they were comfortable leaving their children simply with the nanny. They invited me to live in their home, enjoy their amenities, drive their cars, and watch their children in what in those days was called "sub-parenting." Most of their neighbors lived similarly. The generosity of their payment for my services helped considerably in defraying some of my expenses while I was a seminary student. There are many such homes and families in the large cities of our world, but this is the only one with which I have ever had this extensive firsthand experience.

Now imagine a very different kind of neighborhood, a rat- and cockroach-infested slum. Houses here are made out of cardboard and canvas with corrugated aluminum roofing. Typically they have only one or at the most two rooms. This neighborhood has no swimming pool, not even running water or electricity. Water is purchased from vendors who bring it in on large trucks once a week. Neighbors haul huge barrels or buckets that are filled by a hose from the trucks. They then must dole out the water carefully so that it lasts until the vendors return the next week. This neighborhood has an 80 percent unemployment rate, not because people are lazy but because there are no jobs to be had. Many of these people eat only one healthy, nourishing meal a day and that thanks to a central cooperative soup kitchen where neighbors pool their meager resources, buy in bulk, serve one another, and thus eat more cheaply than they otherwise could. But the organizers of the kitchen have to beware of being perceived as too cooperative or communal in their efforts, lest they be labeled Communists and suddenly disappear one night, never to return again, presumably as victims of the vigilante squads clandestinely supported by the right-wing military regime in power. Believe it or not, I spent considerable time in precisely such neighborhoods for nearly two weeks in 1990 in Lima, Peru, though I retreated to considerably better accommodations (that Americans would call lower middle-class) each evening. Certainly many such neighborhoods exist throughout the Third World, many of them comprising most of the largest cities. But again, this is the only one of which I have such extensive firsthand experience.

Middle-class Western Christians who encounter these discrepancies between rich and poor "up close and personal" initially react in quite different ways. Many are shocked and horrified. How can such injustice be tolerated? Some with very sensitive consciences and high idealism propose a radical overhaul of our social structures, from national health care systems to government-subsidized housing to full-fledged socialist economies. Some would accomplish their ends even by revolutionary violence, if necessary, though the track record of nearly a century of Marxism in various countries discloses only a little success in narrowing the gap between the haves and have-nots of our world.

Other equally concerned Christians argue for exactly the opposite approach. What is needed is more pure capitalism, they argue. The problem is that we, and often other nations, don't have *enough* true free-market economic systems in place. Capitalism is not to be blamed because pure capitalism hasn't yet appeared or been given a chance. The rich and the multinational corporations are taxed too much. There is not enough incentive for workers to get off welfare, and, to use the term that became common in the 1980s in the Reagan years, what is needed is a "trickle-down" economic system. Some even promote police or state violence to accomplish their goals, if necessary. But twelve years of the purest form yet of such capitalist forces in the United States in the 1980s and early 1990s simply led to the greatest disparity between rich and poor in American history.

A third reaction is quite different still. Perhaps as a defense mechanism to cope with the enormity of the problem, perhaps due to misinformation or prejudice or maybe for some other reason, some Christians simply are not prepared to help at all. They would rather blame the poor for their problems, assuming all or most poor people are lazy, many criminal, still more irresponsible, and in general more non-Christian than most rich folks. All who really want to, these believers argue, could pull themselves up by their own bootstraps. Most people who are poor simply get what they deserve.

Now however appropriate this last view may be in isolated situations, perhaps more often in American slums than in the Third World, it's particularly inappropriate as a global generalization, as virtually anyone who knows a large number of poor people on several continents of our planet will attest. Certainly it doesn't fit the two scenes that I outlined reflecting my own experience, because the community in Lima was composed largely of evangelical Christians and the wealthy neighborhood in the suburban Chicago area was a Jewish neighborhood, hostile to Christianity. And yet for most of the last half century the one neighborhood has gotten consistently poorer, while the other has grown increasingly richer.

How would Jesus have reacted if he had seen such socioeconomic discrepancies in his day? The fact is that he did, and usually, as so often today in many parts of the Third World, juxtaposed starkly side by side. Jesus even once told a story about precisely such a situation, and his response fits none of the three models of Christian reaction we have so far sketched. The story begins in Luke 16:19.

We read in verses 19–21,

> There was a rich man who was dressed in purple and fine linen and lived in luxury every day. At his gate was laid a beggar named Lazarus, covered with sores and longing to eat what fell from the rich man's table. Even the dogs came and licked his sores.

Jesus' story begins by epitomizing the extremes of rich and poor in first-century Israel, with one man living on "easy street" and the other suffering in agony. Only a handful of the wealthiest in Jesus' world would have fit the description of this rich man robed in purple, the color of royalty, and dressed in fine linen, a fabric available at that time only to the wealthiest. The expression "lived in luxury" (v. 19) elsewhere often implies sumptuous feasting, which fits well here since Lazarus longed to eat even the leftovers from the rich man's banquet. The beggar's plight was more common, but the depiction of Lazarus is still extreme. He "was laid" at the rich man's gate, suggesting that perhaps he was crippled and unable to get there without help. He is covered with sores—open wounds—reminiscent of the sufferings of Job in the Old Testament, and the dogs who come and lick the sores are not the friendly pets we think of in our culture. The Israelites did not keep dogs as house pets in those days. Rather, these are the scavenger dogs roaming throughout the villages, and licking Lazarus's sores merely increases his torment. The fact that he quickly dies could suggest he was already close to death.

Yet Jesus' audience, or at least a significant part of it, would have been steeped in the belief that riches were a blessing for obedience, with suffering a punishment for sin. And they could point to at least some Old Testament texts to support those beliefs. Jesus' listeners were thus almost certainly astonished, and quite probably even outraged, when they heard the way Jesus continued his story in verses 22–26.

> The time came when the beggar died and the angels carried him to Abraham's side. The rich man also died and was buried. In Hades, where he was in torment, he looked up and saw Abraham far away, with Lazarus by his side. So he called to him, "Father Abraham, have pity on me and send Lazarus to dip the tip of his finger in water and cool my tongue, because I am in agony in this fire."
>
> But Abraham replied, "Son, remember that in your lifetime you received your good things, while Lazarus received bad things, but now he is comforted here and you are in agony. And besides all this, between us and you a great chasm has been set in place, so those who want to go from here to you cannot, nor can anyone cross over from there to us."

Jesus completely reverses the conventional expectation concerning who winds up in heaven and hell, or to use the language of the parable, by Abraham's side (close to the presence of God) and Hades, or Sheol, the shadowy underworld of Old Testament times. Jesus uses the language and imagery of important strands of conventional Jewish folklore. Thus these verses should not be pressed as if they were meant to teach in detail doctrine on the last days or the life to come. But what is crystal clear, even from the metaphorical imagery, is that there is not the slightest possibility of reversal or even alleviation of the rich man's punishment and suffering.

In professing Christianity today, we too occasionally find parallels to the Jewish expectation that Jesus countered. The so-called prosperity gospel (or "health-wealth" movement) claims that, if people just have enough faith, God will heal them of their sicknesses and grant them material riches. But even in the Old Testament that was only part of the story of God's arrangement with Israel. Proverbs, the Book of Job, Ecclesiastes, and many of the psalms speak out about the righteous poor and the unjust rich. God's promise was never so much about individual blessing for one person's faithfulness as about national blessing for the obedience of the people, and especially their leaders, as a whole. Israel could look forward to living in its land in peace and prosperity during those periods in which the country overall lived largely in faithfulness and obedience to God. But that was also a unique arrangement with Israel, which God did not make with any other nation in Old Testament times, and which is conspicuously absent from the New Testament altogether as anything the church can appropriate.

But I suspect that this is not the issue that troubles most of us. We undoubtedly know, or at least know of, many rich people who have not deserved what they got, and many of us perhaps know of at least some poor people who are relatively innocent victims of circumstances outside their control.

More likely a key issue for us is the lack of any reference in this story to anyone's faith. The rich man seems to be condemned simply because he was enormously wealthy. The poor beggar Lazarus seems to have been rewarded in the next life simply to compensate for his horrible poverty and suffering in this world. This does not seem to be the salvation by grace through faith that we know so well from the apostle Paul, and even from Jesus elsewhere, but rather salvation or damnation by socioeconomic bracket! The last five verses of this parable, I suggest, disprove this notion. Look at verses 27–31.

> He answered, "Then I beg you, father, send Lazarus to my family, for I have five brothers. Let him warn them, so that they will not also come to this place of torment."
> Abraham replied, "They have Moses and the Prophets; let them listen to them."
> "No, father Abraham," he said, "but if someone from the dead goes to them, they will repent."
> He said to him, "If they do not listen to Moses and the Prophets, they will not be convinced even if someone rises from the dead."

In his dialogue with Abraham, the rich man pleads for a special revelation to his brothers who are alive on earth and thus still have the chance to "repent" (v. 30). This suggests that he realizes that *his* problem, too, was that he had never repented—never truly had a relationship with God during his lifetime. And that makes the inference reasonable that Lazarus did have such a relationship, though it's never spelled out. It's interesting, though, that this is the only parable of Jesus in which a character is given a name, and for that reason some have wondered if it was not a fictitious story but rather a true account of people Jesus knew. The form of the passage, however, perfectly matches that of many, many other parables of Jesus. There's probably a quite different reason that Lazarus is named here. Lazarus, you see, is the Greek equivalent of the Hebrew Eleazar, which means "God helps." What is more, the best known Eleazar in Old Testament times was Abraham's faithful servant. And isn't it interesting that instead of God speaking here (or a master, king, father, or shepherd figure standing for God, as happens consistently in Jesus' parables), it is Abraham who functions as God's spokesman? A Jewish audience steeped in their Scriptures—our Old Testament—would almost certainly have made the link between Abraham and Lazarus and assumed that Jesus was implying the presence of the poor man's piety.

It still remains striking, though, that Jesus never spells out any of this explicitly. He no doubt assumed that his clues were adequate, particularly regarding the state of the rich man on whom most of his attention is centered.

But what is the tip-off that this man had never repented? When we recall that a full-orbed biblical definition of repentance is a change of action and not merely sorrow for sin, an answer emerges clearly. The rich man was aware of deep human physical suffering in his immediate proximity. He was in a position to offer enormous help, but he refused to lift so much as a finger. As a Jew who knew "Moses and the Prophets"—the legal and the prophetic portions of Scripture—he would have been familiar with the major biblical theme of giving generously to the needy, whether from a text in the law of Moses, like Deuteronomy 15:11 ("There will always be poor people in the land. . . . Therefore I command you to be openhanded toward the poor and needy in your land" [NIV]) or from a classic prophetic text like Micah 6:8 ("Act justly and . . . love mercy and . . . walk humbly with your God" [NIV]). Countless passages of Scripture in between prove equally pointed. Yet this rich man did absolutely nothing to help.

The sting in the tale is that such teaching remains in force in New Testament times, whatever differences appear as one shifts from Old to New Testament teaching. The concern for well-to-do believers to share generously from their surplus remains unchanged. James 2:14–17 says, "What good is it, my brothers and sisters, if people claim to have faith but have no deeds? Can such faith save them? Suppose a brother or sister is without clothes and daily food. If one of you says to them, 'Go in peace; keep warm and well fed,' but does nothing about their physical needs, what good is it? The same way, faith by itself, if it is not accompanied by action, is dead." Just a few short epistles later, 1 John 3:17 declares:

"If any one of you has material possessions and sees a brother or sister in need but has no pity on them, how can the love of God be in you?" And again one could turn to many other like-minded texts.

Now occasionally some extremist in Christian circles declares that it is impossible to be both rich and Christian. That's not what Scripture teaches, or it would eliminate every one of us in middle-class Western Christianity, we who are filthy rich by global standards. What Scripture does consistently teach, however, is that it is impossible to be both rich and Christian without simultaneously being generous and sharing what we have with others. The most extensive teaching passage in the New Testament on the topic is 2 Corinthians 8–9. In 8:13–15, Paul explicitly addresses the question of whether he is asking those who are currently rich to trade places with the poor, and he explicitly denies this. Paul simply calls people to give out of their surplus, but to be ruthlessly honest about how much is surplus!

A husband and wife team of researchers, the founders of empty tomb, inc., in Champaign, Illinois, have tracked American and American Christian expenditures as well as global needs. John and Sylvia Ronsvalle have estimated that $30–50 billion a year could meet the most essential human needs around the world. "Projects for clean water and sanitation, prenatal and infant/maternal care, basic education, immunizations, and long-term development efforts are among the activities that could help overcome the poverty conditions that now kill and maim so many children and adults."[1]

The Ronsvalles go on to write, "That figure of $30 to $50 billion may sound like anything but good news. God may be generous, you may agree, but has he been *that* generous? Consider this: If church members in the United States would increase their giving to 10 percent of their income, there would be more than $65 billion per year available for overseas ministries and $15 billion a year for meeting the needs of our neighbors across town, even while maintaining current congregational programs, including building projects."[2]

The problem, of course, is that most Christians don't and won't give 10 percent to the Lord's work. The current averages for American Christians in general run somewhere between 2 and 3 percent. Evangelicals, at best, give only about one percentage point more. Early in our married life, while living for three years in Scotland in what by American standards could only have been called inner-city conditions, fellowshipping with very fiscally frugal, conservative Scottish Baptists, and reading Ron Sider's *Rich Christians in an Age of Hunger* when it was hot off the press, my wife and I became convinced that passages like 2 Corinthians 8:13–15 led logically to what Sider called a "graduated tithe." We began giving 10 percent to the Lord's work while we were living on a shoestring and giving just about all that we earned (and some that we borrowed) to the university in which I was doing my doctoral studies. We trusted that God would increase our annual income above mere cost-of-living increases so that we could then give a higher percentage. We didn't follow any fixed formula but simply committed to increase that percentage as our income grew. After twenty-three years of marriage, our giving, both to our church and to other Christian organizations and individuals who are concerned to meet the holistic needs of people's bodies and spirits, has topped 40 percent of our family's annual gross income. It can be done, though one has to make choices along the way as to how one spends one's money. We have some inherited investments that have done very well and enabled us to be more generous than many could. But still large numbers of middle- and upper-class Christians in the Western world could do far more than the 3 to 4 percent they currently average. Many could do considerably better than the 10 percent that some churches mandate, though the New Testament never fixes a percentage and though many of the members of those churches never follow the mandates of their leaders.

The point, however, is not the percentage of one's giving but one's attitude. Does a parable or a sermon like this make you ask yourself, "How can I do more?" or do you start to do a slow boil and get upset with the preacher (or perhaps even with Jesus) for having raised the topic in so pointed a fashion? I've titled this sermon "Can I Be Saved without Stewardship?"—that is, without generous Christian giving of many different kinds over a lifetime. I believe it's as logically impossible as saying we've experienced God's forgiveness without forgiving others or that we know his love without loving others. He has been phenomenally generous in giving us eternal life, and when he has blessed us with material abundance on top of that, how can we not share generously from it if his Spirit truly dwells in us and guides us?

We read 1 John 3:17 earlier. It's fitting to close by reading the next two verses in that same context—1 John 3:18–19: "Dear children, let us not love with word or tongue but with actions and in truth. This is how we know that we belong to the truth and how we set our hearts at rest in his presence." May God help us to be obedient and demonstrate that we truly have experienced his love and generosity in our hearts.

Commentary on "Can I Be Saved without Stewardship?"

The parable of the rich man and Lazarus follows a similar structure to the parable of the prodigal son. Abraham represents God as the master figure, while Lazarus and the rich man clearly function as contrasting subordinates. Although the surprise concerning which one turns out to be the good model is not as drastic as in the parable of the prodigal, it remains likely that many in Jesus' audience would have assumed the rich man was blessed by God for his piety and that the dying beggar was being punished for some sin.[3]

Despite the similarities in the structures of the two parables, I have adopted a slightly different structure for my sermon here. I begin with rough, contemporary equivalents to the lifestyles of first the rich man and then Lazarus. Next I proceed sequentially through the text of the parable and conclude with fairly lengthy reflections on contemporary application. Three lessons emerge from this parable, just as they did with the parable of the prodigal: the eternal punishment of the unrepentant rich, the eternal reward for the pious poor, and the revelation of these truths through Abraham, Moses, and the prophets.[4] Each of these points is implicit within my exposition, but I have chosen not to spell them out as I did with the three lessons in the prodigal son or to structure the body of my sermon to correspond to them. Rather I have sought to focus more on the big idea of stewardship: those who call themselves Christians must demonstrate the reality of their profession by giving generously of their surplus resources.[5] That is also the reason for my provocative title, "Can I Be Saved without Stewardship?"

The first two paragraphs of the message form the contemporization. As I point out, these are not the only or even the most extreme examples of the disparities between rich and poor in the world today, but my firsthand involvement with each makes them personally more gripping. Besides, I want my audiences to recognize that I am not speaking abstractly about something I have not intensely wrestled with through personal experience. That the one setting was primarily non-Christian (Jewish) and the other primarily evangelical Christian also creates important parallelism with the rich man and Lazarus, respectively, but I deliberately withhold that information at the outset in hopes of creating the same surprise that Jesus' story did.

I have spoken on stewardship often enough over the years that I can anticipate key reactions of Christian listeners. Hence, I felt it was necessary to discuss the three main ways contemporary believers react to the gap between the haves and have-nots in our world. That discussion forms the bridge between my introductory contemporizations and the comparatively short body of the sermon. I begin with the least common reaction among North Americans (pro-socialist), so that as I criticize it, I will gain the support of and establish common ground with most of my audience. (I have also preached this sermon in Latin America, but only among evangelicals, who, interestingly, were even less inclined to socialism than their North American counterparts.) I pose the second reaction in fairly extreme form (strongly pro-capitalist) and as the diametric opposite of the first reaction so that again a majority of my listeners will stay with me, even if they recognize that I am moving closer to a view that many of them might endorse. Based on current Christian giving patterns, however, I suspected that the largest segment of my listeners would be the most apathetic ones, so I save my description of their approach and my response to it for last. The final paragraph before the body of the sermon then appeals to today's fascination with the question, "What would Jesus do?" and attempts to heighten interest by suggesting that Jesus' response would fall into none of the three previous categories.[6]

As with my focus on the details of the prodigal son, my exposition of the contents of this parable proves fairly short. Given the length of my introduction and the amount of practical application with which I wanted to end, I was forced to be brief at this juncture. But the passage is well known, even if not as well known as the prodigal, and the exegetical issues can be succinctly explained. Breaking the passage into verses 19–21, 22–26, and 27–31 creates a very rough correspondence, in turn, to each of the three main characters, with the circumstances of one individual most highlighted in each section—the plight of Lazarus, the fate of the rich man, and the role of God's spokesmen—even though a strictly inductive focus on the structure of the passage might divide it at other points.[7] Thus, even though I don't spell out three explicit points as in my sermon on the prodigal, the body of the message retains a tripartite structure, with all the rhetorical advantages that go along with it.

Because there are natural, episodic breaks after verses 21 and 26, I read the parable in stages as I proceed through the sermon rather than all at once. My goal in the first segment is to highlight the features that show both the rich man and Lazarus as epitomizing social and economic extremes in their society.[8] I also note the likelihood that at least some in Jesus' audience would assume the rich man was going to be rewarded rather than Lazarus. In the second segment, I highlight the "great reversal"[9] and note in passing that the details, especially about the afterlife, should not be taken too literally. My main concern in applying this segment is to counter the contemporary "health-wealth" heresy.[10] But, as in my exposition of the parable of the prodigal, I am building toward what I believe is the climactic point—the final part of the dialogue between the rich man and Abraham in verses 27–31. It is climactic because it is last, because it is where Jesus entirely diverges from the Egyptian and Jewish folktales that partially paralleled verses 19–26, and because it represents the point that evangelical audiences typically most need to hear.

One of the problems with much evangelical preaching is the interpretation of Scripture as if Paul wrote every book in it! Our simplest presentations of the gospel owe so much to Paul's letters, particularly Romans, rightly stressing justification by faith alone, that we unwittingly assume that other biblical writers have identical emphases. But it is unlikely that anyone who read the parable of the rich man and Lazarus as his or her first exposure to biblical teaching would ever come up with the idea of justification by faith! It is not that I believe Jesus contradicts Paul, as will become clear as the sermon nears its end; it is just that we must hear Jesus in his own right.[11] Thus, although he often talks about faith, his characteristic term for what makes people right with God is "repentance." And it is precisely repentance that has not characterized this rich man and his family (v. 30). Meanwhile there are hints that make it probable that Jesus thought of Lazarus as one of the pious poor. But what hits us over the head is not the inward attitudes of these men toward God, but the outward behavior of the rich man, along with Abraham's climactic emphasis on the sufficiency of the Bible to inculcate our responsibility toward the needy.[12]

I therefore highlight sample Scriptures from *both* testaments to illustrate how true Abraham's remark proves, first for Jews in Jesus' day and then for Christians in ours. I deal with one final, frequent objection to generous stewardship—"Are you calling us to trade places with the poor?" My goal as I begin my conclusion is not to entice large numbers of people to suddenly change their giving patterns drastically. I realize it is highly unlikely that one message will ever accomplish this. Indeed, many folks fail to improve *at all* in their stewardship exactly because all they've ever heard are more radical appeals that, rightly or wrongly, they believe they could never heed.[13] So I quote some statistics that should encourage people about the good that even moving *up* to a tithe could accomplish (without arguing that a tithe is mandated in the New Testament). But then, precisely because I am convinced many could do much more, as well as to demonstrate that I am not calling anyone to do anything I have not already done myself, I share our family's own experience practicing the graduated tithe.[14] Yet I recognize that it is the heart attitude toward giving and not the amount or percentage given that matters most with God. So I include a method for people to diagnose their own attitudes in my closing paragraph. I also allude for the first time to the sermon's title and show how I believe the answer to the question, "Can I be saved without stewardship?" is no, but I do so without violating Paul's (and Jesus') principle of salvation by faith rather than works. It has been encouraging for listeners to tell me that, when they knew in advance I was going to preach on this passage, they expected that they would feel very guilty over their lack of stewardship, but instead they came away more encouraged by what they were already giving and more motivated to share even more.

3

Who Is My Most Important Neighbor?

Luke 10:25–37

Not long ago, a prominent Denver news story related the tragic events of the apparent suicide of Jeannie VanVelkinburgh, a woman who a few years back had been paralyzed by gunshot wounds inflicted on her after she tried unsuccessfully to intervene and save the life of an African immigrant who was being murdered in public on a downtown street corner. Both when the original murder took place as well as after Jeannie's death the media referred to her as a "good Samaritan." In fact, when people intervene to help those in peril in the public arena, our culture regularly refers to them as good Samaritans. Over thirty American states have good Samaritan laws, which protect from prosecution people who attempt to aid victims in such situations and in doing so hurt or injure an attacker. Countless towns throughout the English-speaking world have hospitals that are similarly named Good Samaritan. The very word "Samaritan" has become synonymous in our culture with one who offers compassion or mercy, perhaps at substantial risk to herself or himself.

But should Christians intervene the way Jeannie did? Most would probably agree with her attempts to ward off the murderers. But what about less life-threatening situations? Should Christians stop and offer roadside help to every stranded motorist? What would you do? Certainly the more common pattern—whether in our news reports or in our own experiences—is the situation in which no "good Samaritan" ever appears on the scene. We often hear of muggings during which neighbors didn't even call the police from the safety of their own homes for fear of getting involved. Numerous modern settings raise afresh all the difficult questions that surrounded the original story Jesus told that came to be known as the good Samaritan and from which all subsequent uses of the expression derive. We find the passage in Luke 10:25–37.

> On one occasion an expert in the law stood up to test Jesus. "Teacher," he asked, "what must I do to inherit eternal life?"
>
> "What is written in the law?" he replied. "How do you read it?"
>
> He answered: "'Love the Lord your God with all your heart and with all your soul and with all your strength and with all your mind'; and, 'Love your neighbor as yourself.'"
>
> "You have answered correctly," Jesus replied. "Do this and you will live."
>
> But he wanted to justify himself, so he asked Jesus, "And who is my neighbor?"
>
> In reply Jesus said: "A man was going down from Jerusalem to Jericho, when he fell into the hands of robbers. They stripped him of his clothes, beat him and went away, leaving him half dead. A priest happened to be going down the same road, and when he saw the man, he passed by on the other side. So too, a Levite, when he came to the place and saw him, passed by on the other side. But a Samaritan, as he traveled, came where the man was; and when he saw him, he took pity on him. He went to him and bandaged his wounds, pouring on oil and wine. Then he put the man on his own donkey, brought him to an inn and took care of him. The next day he took out two silver coins and gave them to the innkeeper. 'Look after him,' he said, 'And when I return, I will reimburse you for any extra expense you may have.'
>
> "Which of these three do you think was a neighbor to the man who fell into the hands of the robbers?"
>
> The expert in the law replied, "The one who had mercy on him."
>
> Jesus told him, "Go and do likewise."

A study that has since become famous took place at Princeton Seminary in 1970. It involved forty seminary students as part of a class on religious education and vocation. The students did not know that they were the subjects of a psychological study. They were broken into two groups. One was told that they were to give a talk on possible careers that a degree in religious education could afford. The second group was given the task of expounding on the parable of the good Samaritan. Both groups were told that in a few minutes they would be asked to go to two different buildings on campus and give extemporaneous talks on the topics that had been assigned to them to see how well they thought and spoke on their feet without much advance notice. Each of the two groups was then subdivided further into three subgroups corresponding to the various degrees of haste that they were told they needed. One-third in each half of the class was told that they were already a bit late for their appointments and that they should hurry across campus. A second third of both groups was simply told to go at once and proceed quickly. And a third group was told they had about three to five minutes before they were expected at the next building. Princeton's campus is an urban one, and a man was planted en route in an alleyway that all of the students had to go through. It was winter, the weather was approximately five degrees Fahrenheit outside, and the man was slumped over, coughing and not adequately dressed for the weather. Of the forty seminarians unknowingly being tested, only sixteen offered any kind of help—most of those by telling people in the next building about the man they had seen, a few by actually stopping and seeing if the man was okay. The study determined that there was a direct correlation between those who were told they were in the greatest hurry and those who did not offer any kind of help at all. But there was no correlation between who was most likely to stop and their assigned topics, whether or not they were speaking about the good Samaritan. Nor was there any correlation between the likelihood of their helping and the nature of their religious commitment or maturity as Christians.

Similar studies have been repeated with varying details in a number of parts of the country in the thirty-plus years since the Princeton experiment. Researchers have discovered that rural people are more likely to help than urban folk and that Midwesterners are more likely to help than those from either the East or the West. Religion and personality seemingly affect the nature of the help offered but have no demonstrable influence on the likelihood of whether someone will help at all. What in the world are we to make of such studies? Is this merely an indictment of the sinfulness of all humanity, Christians included? Is it a pointer to the amount of fear our violent society has produced in us, especially among urban dwellers? Or is it possible we have partially misunderstood Jesus' parable? I suspect the answer to all three questions is yes. But today let's focus on the interpretation of the text. I believe that, as with many of Jesus' parables, three key lessons emerge from the good Samaritan based on the three main characters: the Samaritan; the priest and the Levite, treated together as one; and the man who was wounded, robbed, and left for dead. But in my experience, most expositions of this story never get past the first of the three lessons. We'll begin with that one and then try to press further.

Clearly a central lesson of the parable of the good Samaritan is that *believers are called to show compassion to anyone who is in need.* Obviously there is an example here that we are supposed to imitate. The very last line of the passage says that Jesus told the lawyer, "Go and do likewise" (v. 37). But do *what* likewise? Jesus could hardly expect twenty-first-century Americans to find a donkey, secure some oil and wine, look for every needy person, transport them to the local innkeeper, and pay him with two silver coins. We have to ask what a contemporization, what a modern equivalent to this passage might look like. Again, in my experience, by far and away the most common illustration contemporary preachers use is the person whose car is broken down by the side of the road. But I must confess that in thirty-two years of driving I have never stopped to help a stranded motorist. Maybe you'll think I'm just rationalizing, but I think I have some good excuses. The first is not a particularly Christian one: I am so hopeless when it comes to fixing cars that I would seldom be of any help at all. And most of my life requires me to drive in town or on major highways where there are regular ways of receiving help from people who are competent in car repair. More recently, in our high-tech age, it's far more likely that a stranded motorist is going to have a cell phone than I will, since we are still a one-cell-phone family, and usually I make sure it's my wife or daughter who carries it when they drive.

But I remember just a few winters ago visiting a friend in rural Montana not too many miles from Yellowstone Park. And I remember him driving me through the northern entrance to the park and on some of the roads that remained open in the winter. As he navigated one heavily snow-packed road, he suddenly hit a slippery patch, and we spun off into a ditch. I was grateful that at least one rural person in Montana *did* believe in helping stranded motorists, because, on a day when not too many cars were going through Yellowstone, he came by after just a few minutes with a chain and was able to link it to a hook on the back of his pickup and pull us out.

The road that Jesus describes in this parable was probably far more like that semi-isolated, snow-packed, slippery road in Yellowstone in the middle of winter than the highways and streets in and around Denver that I drive most of the time. In fact, the road from Jerusalem to Jericho, the remains of which can still be seen from a modern highway that takes pretty much the same path descending thirty-three hundred feet in just seventeen miles through very rugged desert and wilderness terrain—that Jerusalem-Jericho road was notoriously dangerous, with robbers regularly hiding out and preying on vulnerable individuals who weren't part of a larger caravan of travelers. Perhaps the Samaritan was someone like our helper in Montana and realized there might not be anyone else who would rescue the man who had been attacked. Some of the follow-up studies to the 1970 experiment at Princeton have demonstrated that when people do suspect they are perhaps the only ones who can offer help, they are more likely to intervene than when they think there are other methods of needy people getting the aid they deserve.

But I think we need to reflect much more broadly and imaginatively than just in terms of roadside breakdowns or robberies. Even in Jesus' world, the details of the man's misfortune (v. 30) and the kind of help the Samaritan offered (vv. 34–35) could have been described in dozens of different ways. What is crucial to making the Samaritan such a powerful example was his attitude. Verse 33 says that when the Samaritan saw the injured man "he took pity on him." The expression could also be translated "had compassion on him." And verse 37 confirms that the lawyer picked up this central characteristic when he refers back to the Samaritan simply as "the one who had mercy on" the wounded man. When we look at the story in that light, we are reminded that there are people all around us in our world who are in need of mercy—physically, emotionally, and spiritually. Do we share the Samaritan's compassion for the many needy people in our world, or have we become calloused through a lifetime of watching thousands of acts of violence on television, in the movies, and even in real-life newsreels? Is one of our defense mechanisms against being overwhelmed by the despair of the world that we put up emotional force fields to shield us from their impact? Each of us probably reacts differently to our violent world in light of a whole host of varying personal circumstances and experiences and depending on the particular needs that we encounter. Is it a hitchhiker, a downtown beggar, or a man in the suburbs with a cardboard sign asking for money by a major intersection? Is it a poorly dressed visitor coming to our local church asking for help? And what if any of these situations reflect scams by con artists, as some of them in fact may? In certain cases the most compassionate response may be to refuse the request. As Augustine once commented on the Sermon on the Mount, when Jesus says to give to everyone who asks, he doesn't say to give everything that he or she asks for.

The more important question, therefore, is if we have an ongoing commitment in one fashion or another to supporting ministries that make a priority of the homeless, those who don't qualify for welfare or adequate health care, the physically challenged, the victims of abuse, the forgotten nursing home patients, and so on. Is there at least one area in each of our lives in which we're personally involved in the ministry of compassion for hurting people in our world? For many years in our family it was my wife's volunteering at the Inner City Health Center in the Five Points neighborhood of Denver and the periodic spin-off opportunities that I had to help and to get to know people involved in a whole variety of inner-city ministries. More recently, through our church's involvement with the Denver Rescue Mission, we have helped to lead a service one Friday evening each quarter for several years. Again, Fran has done far more than I have. Our family has also been involved in raising the money, in making preparations, in buying furniture, in renting an apartment, and in doing everything to make it possible for a newly arrived African family from Sierra Leone to begin study at Denver Seminary and to work part-time on our staff at church. These and many other examples that we could cite may never be labeled the work of a good Samaritan by our secular media or culture. They may never even be noticed by the world, but they are every bit as direct an application of the Samaritan's model of compassion for those who are in need as the more highly publicized stories like Jeannie VanVelkinburgh's.

But Jesus could have driven home the point about compassion for the needy without verses 31–32 at all. No need to have had a priest and a Levite go by without offering help to the wounded man. But he does include them, and he creates considerable suspense as first one and then a second individual pass by and do nothing—individuals who by the standards of first-century Jewish culture should have been the very ones to offer help. From them we therefore learn a second lesson. Paradoxical as it may sound, *religion often gets in the way of demonstrating God's compassion for people.* But with Jesus, that's no excuse!

As I just mentioned, these aren't just any two passersby but representatives of the religious leadership, and more specifically the temple authorities. There were so many priests in Jesus' day that not all of them lived in Jerusalem. Some commuted from the town near the Jordan River known as Jericho. Because the man was going *down* from Jerusalem to Jericho, and because the priest is also described as going *down* the same road (literally downhill as they headed away from the capital), we can't excuse these clerics' behavior on the grounds that they were concerned about not making it on time for their temple work. The priest and the Levite would have been going home after their duties had been fulfilled. More likely, we may imagine them concerned with the various Jewish purity laws, many of which went well beyond explicit Old Testament commands. Because the man who was robbed is described as half-dead, he may have been lying motionless. The priest and the Levite may have thought he *was* dead and didn't want to ritually defile themselves by touching a corpse. That would have created the inconvenience of rendering them unclean. The rite of purification that they would have had to undergo a week afterward could have interfered with their temple ministry on a later date. But how much more valuable than all of that religious ritual is a human life! We recall Jesus' attitude in challenging the Jewish leaders on topics like healing on a Sabbath, when he declared that it was always lawful to do good on the day of rest (Matt. 12:12), or when he was debating with the Pharisees and the scribes over the dietary laws (about what foods were clean and unclean) and explained that it was not what goes into people that defiles them but the evil speech and deeds that come out of them (Matt. 15:16–19).

How much of "doing church" in fact gets in the way of really performing the Lord's work in our world? I was first struck by this question in high school after having come to faith through a Campus Life club that regularly saw non-Christian kids accepting Christ. We tried to encourage several Christian friends to join us, but they couldn't because their church or their parents required them to attend events in their local churches even on school nights. Yet when we questioned them, as far as we could tell, nobody outside those churches and certainly no non-Christians ever showed up at their events. I remember a few years ago a new church plant right here in Colorado in Highlands Ranch where, because of the denomination with which that church was affiliated, the pastor felt compelled to appoint about forty prescribed officeholders, committee members, teachers, and other "volunteers," even before there were that many qualified people in the congregation. Almost immediately, the initial momentum, enthusiasm, and growth of the church stopped. Soon the entire effort started to wither on the vine, because instead of continuing to reach out to bring new people in, the members simply became embroiled in filling slots and following conventional denominational programs and thus stopped ministering to anyone outside their four walls. David Prior, for many years pastor of churches in Cape Town, South Africa, and Oxford, England, writes that there is a "desperate need for Christians to excise innumerable church meetings, in order to free their diaries for proper meeting with unbelievers."[1] Those of us who are in full-time Christian work have to strive extra hard just to meet and have the time to build meaningful relationships with non-Christians. Those of you who have secular jobs and are surrounded by non-Christians daily, please count that a blessing, especially if you didn't realize that it was one!

But even this second point, that religion often but unjustifiably gets in the way of showing compassion, doesn't exhaust what I believe Jesus wants to teach us through this story. We haven't yet hit on the most important point of all. You see, many stories in Jesus' day were about two clerics and then an ordinary Jew, sort of like a joke where you have two examples as a foil to set up the punch line. There was an entire body of Jewish lore that had an anticlerical or anti-institutional flavor to it. Jesus' audience no doubt thought that he was setting them up for precisely that kind of a tale. A priest should have offered help, but he didn't. A Levite should have offered help, but he didn't. Now an ordinary Israelite, a simple farmer or construction worker, will come along and turn out to be the hero. Instead, huge shock waves would have surged through Jesus' audience when they recognized that the Samaritan was the hero. We lose the impact of the story altogether if we forget this greatest of oxymora in Jesus' world: a *good* Samaritan. The two terms simply didn't belong together in most people's thinking. A Samaritan was a descendant of the unlawful intermarriages, many of them centuries earlier, between Jews and Gentiles in Israel. Often the person of mixed blood is more despised than the completely other. Jesus himself was once accused of being a Samaritan by Jews disputing his claims (John 8:48), and in the same breath he was called demon-possessed.

Thus appears the third and most dramatic point of today's parable. The lesson that the man in the ditch would have learned, based on who came to rescue him, is that *even my enemy is my neighbor*. Many expositions of this parable have ignored the context or framework of the story altogether. And except for reading it at the beginning of this message, we too have thus far ignored it. Now it's time to remind ourselves that the parable was told to answer the Jewish lawyer's question, "Who is my neighbor?" (v. 29). This question was the follow-up to the preceding dialogue in which the lawyer had asked Jesus what he must do to inherit eternal life (v. 25). In good rabbinic fashion, Jesus had countered a question with a question, asking him what he read in the Law of Moses (v. 26). Quoting two central teachings that Jesus on a later occasion would himself say summed up all of the Law and Prophets (Mark 12:29–31), the lawyer answers with the double love command: "Love the Lord your God with all your heart and with all your soul and with all your strength and with all your mind"; and, "Love your neighbor as yourself" (v. 27). We who know the Sermon on the Mount from earlier in Jesus' ministry perhaps wonder if he is setting the man up for the kind of logic that he used there to show the man that he may have thought he had fulfilled the commandments, but in his internal attitudes he certainly hadn't, nor had he attained God's perfect standards of holiness (cf. Matt. 5:21–48). But for whatever reason, Jesus doesn't adopt that strategy here. Perhaps it was because he recognized that the man himself sensed a deficiency when he asked the follow-up question, "Who is my neighbor?" Perhaps the man recognized that standard first-century Jewish nationalism did not extend that label to the other peoples of the world. Interestingly, when Jesus unequivocally portrays the hated enemy—the Samaritan—as included in the definition of one's neighbor, the lawyer can't even bring himself to pronounce the name "Samaritan." He simply replies to Jesus' closing question regarding who proved neighborly with the words, "The one who had mercy on him" (v. 37).

The best way to re-create the original shock effect of Jesus' story in our twenty-first-century world is to look for those who are the most hated enemies in our global village: Catholics and Protestants in Northern Ireland; warring tribes or governments and their rebel opponents in many countries of sub-Saharan Africa; conservative white male heterosexuals in the United States and people of a different race, gender, or sexual orientation. In Israel today we again have a classic illustration with Muslims and Jews. New Testament scholar Kenneth Bailey, whose books on the parables offer a treasure trove of insights into Mediterranean culture, and who himself was a long-term American missionary first in Lebanon and then in Israel, describes how in twenty years of ministry in the Middle East, he never dared to retell the story of the good Samaritan to a Palestinian audience and have the hero be a Jew. Perhaps he feared doing so might place his life in jeopardy. The best way to generate equivalent tension within an American audience today would probably be to make the hero an Al-Qaeda leader who helped plan the horrors of September 11, 2001. Do we really believe that such people are our neighbors, created in God's image, no less precious to him than we? Those who are not yet Christians among our enemies are no more lost than we once were, and God calls us to bring them the gospel as well. Those of other races and nationalities who are Christians are just as significant a part of the body of Christ as we are. If so, then where are they in our churches? Where are they in our lives? We can no longer use the excuse that they're not in our neighborhoods! Will it be only Promise Keepers that will have trumpeted the theme of racial reconciliation when the history of the last couple of decades of American evangelical Christian life is written? And in the international arena, did the world clearly recognize after September 11 how different the American church's response was compared with our government's, however necessary the war in Afghanistan may or may not have been? If we go to war with Iraq again, will the world then recognize the difference between the evangelical church and the American government? Most first-century Jews could not have imagined calling Samaritans their neighbors. By making the Samaritan the hero of this passage, Jesus may be answering the question posed in the title of this sermon by saying that *one's enemy is the most important neighbor of all,* especially if one wants to determine if Christianity has turned us into people who are significantly different from the unredeemed.

But there is a further dynamic here, as the wounded man receives help from the Samaritan. With the Samaritan, we were given a model of compassionate behavior to imitate. With the priest and the Levite, we were warned against allowing religious duty to make us unloving. From the man in the ditch, we learn the lesson of our need to be willing to receive help. One of the ironies in many Christian churches is that many folks who do a pretty fair job of ministering to others have never learned how to ask for and receive help when they're in need. One of the frustrations of countless Christian pastors comes from discovering people in their own congregations who are extremely needy and hurting, and have been so for some time, but no one has been aware of their situation because they refuse to tell anyone. "I don't want to be a bother," they say. "I can manage on my own," others retort. Or, "I don't want people to think I have to ask for help." These and other excuses are all really cover-ups for the sin of pride, for refusing to let the body work the way Christ designed it to, with each one ministering to someone else, grieving with those who grieve as well as rejoicing with those who rejoice (1 Cor. 12:26). Our rugged Western individualism makes it tougher to do this in twenty-first-century America than in many cultures around the globe. But we must swallow our pride and admit our needs. Otherwise, the irony will only increase, when we eventually reach the point where we realize we do want help and then complain that the church has never given it!

There is an interpretation of the parable of the good Samaritan that is very different from anything that we've talked about this morning, one made famous by no less than Augustine in the early fifth century. For him the story was a detailed allegory of the fall of humanity. Jerusalem stood for the heavenly city; the man who was wounded for Adam, who fell into sin just as this man fell into the hands of robbers; the priest and the Levite who passed by stood for the Law and Prophets, who were unable to save; and the Samaritan stood for Christ, who did come and offer salvation. The inn stood for the church, where healing could occur, while oil and wine were the sacraments of baptism and the Lord's Supper. Even the innkeeper was symbolic; for Augustine, he stood for the apostle Paul! We laugh today at how anachronistic this interpretation seems, not to mention that it ignores the context in Luke altogether. Jesus' story was not an allegory about the fall of humanity into sin but an answer to the question, "Who is my neighbor?" But one insight that Augustine received, one that many others agree is worth pondering, is the Samaritan as a picture of Christ. Even that was probably not Jesus' primary intention, in light of everything we've already said about the passage. But it's certainly true that Jesus himself was the one and only perfect model of compassion for those in need of mercy in his day, and in every day, and only he will ever show us complete and perfect mercy. Jesus, even more than the Samaritan, is the model worth imitating. And when we do find, for whatever reason, that God's people prove less than fully supportive or even indifferent, we should remember that we can find all the strength we need in Christ.

Who needs your mercy this week, even if you have to slow down from your hurry to show it? Who do you need to recognize as your neighbor, whom you may have been ignoring or even despising? What need might you have to allow someone else to minister to you, even if that person may not be a fellow believer?

Commentary on "Who Is My Most Important Neighbor?"

We turn now from Jesus' common triangular or monarchic parable structure to the one parable that yields a straight-line horizontal diagram. Instead of a powerful master figure with contrasting subordinates, we encounter a powerless figure in the person of the man who was robbed and left half-dead. But he remains the unifying figure in the story in that he can clearly distinguish between the priest and the Levite, on the one hand, and the Samaritan, on the other, and recognize who offers him the help he needs. Moreover, we have a dramatic reversal of expectation as to who that individual turns out to be. Everyone in Jesus' audience would have assumed either a priest or a Levite would offer aid long before a despised Samaritan.[2] But today, precisely the opposite is the case, even among people with very little church background. As I emphasize at the beginning of the sermon, people now think Samaritans are "good guys," while enough latent anti-Semitism (or at least anticlericalism) remains in our world that the priest and the Levite are not necessarily looked upon as potential heroes.

When I first composed this message several years ago, the murder of the African man in downtown Denver was recent news. I could thus appeal to the story of Jeannie VanVelkinburgh and expect almost everyone in my congregation to be familiar with it. When I recently revised the sermon for use in a new Denver-area context, I thought about looking for a different, more current "good Samaritan" example, but I knew of none that was nearly as widely publicized. So, because of Jeannie's tragic apparent suicide, I kept the original illustration, knowing that those who did not yet live in Denver at the time of her injuries would probably have heard the story more recently anyway.[3]

The story also acutely focuses attention on the serious danger a "good Samaritan" can face, an element not always present in cases where the media apply that label to individuals, but one that was clearly present in Jesus' story. Thus my second introductory paragraph transitions to the hard questions these accounts, ancient and modern, raise, questions many Christian readers don't feel comfortable posing of the biblical text, at least not publicly, even though many have thought about them. I am then ready to read the text from Scripture, and because the body of my sermon does not break down the passage episodically, I read the text all at once.

The discussion of the famous study at Princeton Seminary[4] and of similar follow-up studies[5] is still introductory in the sense that I am not yet commenting on details of Jesus' parable. But because of its length, along with the fact that it presupposes some familiarity with the story from Scripture, I don't want to delay reading the parable any longer. While the story in its broad contours is very familiar to most people, including many unchurched folks, I can't presuppose that everyone in my audience recalls all the details.

The modern sociological and psychological studies I cite prepare the way for a discussion of the hard questions surrounding the parable, including the most directly exegetical question: "Is it possible we have partially misunderstood Jesus' parable?" Most listeners are so familiar with the parable as a model of compassion that more elaborate and distinctive preparation is needed to open the door for the suggestion that there are additional points, and that the model of compassion may be the least significant of the main points Jesus made here. Again, I do not attempt methodologically to defend in advance my theory of three points, one per main character or main groups of characters, but allow each to emerge naturally as we consider the passage: the presence of the priest and the Levite requires more than just the Samaritan's model of compassion; the choice of the Samaritan requires us to come to grips with the ancient enmity between most Jews and most Samaritans.

The order in which the three points are presented is thus a deliberate choice. To show that I am not denying the conventional interpretation and to build on common ground and establish the good will of my audience, I start with the general message of mercy. It is, after all, what Jesus highlights in his closing half verse: "Go and do likewise" (v. 37b). But, as the larger context of the parable makes clear, that is not all that Jesus is trying to teach, since he tells the parable to help the lawyer answer his question about who qualifies as his neighbor (vv. 29, 36–37a).[6] Additional points will emerge from both the bad and the good models of neighborliness depicted.

Instead of dealing exclusively with the meaning of the parable in its original context under the three subdivisions of the body of the sermon, as I did in the sermons on the prodigal and the rich man and Lazarus, I intersperse a heavy dose of application in each part. The example of the stranded roadside motorist is so commonly employed, often as the only kind of application,[7] that I want to get people thinking early on about other situations in which to apply the parable, as well as noting ways in which the standard application may in fact not be a very good one. The issue of genuine danger or risk needs to appear in any contemporization. And given the probable abuses of our aid in certain contexts, we need to think carefully about how we offer help to the needy. Without becoming cynical and thus avoiding getting involved altogether, we need to analyze situations astutely and not intentionally set ourselves up to be taken advantage of.

As with my opening reference to a well-publicized local "Samaritan," I continue to refer specifically to situations within the Denver area. If I were preaching this parable in other communities and knew of equivalents in those settings, I would appeal to them. But when I have used this message in other parts of the country, and in other countries, I typically have not been that familiar with the local scene, so I have preserved the references to Denver to show that I know what the nuts-and-bolts application looks like in at least one setting. Then I challenge my congregation to become equally informed, if they are not already, about equivalent helping mechanisms in their area. As with the sermon on stewardship from the parable of the rich man and Lazarus, I also include a tool for attitudinal self-diagnosis. We may debate what are the most appropriate or effective helping mechanisms, but are we at least asking the question because we sympathize with the desperately needy enough to want to help in *some* way?

The parable's second main point requires more detailed historical study. It is not entirely self-evident why the two clerics passed by the injured man without helping, so certain educated guesses must be made. But the analysis presented reflects a fair consensus of current scholarly opinion.[8] My applications continue to reflect my own experience, but I appeal to David Prior's trenchant quote in order to generalize and to suggest the widely applicable nature of such illustrations.

The third and climactic point turns to the dynamic of enemy-love, which must form the heart of any exposition of the parable.[9] This explains my sermon title, "Who Is My Most Important Neighbor?" The implied contrast between an ordinary Israelite and the Samaritan as the expected hero of the passage has recently been disputed,[10] but still seems to fit well.[11] The reversal between the lawyer's question and Jesus' counterquestion at the end of the passage has often been noted, as has the man's seeming inability to answer Jesus by explicitly referring to a "Samaritan."[12]

The sermon's fairly lengthy conclusion returns to the task of contemporization, attempting to construct highly shocking modern equivalents. Centuries of domestication of this parable have made it virtually impossible for preachers to recreate the outrage that would have accompanied Jesus' original telling. Kenneth Bailey's admission of his lack of courage (despite very courageously ministering in the most dangerous parts of the Middle East for decades!) brings this point home dramatically,[13] as I hope does the discussion of September 11 and beyond.

The sermon could easily have concluded at this point, but my experience (and frustration!) with folks who are unwilling to let others even know of their needs pushes me to add a paragraph on transparency and vulnerability. The long history of the Christological interpretation of the passage, which I suspect at least a few in the churches in which I preach will know,[14] leads to the final detailed paragraph. I then conclude, much more concisely, by rephrasing the three main points as questions for immediate application.

4

Can I Be Saved If I Refuse to Forgive Others?

Matthew 18:23–35

Once upon a time there was a multibillionaire in Washington, D.C., who ran afoul of the law for insider trading. Worse still, he saw his entire fortune dwindle due to his investment in junk bonds. Faced with bankruptcy and with jail, he begged the president of the country, for whom he had worked on a special project, for leniency. To his astonishment and to that of the country, the president announced he would request a full pardon and set him free. As the billionaire was going back home from his meeting with the president, he met a low-echelon accountant of his former corporation who had been caught altering his books, so that over a four-month period he had stolen about four thousand dollars. Awaiting trial and faced with possible short-term imprisonment, the accountant begged his former CEO to intervene in the plea-bargaining process. Coldly and callously, the billionaire replied, "I will press for the maximum sentence." Some of the accountant's colleagues heard about what happened and sent word through a congressional friend to the president. He was outraged. "I haven't signed the pardon yet," he responded, "and now I certainly won't! That ingrate can rot for the rest of his life in jail for all I care." And so he did.

As you've probably guessed, this story is fictional, though many elements in it unfortunately parallel various public events of recent years. But my story is a modern-day counterpart to the parable of the unforgiving servant in Matthew 18:23–25. That text reads,

Therefore, the kingdom of heaven is like a king who wanted to settle accounts with his servants. As he began the settlement, a man who owed him billions of dollars was brought to him. Since he was not able to pay, the master ordered that he and his wife and his children and all that he had be sold to repay the debt.

The servant fell on his knees before him. "Be patient with me," he begged, "and I will pay back everything." The servant's master took pity on him, canceled the debt and let him go.

But when that servant went out, he found one of his fellow servants who owed him a few hundred dollars. He grabbed him and began to choke him, "Pay back what you owe me!" he demanded.

His fellow servant fell to his knees and begged him, "Be patient with me, and I will pay you back."

But he refused. Instead, he went off and had the man thrown into prison until he could pay the debt. When the other servants saw what had happened, they were greatly distressed and went and told their master everything that had happened.

Then the master called the servant in. "You wicked servant," he said, "I canceled all that debt of yours because you begged me to. Shouldn't you have had mercy on your fellow servant just as I had on you?" In his anger his master handed him over to the jailers to be tortured, until he should pay back all he owed.

This is how my heavenly Father will treat each of you unless you forgive a brother or sister from your heart.

Not all of the details of my modern-day contemporization of the parable prove exactly parallel. It's probably not possible to make the two stories match exactly, given the shift from monarchies in Jesus' day to contemporary democracies. But hopefully the overall effect of the two accounts is relatively similar. The Greek literally describes the first servant as owing ten thousand talents. The talent was the highest denomination of currency in the ancient Greco-Roman world. The Greek word translated "ten thousand" was the highest named numeral, the word from which we derive our English "myriad." The TNIV is the first translation to fully capture the enormity of this sum by rendering it "billions of dollars." Apart from kings, only a very few in the ancient world would ever come close to owning this amount of money, much less owing it to anyone else. These were truly the Bill Gateses and Warren Buffetts of Jesus' world. Like my story, Jesus' parable was just realistic enough to be barely conceivable, but it stretched the boundaries of his audience's imagination.

The sum that the second servant owed, on the other hand, was literally one hundred denarii, that is, one hundred days' minimum wages. The TNIV's "few hundred dollars" is an improvement over the old NIV's "a few dollars." But even at as low a rate as five dollars an hour, lower than most states' minimum wage today, a hundred days' earnings would come to four thousand dollars. The sum in its own right is significant enough. It's just that it's ludicrously small compared with the first servant's debt. Jesus intends for his story to enrage his audience. He also teaches about God and his ways with humanity, and that leads us to the parable's three central lessons. These lessons emerge both from the three principal characters in the story and from the three main scenes into which it divides.

The first lesson deals with *the king's lavish grace in forgiving debts*. The king's behavior leads to the central focus of the first episode, which spans verses 23–27. Clearly the point of the king's canceling so massive a debt is to display his enormous grace. That's why Jesus created the story with a servant owing such a huge debt in the first place. That the king wanted to settle accounts was realistic enough (v. 23), but as soon as we are told that a man comes owing "billions of dollars" (v. 24), we are meant to imagine that there is no way he could ever repay his debt. Verse 25 suggests that the king, even before forgiving the man's debt, is a generous man, because he proposes only that the servant and his family be sold into slavery. Sadly enough, selling people into slavery to recoup debts was common enough in first-century Israel. Sometimes Jews who were bankrupt voluntarily sold themselves into slavery, so at least they would be cared for. But the sum such a sale would net could hardly have equaled even a tiny fraction of this servant's stupendous debt. A harsher monarch could easily have ordered that the man and/or his family be sent to debtors' prison or even to their execution. Nor is it likely that the extra time the servant attempts to negotiate in verse 26 would have changed his situation. Again, he might have been able to earn back a little bit of the amount he owed, but no form of employment could have made a large dent in a total bill of "billions of dollars." The king's magnanimity stands out on every count. Clearly his behavior depicts God's grace in forgiving our sins, when we add up all the things we have done to fall short of his infinitely perfect and holy standards, combined with all the things we have not done that could have pleased him. Our sins are as enormous in God's eyes as a billion-dollar debt to the government. There is no way in the world we can ever repay it. If it is to be forgiven, it must be wholly of God's magnificent grace.

The second lesson, jarringly juxtaposed with the first, deals with *the absurdity of spurning such grace*. The treatment of the second servant forms the heart of this scene or episode. Almost as unimaginable as the king's forgiveness is the first servant's response. Jesus highlights the contrast between the two men by using very closely parallel wording in verses 26 and 29. Both servants approach their masters by falling on their knees. Both beg their masters with the words, "Be patient with me, and I will pay you back." But verses 27 and 30 reflect as diametrically opposite a pair of reactions to the pleas as Jesus could have portrayed. The king forgives the enormous, unpayable debt. The servant just forgiven that debt has his underling thrown into prison. Little wonder that the second man's fellow servants were "greatly distressed" (v. 31). The word used here could also be translated "outraged." We're meant to react to Jesus' story with distress and anger as well. This is an example of appropriate tattling, and we are supposed to sympathize.

The aftermath of the tattling leads to the third episode in verses 32–34 and to the ultimate destiny of the first servant. The third lesson that the parable teaches deals with *the frightful fate awaiting the unforgiving.* Now we see another side of the king as well. He can exhibit lavish, unprecedented love, but he can also unleash righteous anger and punishment. Here that anger seems unmitigated. The logic of verses 32–33 is inescapable. One man was forgiven so enormous a debt. How could he possibly refuse to show mercy to his fellow servant, who owed a comparatively paltry debt? Nor does verse 34 offer any prospect of an end to the sentence, as in the Roman Catholic doctrine of purgatory, which argues that most people spend time after their deaths in an intermediate state that is neither heaven nor hell until they have atoned for their sins in this life, after which point they may proceed to heaven. It is true this verse is often used as a proof text for purgatory because of the line "until he should pay back all he owed." But when we remind ourselves that it was next to impossible for someone in a Roman prison to earn any money, it would have been completely impossible for a man owing billions of dollars ever to have any way to pay back his debt while being tortured in jail. D. A. Carson, in his commentary on Matthew, correctly captures the balance of mercy and judgment reflected here: "Jesus sees no incongruity in the actions of a heavenly Father who forgives so bountifully and punishes so ruthlessly, and neither should we. Indeed, it is precisely because he is a God of such compassion and mercy that he cannot possibly accept as his those devoid of compassion and mercy."[1]

So far, so good, perhaps. The parable seems to have resolved itself in a satisfactory way that fits our sense of justice. But then comes Jesus' concluding application in verse 35, which makes plain the spiritual lesson behind it all. Let's read it again: "This is how my heavenly Father will treat each of you unless you forgive a brother or sister from your heart." Jesus makes it clear that the king represents God, the heavenly Father. The disciples would have understood this, because kings in the parables of the rabbis regularly stood for God. The servants then naturally stand for the people of this world, every potential disciple or follower of God, as he has now revealed himself in Jesus Christ. Each would-be disciple must identify with the greatly indebted servant, and the people who wrong us are like the first man's fellow servants. To sum up the parable, Jesus is essentially declaring that the spiritual debt God has forgiven us is so enormous that any refusal on our part to forgive other people is as ludicrous in comparison as this man's behavior in the parable and that God will be equally stern in his punishment of such lack of forgiveness. Now the story has become uncomfortable. In fact, it raises three crucial theological questions.

The first question is "What kind of judgment is this?" This is the easiest of the three to answer. Jesus almost certainly is referring to what we today call hell—eternal punishment—conscious, agonizing separation from God and all things good. Every other scriptural reference to jailers or to torture in the context of God's judgment clearly points in this direction.

But that leads to the second issue. Does Jesus' story then call into question the doctrine we popularly call "eternal security"? Not necessarily. Jesus has already said something quite similar in the Gospel of Matthew, which his disciples could well have been expected to remember. After giving the Lord's Prayer in the Sermon on the Mount, Jesus declares, "For if you forgive others when they sin against you, your heavenly Father will also forgive you. But if you do not forgive others their sins, your Father will not forgive your sins" (Matt. 6:14–15). One chapter later in his great sermon, in 7:21–23, Jesus goes on to explain, "Not everyone who says to me, 'Lord, Lord,' will enter the kingdom of heaven, but only those who do the will of my Father who is in heaven. Many will say to me on that day, 'Lord, Lord, did we not prophesy in your name and in your name drive out demons and in your name perform many miracles?' Then I will tell them plainly, 'I never knew you. Away from me, you evildoers!'" It is significant that Jesus does not say, "I no longer know you" or "you lost your salvation" but rather, "I never knew you." You were never truly one of my followers, even though you may have fooled some, perhaps even fooled yourself. The Dutch Calvinist Herman Ridderbos puts it this way in his commentary on Matthew: "Whoever tries to separate man's forgiveness from God's will no longer be able to count on God's mercy. In so doing he not merely forfeits this, like the servant in the parable. Rather he shows that he never had a part in it. God's mercy is not something cut and dried that is only received once. It is a persistent power that pervades all of life. If it does not become manifest as such a power, then it was never received at all."[2] First John 2:19 seems to reinforce this perspective. As John analyzes what went wrong when certain false teachers left his churches in and around Ephesus at the end of the first century, he writes, "They went out from us, but they did not really belong to us. For if they had belonged to us, they would have remained with us; but their going showed that none of them belonged to us."

A third question is perhaps the hardest of all. What about forgiveness for the unrepentant—for those who don't seek our forgiveness as the two servants in this parable do? To be fair to the text, we must admit that Jesus does not explicitly address that question in this parable. Its context, however, in Matthew 18 proves highly significant. The entire chapter is a collection of Jesus' teachings for the disciples, which include in verses 15–20 the famous passage on church discipline. When a brother or sister sins against another believer, there is a process to be followed in hopes of bringing about repentance and restoration. But at each stage, if the offending person refuses to repent, the next level of discipline is initiated. At the end of the process, if nothing else works, Jesus concludes, "treat them as you would a pagan or a tax collector" (v. 17b), that is, as a non-Christian. This is where the concept of disfellowshipping or excommunication comes from.

When we understand that verses 15–20 describe what to do with the unrepentant, then we are in a position to understand the other two verses that precede the parable of the unforgiving servant—verses 21 and 22. These two little verses narrate the famous exchange between Peter and Jesus on how many times disciples should forgive someone who sins against them. Peter thought he was being gracious in suggesting "up to seven times" (v. 21), but Jesus replies, "I tell you, not seven times, but seventy-seven times" (v. 22). These verses are often cited out of context, so that the contrast with verses 15–20 is lost. But unless Jesus is flatly contradicting himself here, we have to understand verses 21–22 as meaning what disciples are to do when someone sins against them and truly repents. This is confirmed by a partially parallel text in Luke 17:3–4 in which Jesus more directly declares, "If any brother or sister sins against you, rebuke the offender; and if they repent, forgive them. Even if they sin against you seven times in a day and seven times come back to you saying 'I repent,' you must forgive them."

It is also crucial to remind ourselves of the biblical definition of repentance. Far more than merely saying one is sorry, the Hebrew and Greek words for repentance throughout both testaments regularly refer to a 180-degree about-face, a change of action so that one no longer commits the sins in question. One may sin in new areas, thus leading to the frequent need for forgiveness, but continuing to commit the same sin repeatedly against another person usually demonstrates that no true repentance has ever occurred. So it is both invalid and very damaging to apply biblical calls for forgiveness to situations of chronic abuse, in which repeated patterns of destructive behavior continue without any change, no matter how sorry a person claims to feel. To continue to offer forgiveness without intervention in such situations creates what psychologists call the "enabling" process. The perpetrators are not helped but unwittingly encouraged to continue their destructive behavior, and the victims set themselves up for further abuse. Such situations require intervention by fellow Christians, pastors, often even professional counselors, so that everything possible might be done to help the perpetrator abandon the addictive or hurtful behavior.

But there are still plenty of situations in which Jesus' words to Peter and the parable that illustrates them prove more than applicable. The vast majority of little and even big offenses against most of us, on most days, fall into the category of sins we are called to forgive. And even when we may need to remove fellowship from a person or to separate ourselves for the sake of our safety from someone whose behavior may prove hurtful to us, we still must seek God's help in not harboring a grudge, musing how we can retaliate, or even plotting vindictive behavior in return. We do not want to water down the parable so that it loses the shocking effect on us that it surely had on the disciples, Jesus' original audience.

I began with a fictitious story. I end with a true one about former friends of mine. Only the names and a few minor details are changed to protect the guilty.

I first got to know Michelle in a small church fellowship group. She had been raised in a conservative Southern home, had gone to Christian schools and a Christian college, and had married a would-be preacher by the name of Joe. Michelle was pretty, reasonably friendly, but at times quite withdrawn. Joe never actually became a preacher because Michelle couldn't imagine ever being a preacher's wife. As I got to know Joe and Michelle, I soon sensed that theirs was a fairly fragile marriage. She was used to an upper-middle-class, comfortable lifestyle with many possessions, a small clique of close friends, and was largely unwilling to do anything that would jeopardize this security.

One day in our group, I taught on this very parable. Afterward Michelle accosted me. "You don't know what my father was like," she said, "overbearing, demanding, never giving me enough freedom, stifling my creativity, my independence, quashing most of my desires. I can never forgive him. I *will* never forgive him." She pronounced her words slowly and carefully. A brief conversation got me nowhere, and I went away distressed.

It has been more than a decade now since I've seen Michelle. I see Joe once every year or two. I learned from him that not long after our confrontation the two of them broke up. Joe told me that at the time Michelle didn't show much interest in church or spiritual things anymore. She wasn't even sure that she believed in Christ. I'm afraid Jesus might say she never had believed in him. Of course, only God knows her spiritual state, and we are grateful that we don't have to judge. He flawlessly discerns every human heart. But the sad sequel to my conversation with Michelle simply reinforces the power and profundity of Jesus' words here about the link between true Christian salvation and an ability and willingness to forgive others.

Please hear me carefully. I'm not talking about somebody who struggles to forgive but keeps on trying. I'm not talking about someone who knows he or she needs to forgive, even wants to, but finds it very, very difficult. Again we may need the help of Christian friends and even professional counselors to fully forgive people who have deeply wounded us. What I am talking about is an attitude that doesn't even care, that refuses even to try to forgive, as is seemingly the case with Michelle. Is there someone that you need to forgive today? If so, please realize the great urgency of doing so. To return again to the Sermon on the Mount, this time to Matthew 5:23–26, Jesus says, "Therefore, if you are offering your gift at the altar and there remember that the brother or sister has something against you, leave your gift there in front of the altar. First go and be reconciled to that person; then come and offer your gift. Settle matters quickly with your adversary who is taking you to court. Do it while you are still together on the way, or your adversary may hand you over to the judge, and the judge may hand you over to the officer, and you may be thrown into prison. Truly I tell you, you will not get out until you have paid the last penny." Once again we see imagery identical to that of our parable in chapter 18. And once again, no one will ever pay the last penny, so there is no hope of getting out at all.

The title of this sermon is "Can I Be Saved If I Refuse to Forgive Others?" After what God in Christ has done for us, could we ever absolutely refuse to make any attempt to forgive those who have sinned against us? I believe the point of Jesus' parable of the unforgiving servant, as harsh as it may sound, is that the answer to that question is "no," for no one who has truly sensed how much he has owed God, how much she has offended God, how much his sin has separated him from an infinitely holy and loving creator, and who also recognizes that God in Christ has forgiven her, through no merit of her own—no one who truly understands these concepts and thus has received and appropriated that forgiveness could ever act in such a way as the servant in this parable. True Christians could never absolutely refuse to forgive one another, choosing instead to inflict the worst possible vengeance. May God guard all of us from ever behaving like the servant in Jesus' story.

Commentary on "Can I Be Saved If I Refuse to Forgive Others?"

This is the second in a series of sermons I preached, all titled, "Can I Be Saved . . . ?" (recall the message on the rich man and Lazarus in chap. 2). The deliberately provocative titles are intended to highlight that transformed living must flow from professions of faith if God is to deem them genuine. But within the messages, I try to reassure audiences that I do believe in the perseverance of the saints (or what is popularly, though at times misleadingly, called eternal security) and of salvation by grace through faith. I just want to be faithful to *Jesus'* original message and its impact rather than jumping immediately to a Pauline interpretation of Christianity.

The parable of the unforgiving servant is one of two that have a master figure, in this case a king, but, instead of contrasting subordinates underneath him, present a single servant with additional servants under him. Thus the diagram is a straight top-down, vertical line. Again, three points may be associated with the three main characters, though in this instance, they emerge even more directly from the three successive scenes of the passage: the master and first servant (vv. 23–27); the first servant and his servant (vv. 28–31); and the master and the first servant again (vv. 32–35).[3]

The introduction to the sermon is the shortest of those thus far displayed. It is also the first purely fictional contemporization that I have created, though, as I note, it does contain various parallels to the recent scandals in corporate America. As a result, I have the freedom to approximate the brevity of Jesus' own parable and to juxtapose the two back-to-back. Thus, my reading of the parable, in its entirety, comes immediately after the brief contemporization, so that readers can more easily compare and contrast the two stories.

As a bridge to the commentary proper on the parable, two paragraphs reflect on the ways in which my made-up story does or doesn't match Jesus' narrative. The most important elements needing explanation are the equivalents to the amounts of money employed, particularly because modern translations (and/or accompanying explanatory footnotes) often do not come even close to getting the numbers right![4] Again, I do not attempt to defend my three-main-point approach but simply build on the homiletical tradition of dividing a message into three parts to suggest that the points will emerge as we consider the passage scene-by-scene and character-by-character.[5]

There are two highly unrealistic features of this parable that provide key indications of its symbolic or spiritual meaning. They lead directly to the first two main points of the passage. The king's lavish grace fits God far better than typical, earthly rulers. The servant's hardheartedness proves so incongruous after his forgiveness that it, too, makes better sense with a spiritual referent. A bit of historical background to the possible punishments for ancient indebtedness is needed to unpack the first point and to help the king's magnanimity emerge with utter clarity.[6] The literary parallelism between the first and the second scene must be highlighted to bring out the inconsistency and ingratitude of the first servant's behavior in stark contrast.[7]

The third scene raises the most acute theological problems in the passage. The first emerges from the parable itself—Does verse 34 suggest a possible end to the period of punishment for the servant? Given that typical North American evangelical congregations have a fair number of ex-Catholics in their midst, and given that this is the one New Testament text most often used to buttress the Catholic doctrine of purgatory, I feel the need to rebut that proof-texting, even if briefly.[8] But if Jesus is talking about hell and not purgatory, then I must address the severity of the punishment, and the quotation from Carson's commentary proves helpful. The second issue is more difficult and appears pointedly in the concluding verse, which spells out Jesus' spiritual application explicitly. I create some temporary closure ("So far, so good, perhaps"), therefore, before turning to this more difficult problem, which actually heightens the impact of verse 35 and the issue it raises: Is Jesus more Arminian than Calvinist with respect to "eternal security"?

What I subdivide into two separate questions could also be viewed as the flip side of the same question. No, the passage does not teach the possible loss of salvation, but it does teach that true forgiveness when appropriated will lead to believers forgiving others. The larger narrative flow of Matthew's Gospel is important at this point, given the similarities of our parable to 7:21–23, which Matthew could have assumed would inform his hearers' understanding of 18:35. First John 2:19, in my opinion, offers the clearest biblical explanation of how to reconcile the promises of the security of the believer with the reality of some who commit apostasy.[9] Ridderbos's quote also proves helpful, although I typically don't quote academic commentaries back-to-back in my sermons, preferring instead to simplify and put their thoughts into my own words. Still, here I have preserved the memorable wording of two key citations.

In preparing the way for my concluding illustration, larger contextual considerations must be addressed. In a series of sermons preached from consecutive texts of Matthew, one could include this portion in the exposition of verses 15–22. As a stand-alone sermon on this parable, however, one has to go beyond the specific text of the day. One could also choose to preach on all of verses 15–35 together as a self-contained unit, but then other important issues emerging from the earlier verses might make the message too long or unwieldy. In my chosen format, however, I want merely to stress the implications for forgiveness that the larger context of the parable presents. Verses 15–20, on the theme of church discipline, describe a process of restoration that implicitly calls for forgiveness whenever there is true repentance but that requires disfellowshipping if all other means to achieve repentance have been tried without success. Verses 21–22 by themselves appear to teach unlimited forgiveness, but the parallel in Luke 17:3–4 includes repentance as a condition. The unforgiving servant depicts the king both granting and withholding (or retracting) forgiveness. Thus a mediating position is needed between the common extremes of "wiping the slate clean" in all circumstances and vindictively harboring grudges in certain instances.[10]

Still, the parable would have shocked Jesus' original audience, and, as I state explicitly, I do not want to lose the shock effect for today, even while I don't want people misusing the text to support psychological "enabling."[11] To that end, I close with a fairly detailed real-life story. Precisely because my introduction was both brief and fictional, I balance that at the end of the sermon with a somewhat lengthier true-life case study in which I was personally involved. As is important in all such case studies, the names are changed, as are enough incidental details, so that the true identities of the characters are not likely to be surmised. Because there is such a delicate balance, theologically and pragmatically, between giving people too little or too much assurance of salvation, I take the time after completing the case study to include one more paragraph explaining my larger theological understanding. In virtually every moderately sized audience, there will be genuine Christians who have wrestled intensely with forgiving difficult people and who thus could easily imagine me to be claiming they are not saved. That misunderstanding may result no matter how many caveats the message includes, but I want to forestall it as much as possible. Still, "Michelle" is not the only person I have known who has abandoned Christianity altogether after repeatedly refusing to forgive someone. I dare not rule out the possibility that some people in Christian congregations hearing this message may be fooling others (and even possibly themselves) in appearing to be Christians when they are not. How one responds to offenses against oneself, even when they hurt deeply, becomes an important tool for self-diagnosis.[12]

As with the sermon on the parable of the rich man and Lazarus, I call particular attention to the sermon title only in my closing paragraph. Most people in the audience will have noticed it earlier and begun to wonder if I am denying salvation by grace through faith alone. I leave that tension with them until the very end of the message, at which point I have also paved the way theologically to answer the question about salvation apart from forgiving others, without making Jesus promote a works righteousness. The last sentence of the sermon is part prayer, part plea. The message thus closes with an emphasis on the seriousness of the matter, on how much is at stake in the arena of forgiveness.

5

Shrewd Stewards

Luke 16:1–13

Did you hear about the IRS worker who was given notice that he was being laid off and who then mailed twenty good friends large, undeserved tax refund checks? Or did you hear about the hospital administrator, about to lose his job, who reduced the bills of several prominent patients by several thousand dollars? Or how about the just-fired defense contractor who changed five-hundred-dollar screw orders to five dollars? Each made many new friends as a result and thereby received several new job offers.

I don't know if those events ever really happened. But they are somewhat parallel to a story Jesus once told. It's found in Luke 16, beginning with the first verse:

> Jesus told his disciples: "There was a rich man whose manager was accused of wasting his possessions. So he called him in and asked him, 'What is this I hear about you? Give an account of your management, because you cannot be manager any longer.'
>
> "The manager said to himself, 'What shall I do now? My master is taking away my job. I'm not strong enough to dig, and I'm ashamed to beg—I know what I'll do so that, when I lose my job here, people will welcome me into their houses.'
>
> "So he called in each one of his master's debtors. He asked the first, 'How much do you owe my master?'
>
> "'Eight hundred gallons of olive oil,' he replied.
>
> "The manager told him, 'Take your bill, sit down quickly, and make it four hundred.'
>
> "Then he asked the second, 'And how much do you owe?'

"'A thousand bushels of wheat,' he replied.

"He told him, 'Take your bill and make it eight hundred.'

"The master commended the dishonest manager because he had acted shrewdly. For the people of this world are more shrewd in dealing with their own kind than are the people of the light. I tell you, use worldly wealth to gain friends for yourselves, so that when it is gone, you will be welcomed into eternal dwellings.

"Whoever can be trusted with very little can also be trusted with much, and whoever is dishonest with very little will also be dishonest with much. So if you have not been trustworthy in handling worldly wealth, who will trust you with true riches? And if you have not been trustworthy with someone else's property, who will give you property of your own?

"No one can be a slave to two masters. Either you will hate the one and love the other, or you will be devoted to the one and despise the other. You cannot be a slave to both God and Money."

The story Jesus tells is about a manager who was put in charge of a large estate, as often happened in the first century, with all the legal privileges and responsibilities to take care of his master's money. This particular manager was given notice that he was going to lose his job for some unspecified financial mismanagement. Because he couldn't see himself in any other line of work or unemployed, he went around reducing the bills of his master's debtors, so that, in a society in which one favor very much deserved a favor in return, the debtors he had treated generously would look after the manager and help him find new employment.

Of all of Jesus' parables, this is probably the most puzzling. It is certainly the one on which more scholarly ink has been spilled than any other. It deals with one of Jesus' favorite themes—the right use of riches. But that, too, makes it particularly difficult to preach on in the twenty-first-century Western world, in which so many Christian leaders who talk about money simply harangue their listeners for more, abuse the Scriptures' teaching on the topic, or (precisely because of others' abuse) think that finances are not a topic to be discussed in public at all. Jesus avoided the twin dangers of abuse and silence. Approximately one-fifth of all his teaching was about money matters. And so, despite the difficulty of the passage, despite the possible unpopularity of the theme, it's one we dare not run away from.

The difficulty of the story is compounded, however, when we try to determine what precisely is the point that Jesus drew from it. Some commentators have observed that it seems he makes three separate points in the first part of verse 8, the second part of verse 8, and verse 9, respectively. I happen to think that about two-thirds of Jesus' parables, in fact, teach three points, which often line up very closely with the main characters or elements in the parable. This parable provides a classic example of that phenomenon. In verse 8a, we read about the *praise of the master;* in verse 8b, about *the naiveté of disciples;* and in verse 9, about the *welcome of the debtors.* Shall we look at each of these three points in turn?

One reason that scholars have debated so many different approaches to interpreting this passage has to do with the fact that in the first half of verse 8 the master commends the dishonest manager. A superficial reading might suggest that he is somehow praising the man's dishonesty. But a more careful look suggests otherwise. Actually, Jesus often appeals to somewhat unscrupulous characters to illustrate spiritual lessons based on some other aspect of their behavior—the unjust judge who grants justice to a persistent widow; the thief who surprises people in the night; and the strong man who must be bound before his house can be plundered. Verse 8 does not say that the master commended the manager for his dishonesty, merely that he commended the manager because, after he was caught for whatever dishonest dealings he had done, he acted shrewdly.

Jesus, in fact, regularly employs the imagery of a scene of reckoning or accounting between masters and servants as a metaphor for final judgment. We think especially of the parables of the talents and the pounds in which good and wicked servants are praised or censured. Clearly, there are a number of stories in which Jesus teaches those who want to be prepared for final judgment to behave wisely in this life. Some commentators have tried to make the steward in this passage appear better than he does at first glance. Some argue that all he was doing in reducing the bills of the debtors was eliminating the legal but unethical personal profit that he had added to the actual amount of the bills in order to line his own coffers. Others have suggested that he equally legally reduced an excess profit that the master was skimming off the top of a much smaller amount that was genuinely owed. There is some evidence from the writings of the rabbis in at least a couple of centuries after the time of Christ that Jesus might have had one or both of these models in mind. But if so, neither is explicitly described. It's safest to take Jesus' words simply at face value—that the master of the dishonest manager praised him not for his dishonesty, not for a clever ploy that in fact demonstrated some morality on the part of the steward, but simply, as we read, because he had acted shrewdly. We are not to imitate his unjust behavior, but rather his wise, clever, resourceful, intelligent action, while remaining innocent of all evil. Matthew 10:16, in a quite different context, may in fact be the best one-sentence commentary on Jesus' parable found anywhere. There Jesus commanded his followers to be "as shrewd as snakes," but "as innocent as doves."

There are a great number of ways in which Christians need to be more shrewd. For churches, shrewdness includes knowing and obeying the law, retaining counsel to help leadership with difficult legal situations, particularly if church disciplinary action is ever taken, or in the event of a church member suing that congregation. Shrewdness and the creativity that comes along with it are needed in church programming and in outreach efforts. What will really attract adult unbelievers or nurture believers without compromising the gospel message, on the one hand, but without making it seemingly irrelevant, on the other? So many youth groups and parachurch organizations that target adolescents, like Young Life and Campus Life, exhibit enormously creative methods of outreach and discipleship from which adult ministries could learn much. For individual Christians in secular jobs, shrewdness includes fully understanding legal and ethical ways of witnessing, which also need to be matched by the highest reputation for integrity and hard work in performing one's job itself. Shrewdness extends to sharing one's faith in other contexts as well, even if those creative methods sometimes receive criticism, as when I engaged in a dialogue with a Mormon colleague at Brigham Young University, which led to our writing an entire book on the divide between Mormons and evangelicals. Despite severe criticism from certain quarters, both of us shared with each other our beliefs in more detail than could ever have occurred in an overtly evangelistic setting.

Sadly, Christians often act in diametrically opposite ways. Instead of being as shrewd as serpents and as innocent as doves, we become as wicked as serpents and as dumb as doves! And that leads directly to Jesus' second point in the second sentence of Luke 16:8, an ironic aside: "For the people of this world are more shrewd in dealing with their own kind than are the people of the light." Sadly, Christians are often more naive than non-Christians, precisely in those situations where they need a greater dose of shrewdness. Many Christians typically give far less thought and planning to teaching Sunday school lessons than to teaching in "real schools." Or they think the church will simply administer itself, or that it's acceptable to have haphazardly run committee meetings, rather than insisting on at least the same quality of professional standards they would employ in their secular workplace. If we had truly imbibed the biblical understanding of how, even for lay people, involvement in Christian things is the most significant aspect of our lives from God's perspective, then we'd put more effort into Sunday school, church administration, committee meetings, and programs than into any of their secular equivalents. Again, there are almost countless areas in which we could apply this principle. But perhaps three others are particularly crucial.

The first involves Christians and their political or social activity. It's interesting to trace the swings of the conservative evangelical church in America over the past quarter century. Before 1976, which *Time* magazine dubbed the year of the evangelical, most Christians somewhat naively thought that direct social action or political involvement was not a task for Christian believers. From the 1980s into the early 1990s, in the Reagan and Bush years, many swung the pendulum to the opposite extreme and pinned their hopes of God's working in our land on the fact that we had seemingly conservative Christian presidents in office. Many were then shocked at how little was actually accomplished, spiritually speaking, in those twelve years. Under the Clinton administration, and particularly because of the scandals that rocked his presidency, the pendulum swung again, and even basic forms of respect owed our government, so loudly trumpeted during other administrations, were routinely ignored or violated by evangelicals. Now we again have an even more unabashedly conservative Christian president, and the pendulum swings once more. But neither extreme, neither divorcing the church from the political arena nor pinning one's hopes entirely on the political process, is ever justified. Nor is any uncritical alignment with just one political party or single-interest agenda. If one looks at all the issues about which the Bible speaks, one discovers that a Christian political agenda cuts right across traditional Republican and Democratic party platforms.

Second, we need greater shrewdness and less naiveté in the whole area of holiness and morality. There's a fine balance between censorship, on the one hand, and indulgence, on the other. It's so easy for us to impose our rigid standards of behavior on everyone, even when they go far beyond the comparatively small number of ethical absolutes of Scripture. Those who don't need to have certain things completely forbidden them find that they must kowtow to our detailed rules and regulations, which actually sometimes push people to want to do what in fact *is* forbidden in Scripture. It's much harder to stop looking at others and ruthlessly examine ourselves and determine where *our* boundaries must be and then stop well short of them. It's comparable to the teenager asking, "How far can I go on a date?" It's the wrong question. That young person should instead be asking, "What can I be doing to build a wholesome interpersonal relationship that makes my date a better friend, a better Christian?" Adults should ask similar questions about their relationships, including their relationship with God, as they engage in recreation, entertainment, and other discretionary-time activities.

Third, the whole area of finances remains extremely crucial for Christian stewardship. The baby boomers form the first generation in American history that has not been taught to save and to give generously to charitable causes. Instead they find themselves in debt up to their eyeballs. The so-called baby busters (or Generation X) don't even have the money that the baby boomers could be giving away. Churches and parachurch organizations are paying the price. With an aging donor base, many will not survive into the next generation unless giving patterns change radically. And with rare exceptions, even those who do give do not give primarily to the poor, as the New Testament regularly commands. In fact, loans by first-century Jews were exclusively offered to the poor to help them get out of poverty. That probably is the situation envisioned in the imagery that Jesus uses in this parable.

For those who *are* prepared to use money wisely and receive God's praise, there is a third lesson and a promise that comes with it, found in verse 9. Jesus concludes the story, "I tell you, use worldly wealth to gain friends for yourselves, so that when it is gone, you will be welcomed into eternal dwellings." This is perhaps the most difficult verse in the passage to translate. "Worldly wealth" was simply a stock expression for money of any kind, not specifically ill-gotten gain. It was somewhat equivalent to our slang expression "filthy lucre." Sooner or later money passes through so many hands that it is tainted by some sin. To gain friends for oneself does not mean to use money to buy friendship but, at the spiritual level of the story, to use one's material resources for kingdom priorities—to win and disciple believers. Then, indeed, we will be welcomed by those who have preceded us into heaven when we arrive at our eternal dwelling place. Thus verse 9 does not contradict the principle of salvation by faith but reminds us that true faith works, especially in the area of giving. Jesus' words here may well have inspired (and certainly resemble) what his half-brother James taught in James 2:14–17 when he wrote, "What good is it, my brothers and sisters, if people claim to have faith but have no deeds? Can such faith save them? Suppose a brother or sister is without clothes and daily food. If one of you says to them, 'Go in peace; keep warm and well fed,' but does nothing about their physical needs, what good is it? In the same way, faith by itself, if it is not accompanied by action, is dead." Or again just a few short epistles further on, in 1 John 3:17–18, we read, "If any one of you has material possessions and sees a brother or a sister in need but has no pity on them, how can the love of God be in you? Dear children, let us not love with words or tongue but with actions and in truth." Even right here in Luke 16, the very next main passage after a few miscellaneous teachings is the parable of the rich man and Lazarus in verses 19–31, an illustration of the wrong use of material possessions and the devastating eternal consequences to which it leads.

Neither Jesus nor any New Testament writer ever quantifies how much a true disciple must give, although some Christians still support the Old Testament model of tithing even in the New Testament age. From one perspective, all belongs to God. We're called to be good stewards of 100 percent of what he has loaned to us. As for a specific amount to be given away, the poor in our society at times can't afford 10 percent, whereas almost all of us in the middle class or above could probably do much more. Second Corinthians 8–9, with its model of proportional giving, suggests that perhaps the New Testament mandate is what some authors have called a graduated tithe. The higher one's income, the higher percentage one gives. At least that's what our family has tried to model in the twenty-three years that my wife and I have been married. Also crucial is to whom we give, since even in the most missions-minded of churches 10 percent to one's local congregation typically implies at most 2 percent to missions and less than 1 percent to ministries directly involved with the financially needy.

But some people may say, "You don't know my budget. I just don't have any extra money for anything." I would love to ask those people some questions about how often they eat out, or how much they spend just on eating in general, or on their cars, or their houses, or recreation, or a home entertainment center. From 1980 to 2000, in twenty short years, Americans went from eating 10 percent of their meals out to eating 29 percent of their meals out.[1] An eighteen-year-old granddaughter of our neighbors, now trying to set up an apartment with some friends and live independently for the first time, came to the staggering realization that it was cheaper to buy food in a supermarket and prepare it at home rather than eat out. And when she reported on this to her grandmother, she explained, "My parents almost always ate out, so I just assumed that that was cheaper, since it never seemed like we had a lot of money." Truly amazing!

How crucial is stewardship? The world's need is staggering. Conservatively, one billion people live below the United Nations' poverty line, which is considerably lower than the American poverty line. Conservatively, at least 200 million of them are evangelical Christian brothers and sisters; 20 million are displaced refugees outside their homeland, 24 million within, with many more who are innocent victims of wars and natural disasters. Why is it that some conservative Christians launch passionate boycotts of Disney because of its apparent promotion of the gay lifestyle in certain settings but care not a whit that Nike employs countless factory workers in the Third World and pays them virtual slave wages? Yet, as Ron Sider reports in the most recent edition of *Rich Christians in an Age of Hunger*, in one year Nike paid Michael Jordan as much for promoting its sneakers as they paid their entire eighteen-thousand-member Indonesian workforce that produced them.[2]

But not only are global injustices great. Jesus goes on to note that spiritual maturity directly depends on how we handle our finances. He makes basically the same point three times in Luke 16:10–12. Whoever can be trusted with very "little" (that is, money or material possessions) can also be trusted with "much" (that is, spiritual treasures). Conversely, whoever is dishonest with worldly goods will also be dishonest with spiritual wealth. Jesus says it again, a second way, in verse 11: "if you have not been trustworthy in handling worldly wealth, who will trust you with true riches?" And once more in verse 12, "if you have not been trustworthy with someone else's property," namely, the goods of this life simply on loan from God, "who will give you property of your own"—true everlasting treasure? Thus the passage climaxes in verse 13 with a principle Jesus elsewhere employs in the Sermon on the Mount. No one can be a slave to two masters. In a world where we often work several jobs, we need to recall that a slave was owned by one master and indentured to him in every arena of life. If in that kind of context you attempted to serve two masters, you would wind up either hating one and loving the other or being devoted to one and despising the other. And then comes the application to our theme. "You cannot be a slave to both God and Money" (Luke 16:13; cf. Matt. 6:24).

So who is your master? I hope and pray that it is God, the God of our Lord Jesus Christ, and that an objective outsider, say an accountant, could recognize that fact if he or she were to examine your family budget, your checkbook ledger, and your credit card statements, particularly in comparison with your average non-Christian neighbor. We have recovery groups for people struggling with addictions of all different kinds. We have accountability groups for people who are not addicted but need fellow believers to keep them on the right track with respect to sex or alcohol or eating. Perhaps we need to begin to add to our recovery and accountability groups people who will ask us the hard questions about our expenditures, about our shopping, about how much we don't really need to have. That would free up enormous resources for kingdom work. That would truly make us shrewd stewards.

Commentary on "Shrewd Stewards"

The parable of the unjust steward is the second of the two parables of Jesus with a top-down vertical-line structure (along with the unforgiving servant; see chap. 4). A master figure interacts with a servant, who in turn is responsible for interacting with the master's debtors. The parable does not fall as neatly into three evenly sized scenes as does the parable of the unforgiving servant, although one could subdivide it into the master and his steward (vv. 1–2); the steward and the debtors (vv. 3–7); and the master's concluding reaction (v. 8). But the parable does include something not found with the unforgiving servant—three closing statements that aptly encapsulate the three lessons that are associated with each of the main characters: the master's praise (v. 8a); the disciples' naiveté (v. 8b); and the debtors' welcome (v. 9). As a result, I deal with the parable proper all at once and fairly rapidly. I then slow down to focus more leisurely on the three lessons summed up in these three closing statements. Because I take verses 10–13 to be integrally connected with Jesus' original parable, I also comment on them briefly toward the end of the message.[3]

The introduction to the sermon is the shortest of any presented thus far. Instead of developing one or more contemporary narratives equivalent in dynamics to Jesus' parable, I sum up in several one-line questions what the skeleton of such narratives might look like. The "Did you hear about . . . ?" form of the questions could suggest to some listeners that these are fictitious situations, because today that introduction is often used at the beginning of a joke. But I didn't say, "Did you hear *the one* about . . . ?" which almost guarantees that a joke is coming, so some listeners will probably wonder if these are real situations or not. As with Jesus' parables, they are close enough to reality to be believable, even with certain twists that go beyond what is common.[4] The final rhetorical question about the five-hundred-dollar screw orders was directly inspired by the true accounts of several years back when American defense contractors were charging and receiving outrageous sums for hardware until the media exposed the scandal.[5] By ending the introduction with an illustration that might remind others of that practice, I keep the listener in suspense, however briefly. But I quickly disclose my purpose: to contemporize the parable of the unjust steward, which I then proceed to read.

Before I move to the main lessons, three preliminary issues must be addressed. The first introduces the touchy issue of finances. By retelling the story briefly, incorporating the historical background on which commentators agree, it becomes clear that faithful exposition cannot avoid this central theme. Because of the ways in which the topic of stewardship has been alternately abused or neglected, I stress that it is my intention to do neither. I also remind listeners of how central the theme is throughout Jesus' ministry so that it must be tackled head on.[6]

The second preliminary issue involves hermeneutics. C. H. Dodd's comment on verses 8a, 8b, and 9 that "we can almost see here notes for three separate sermons on the parable as text" has been so widely quoted that it wouldn't surprise me if someone in the congregations to which I preach had heard of it.[7] Or given the number of Christian college or seminary students in most of those churches, some of *them* at least will recognize this as a classic example of the form critic's dictum that while Jesus made only one main point per parable, the early church tradition added extra points.[8] I still don't want to get into a full-orbed hermeneutical discussion, as I might if I were preaching the first in a prolonged series of sermons on just the parables, but I at least tip my hand as to the interpretive procedure I'm adopting.

The third preliminary issue also provides the transition to a discussion of the first point of the passage, so I save it until after I have stated the three points briefly. (Because I have summed them up in short phrases rather than entire sentences, as I sometimes do elsewhere, it is easy to mention them all at once, without distracting the audience too much from my main focus.) This third issue involves the major debate between commentators who think the steward is attempting to act honorably by reducing the debtors' bills and those who see his behavior as continuing to be unjust. The former position in fact subdivides into two parts. Some think the steward is reducing his own profit;[9] others, that he is reducing the master's profit.[10] It is obvious why he would be praised in the former instance; in the latter case, the argument is that the debtors would assume the steward was carrying out the master's wishes, so they would praise the master for his generosity. Though the master would lose some of the profit, he would look good in the eyes of the community. In a culture obsessed with the acquisition of honor and the avoidance of shame, the master would come out way ahead in terms of his reputation even if he lost a little money in the process.

The exegetical issues are complex, and I elaborate only enough to explain why, in the final analysis, I don't adopt this approach. But, again, I have run into just enough lay Christians who have heard of the alternate interpretation that I don't want to ignore it altogether.[11] Otherwise, the unpacking of the master's praise focuses on what both positions can agree on: the master is not praising the steward for his injustice; this parable fits Jesus' larger pattern of appealing to partially unscrupulous behavior with a "from the lesser to the greater" kind of logic; what the servant is explicitly commended for is his shrewdness; and Matthew 10:16 provides a wonderful cross reference to show Jesus teaching a similar lesson elsewhere.[12]

Given verse 8b, the function of the master's praise is not primarily as a model for Christians to emulate. We don't usurp God's role on Judgment Day, which is what the master's verdict reflects. Rather disciples should imitate the servant's shrewdness, which triggered the master's praise, without simultaneously imitating his injustice. The function of the parable's second point will then be to lament how often Christians do the opposite. Because contemporary Christians do not always look on shrewdness as a positive trait and reflect on how they should practice it, I offer a detailed paragraph of wide-ranging, potential current applications. Because the line between innocent shrewdness and tainted wisdom is a fine one, I include an example where severe but inappropriate criticism resulted. As a personal illustration, it also allows me to give a pointed example of my attempt to apply my own message and the consequences that resulted.[13]

The second point is likewise not one of straightforward imitation. Once one recognizes the a fortiori logic of verse 8b and the irony that it reflects, Jesus' point becomes clear, namely, that while it is often true that unbelievers are more shrewd in their dealings than believers, *it ought not be this way*.[14] Thus contemporary application, to which I almost immediately turn, should look for examples of inappropriate Christian naiveté to be avoided. In my opinion, this is the least recognized and most needed of the three points of the parable for most Western evangelical Christians today (and also for those many Third World evangelicals who largely imitate Western ecclesial patterns rather than forging independent, indigenous reflection and practice). Despite the progress made in some quarters with respect to a balanced social ethic, much American evangelical political thought has scarcely reflected on the full range of biblical data that should inform it, focusing instead on just a few key texts and themes.[15] The low standards of morality, often indistinguishable from the non-Christian culture, are well documented, but the tide of behavior has not yet turned. Patterns of giving have begun to improve slightly,[16] but we have such a long way to go that one can scarcely overemphasize this point. It is also worth noting that I have never preached sermons on parables at more than three or four consecutive church services; if I did, I probably would back off the recurring financial applications. But this sermon, like the majority in this book, was originally crafted for a "one-off" setting, for people who had not heard much recently on stewardship. So I felt free to stress the topic.[17]

The financial application of the second point of the passage creates a natural transition to the third point, which explicitly involves using "worldly wealth."[18] Virtually every phrase in verse 9 requires explanation, so here I spend more time with original meaning. While there are other ways besides the use of money to win and nurture Christians who will welcome us into heaven if they have preceded us there, that is Jesus' explicit focus here, so contemporary application would largely overlap with the points I have already made about stewardship in applying verse 8b. Instead of still further application, which might seem excessive and thus be counterproductive, I take the time to show how the suggested interpretation of verse 9 does not contradict salvation by faith and how it in fact fits in with the New Testament's recurring emphasis on the use of money as a key exhibit of the works that demonstrate true, saving faith.

At the same time, Jesus' climactic point in his sequence of three is about the right use of material possessions. So before concluding, I press home this point further, but in the context of avoiding as many misunderstandings as possible. In a Christian world in which many still think the New Testament teaches tithing, or giving 10 percent of one's income (though comparatively few actually practice it), I want to make clear that is not what I'm asking for. For some, a tithe is too demanding; for many, it is too little. I take the opportunity to suggest the graduated tithe as a model that better reflects New Testament teaching and describe how our family practices it.[19] I also want to forestall the most common reply I've received when I've taught on this topic more interactively—hence the protest and my reply concerning budgetary requirements. Because even small improvements in spending habits seem so difficult for many people, I feel compelled to stress the importance of the issue—how much is at stake.

This last topic produces the link to discussing verses 10–13 briefly, since one of the answers to "What's at stake?" is "spiritual blessing." Verses 10–12 are cryptic enough to require some unpacking, but I move rapidly to the climax in verse 13 about serving either God or mammon. Once a person understands that he or she can have only one absolute master, Jesus' closing pronouncement focuses the issue as pointedly as possible. The conclusion should unfold quickly at this point so as not to lose the force of that climax. To that end, I ask a series of questions for self-diagnosis and build on the current popularity of accountability groups in other areas of Christian living to drive home the need for responsibility in this arena. The final sentence contains the only exact replication of the sermon title in the message itself, to emphasize the big idea that unifies all three lessons.

6

Let's Play Wedding, Let's Play Funeral

Matthew 11:16–19

Good morning. My name is Eleazar ben Judah. Thank you for your kind invitation to join you this morning. I understand that you're interested in my experiences with two famous men from my country, whom I met several years ago. Neither lived very long, but both had great impact on our nation. I'm happy to be here and tell you things as I remember them.

The first was named John. I first heard about him when I was with a large crowd that went out from my hometown of Jerusalem to the Jordan River valley to hear him preach. They called him the Baptist because he told our people that they should be immersed in the river, symbolizing that they were repenting from their sins. We Jews were familiar with the practice of baptism. It was a requirement for Gentile proselytes, those who were not born Jewish but wanted to convert to our religion. And one of our monastic sects known as the Essenes practiced daily baptism among their membership as a way to symbolize purification from the last twenty-four hours' worth of sins that they might have committed. But John made it a requirement for all of us Jewish people, as if being God's elect, his chosen nation, and obeying the laws which he gave uniquely to our country weren't enough. And that really irked our religious authorities.

John was also unusual in his appearance. He wore clothing made of camel's hair, and a leather belt around his waist that made him look very much like our ancient prophet Elijah. But when some of our leaders asked him if he was claiming to be Elijah, he said no, he wasn't. I guess he interpreted their question to mean they were asking if he was the literal Elijah returned from heaven. After all, Elijah was one of two characters in our Scriptures who never actually died but who were taken immediately into God's presence at the end of their lives. So some of our Bible scholars believed that the literal Elijah now enjoying God's company in heaven would one day return, in fulfillment of the prophecies in the book of Malachi that describe Elijah coming and turning the hearts of our people back to their God just before what he calls "that great and dreadful day of the Lord" at the end of human history (Mal. 4:5 niv). But whatever John thought of their question, he definitely acted like a prophet and very much like Elijah. He was also an ascetic, eating that desert food—locusts and wild honey. He resembled other hermits and supposedly holy men, would-be messiahs and rabble-rousers who were little more than social bandits. And yet John was different. His message focused on a simple moral life, lived in the light of the imminent coming of the day of God's judgment. He told people who had extra clothes to give them away to help those who didn't have enough. He urged the tax collectors to stop skimming extra profits off the top as they collected their tolls. He even dared to confront Roman soldiers regarding their frequent practices of falsely accusing or extorting money from the people of subjugated nations like Israel.

I always thought that was pretty daring. So it didn't surprise me when, a few months after the crowds had assembled to hear him down by the Jordan River, news came that Herod Antipas up in Perea had arrested him, particularly because he had preached out boldly against Herod's having married his brother Philip's ex-wife. Word eventually got back to us in Jerusalem about the gruesome nature of John's subsequent execution. It seems Herod's new wife, Herodias, had her teenage daughter, Salome, dancing for him and a lot of his wealthy friends at one of those lavish banquets they liked to throw in the Herodian palaces. It seems the girl danced a little too suggestively or sensuously; at least those were the rumors that always surrounded parties in the palaces. Herod was half-drunk and, in his rash eagerness to reward the girl, vowed to give her whatever she wanted, up to half his kingdom. Salome went in and consulted with her mother. When she came back, she didn't ask for any money or land but for the head of John the Baptist on a platter. It makes me sick just to think about that happening, in the midst of a feast no less. But Herod was too embarrassed to let himself be seen as reneging on his vows with such lofty company present, so he agreed, and the dirty deed was done.

It's really interesting, reflecting back on the life of John, how he appealed to the masses. You wouldn't have thought someone whose message was in so many ways so harsh would turn out to be so popular. John really told it straight, like our prophets Isaiah and Jeremiah from centuries ago. But those prophets hadn't been nearly so popular. I think the difference with John was that he was pointing to someone he called "the Coming One" who would not baptize merely in water as John did but with God's Holy Spirit. John said he was preparing the way for that Coming One, preparing the way of the Lord. Word spread that he had actually pointed out a distant cousin of his as the very "Lamb of God"—God's prophesied sacrifice for the sins of the world. Messianic excitement began to spread, and that brings me to the second person you're interested in hearing me talk about this morning.

His name was Jesus. They said he came from Nazareth in Galilee. Not long after John was imprisoned, rumors flew about spectacular miracles that Jesus performed—turning water into wine, providing miraculous catches of fish, healing lepers, and similar remarkable accomplishments. Jesus came to Jerusalem a few times for the large annual festivals to which all faithful Jewish men who could were supposed to make pilgrimage, but I was never in the right place at the right time to hear him firsthand. Most of his ministry took place up north in Galilee, so I really wasn't sure what to believe about him.

But there was one common theme that wove its way through most all of the reports about Jesus that almost certainly would have been true, because his followers wouldn't have made it up if it weren't true. They said he associated with the riffraff of society. And that association really angered our leaders. He called a tax collector to be one of his twelve closest followers and then threw a party for him and all his friends, friends who hadn't even repented—which would have meant confessing their extortionary practices and promising to make restitution. Jesus certainly didn't pay enough attention to our practice of keeping a kosher table or our other laws of ritual purity regarding things one touched that would defile a person. Still other reports told about Jesus hanging around with the poor, with Samaritans, even with women, in public no less, and allowing them to learn from him just like his male disciples did. Who did he think he was, anyway?

Well, you could imagine his popularity with the lowbrows of our society. But his following was wider. His appeal was greater than that. Everywhere he went he seemed to be surrounded by crowds who hung on his every word, probably waiting for something new and even miraculous to occur. I think that a number of people began to suspect that he was our Messiah.

Then one day I had business up north in Galilee. It was after John was arrested but before he was beheaded. I was walking along a dusty country road when I came over the brow of a small hill and saw a huge crowd milling in the distance. As I got close enough to speak to people on the edge of the crowd, I asked them what was happening. Some said it was Jesus of Nazareth teaching the people. It seems some of John's followers had come from visiting him in prison, and they had asked on John's behalf if Jesus really was the Messiah, a natural enough question if John had thought he was but now found himself languishing in prison. Apparently Jesus hadn't given a direct answer but had simply told those followers of John to remind him about the miracles that Jesus had worked. I'm not exactly sure what else he had said, but when I was close enough to hear his words for myself, this is what I heard!

> To what can I compare this generation? They are like children sitting in the marketplaces and calling out to others:
>> "We played the flute for you,
>>> and you did not dance;
>> we sang a dirge,
>>> and you did not mourn."
>
> For John came neither eating nor drinking, and they say, "He has a demon." The Son of Man came eating and drinking and they say, "Here is a glutton and a drunkard, a friend of tax collectors and 'sinners.'" But wisdom is proved right by her actions. (Matt. 11:16–19)

I've mulled those words over and over. They've stuck in my mind throughout the years that have elapsed since then. Obviously Jesus was telling a short parable. Our rabbis did it all the time. First, they created a short story from everyday life to illustrate some passage of Scripture, and then they explained the spiritual lessons of the story they wanted people to learn. But Jesus wasn't explaining Scripture; he was describing people's responses to himself and to John.

I never have been quite sure what to make of his expression "this generation." It sounded like he was criticizing all our people, us Jews. But that couldn't be. He had quite a few committed followers from among our folk and hordes of other superficial hangers-on. Probably he had our leaders, particularly the Pharisees and the Sadducees, in mind, since most of them had never really liked him, or John, for that matter. Maybe, too, he realized that a large number of those in the crowds were pretty fickle, because later they did desert him. Even some of his closest followers would turn against him, one denying that he even knew him, another handing him over to our authorities to be arrested.

Be that as it may, Jesus used a quite clever little comparison on this occasion. "This generation"—our people in general—were like two groups of playmates. One keeps proposing games, but the other simply refuses to accept any of the suggestions and join in and play. First, the proposal is "let's play wedding," but the other group refuses to celebrate. "Well, then, let's play funeral," the first playmates suggest, but the others also refuse to mourn. It is all very similar to our leaders' reactions to Jesus and John and their followers. On the one hand, they rejected the stern, austere call to repentance that typified John's preaching. But they were equally outraged by Jesus' happy-go-lucky partying with the unclean people of our land.

That much of the parable all made pretty good sense to me. But Jesus' concluding words were a bit more puzzling, "But wisdom is proved right by her actions"—"vindicated," you might say. Our Scriptures sometimes personified God as Lady Wisdom. Proverbs 8–9 offers a classic example, portraying God's wisdom as a woman calling out to the people from the streets and squares of the city to come and learn from her, and to avoid giving in to the temptations of another woman, the prostitute, who wants to seduce them to commit sexual sin or its religious equivalent, idolatry. Maybe that's what Jesus meant, that God and his wisdom would be vindicated by the actions of John and Jesus. After all, they were clearly claiming to be his messengers or spokesmen.

The funny thing is, a couple of years after the day I had the chance to hear Jesus preach, he was executed just like John had been. It even happened in my city, in Jerusalem, in spring during the Passover feast. Our leaders had had enough of his subversive message undermining their authority. The crowds had fallen away, too. He apparently still claimed to be our Messiah, but it was obvious he wasn't interested in trying to overthrow the Romans, as we had hoped. And his execution clinched the fact that he couldn't have been our Messiah, because he was crucified. Everyone knows Messiahs don't die, much less the way he did. Our own Law, in Deuteronomy 21:23, made it very clear that anyone who was "hung on a tree" was cursed by God, and our religious leaders had already determined that crucifixion on a cross of wood with a person's arms outstretched was similar enough in appearance to a literal hanging for the same laws to apply. Whatever hopes people had placed in Jesus had to have been dashed by his crucifixion.

You would have expected that to be the end of John's and Jesus' supporters. Strangely, it wasn't. A number claimed they saw Jesus alive again after his death. In fact, another sect grew up among our people called "the Way." I never joined them but had a couple of distant friends who did. They've always intrigued me, though. They carried on John's tradition of moral living and Jesus' tradition of associating with everybody, including the most marginalized members of society. They even went to the Gentiles. The fact is that today in Jerusalem we hear that far more Gentiles have joined their movement around the empire than we Jews ever did.

I guess if you had to boil it all down to one idea, to combine John's and Jesus' message together, "the Way" was teaching *separation from sin but association with sinners.* And that really didn't fit our world, because if you were religious, well, obviously you separated from sin along with the notorious sinners involved in that sin. And if you weren't religious, then you had no compunctions about associating with sinners, but you also participated in their sinful behavior. Is it really possible to be close to God and yet love and even get close to the most sinful people of our world and influence them in a good way? Won't you just wind up being corrupted by them?

We Jews have been a people for about two thousand years now, from the days of Abraham down to my lifetime. We've lived as free people from time to time, but we've also suffered under Egypt, Canaan, Assyria, Babylon, Persia, Greece, and now Rome. We haven't seen many people with the ideas that this group called the Way has, though I suppose some of our kings and prophets tried off and on in their better moments to inculcate similar ideas. These ideas certainly never worked for any length of time, however. I wonder if the Way can do any better. I wonder what these people will look like in two thousand years, if the Messiah hasn't come by then.

If they are still in existence after that long a time and are still welcoming sinners but without sinning themselves, now that would be enough to make me believe. But, of course, I'll never live anywhere close to that long, and I seriously doubt it could ever happen. What do you think? At any rate, that's my story. Thanks so much for listening. I'll be going now. Shabbat shalom. Have a good Sabbath!

Commentary on "Let's Play Wedding, Let's Play Funeral"

Narrative sermons require more time and creativity than I usually have! So, despite the fact that parables lend themselves naturally to narrative exposition (see pp. 20–21), this is the only entirely narrative sermon on a parable that I have written. But the contemporizations and true-life applications in a majority of the other sermons in this book demonstrate the potential for including narrative elements in expository sermons that at times occupy a considerable percentage of the message.

From one point of view, the longer the parable—or any other story, for that matter—the more readily it lends itself to narrative preaching. For example, one could easily spend a fair amount of time telling the comparatively lengthy story of the prodigal son from the perspective of any or all of the three main characters, adding details that fit both the culture and the text. In this case, however, it was precisely because the parable of the children in the marketplace is so short that I first thought about composing a narrative sermon. To focus merely on the details in the text would not take that long. If I were going to preach a message on the parable alone, how would I fill the time allotted to me? That led me to create the sermon that appears in this chapter. (Even then it is the shortest sermon included in this volume.) The format also afforded me the opportunity to include information from elsewhere in the Gospels about John the Baptist. It is interesting that we know more about John than any other character in the Gospels except for Jesus himself, yet evangelical preaching rarely discusses him. This message gave me the chance to begin to redress that imbalance a little.[1]

Because this sermon is a single message, not part of a longer series, I could preach it from either Matthew's or Luke's version of the parable. Luke 7:31–35 is almost word-for-word identical to Matthew, and both evangelists set the passage in the identical context—Jesus' response to messengers who came to him from John after the Baptist was imprisoned, along with Jesus' additional teachings to the crowds about John.[2]

The parable does not quite fit the classic triangular structure of many of Jesus' parables, even though I would classify it as a three-point parable. One way of analyzing the characters is to see the uncooperative playmates as akin to the master or judge figure. But instead of choosing between contrasting subordinates—their companions who first suggest playing wedding and then propose to play funeral—they reject both options.[3] From another perspective, however, one could imagine the playmates who make the various suggestions being at the apex of the triangle, with the double rejections by the recalcitrant children at the two lower vertices. Since the children who propose the two games stand for John and Jesus, they will be the ones who ultimately judge the others—in this case, the listeners who have rejected God's two spokesmen.

Either way, it seems there are three lessons to be derived from the passage—the need to respond to John's message with repentance, the importance of rejoicing with Jesus, and the vindication of God's plan through both men despite the many who reject it. As in the story of the unjust steward, these three points are spelled out sequentially in the comments Jesus appends to the parable proper—verse 18, verse 19a, and verse 19b. If I were composing more traditional exposition, those three points would form my outline.

But the three points can be easily combined into a single big idea—that God's true will, despite the ways humans have so often perverted it, involves separation from sin but association with sinners. So, while I discuss all three points in the message, they do not form the backbone of the sermon's structure. I deal with John and Jesus, in turn, but from the fictional perspective of someone who has heard both men preach.

As with all good first-person narrative preaching in which the persona is a biblical (or biblical-era) character, a fair amount of historical homework is needed so that the invented details ring true to the time and place depicted in the original text. They must also support, rather than contradict or distract from, the material contained within the text.

I imagine myself as a Jewish layman with a common Hebrew name from that day, drawn from biblical characters—Eleazar ben (i.e., "son of") Judah. When possible, I dress in a simple costume—a robe with sleeves resembling a Jewish prayer shawl. At times when I have been a guest speaker in a setting in which I am initially introduced, I then explain that in fact I am not going to speak but have a friend with me who is. I quickly go offstage, put on the robe, and return. It usually draws a chuckle and breaks the ice.

The interpretation of the parable is disputed because the "happy" game is proposed first, but John the Baptist appears first in the explanation.[4] I believe the passage is a chiasm, constructed in a-b-b'-a' fashion so as to present the following structure, after the introduction in verse 16:

  a Jesus' joyous ministry (v. 17a)
   b John's austere ministry (v. 17b)
   b' John's ministry again (v. 18)
  a' Jesus' ministry again (v. 19a)

This is followed, of course, by the conclusion and final point (v. 19b).[5] One might expect me, therefore, to begin with Jesus, but, since Jesus far outstrips John in importance, I spend more time with him and save him for the climactic final position in the sermon. I thus begin with John, which also fits the chronological sequence of the ministries of the two men.

As an imaginary Jerusalemite, Eleazar could easily have heard John when crowds from Israel's capital city flocked to the Jordan River valley. Two paragraphs thus sum up the material found in all three Synoptic Gospels about John just prior to the beginning of Jesus' public ministry (Matt. 3:1–12; Mark 1:1–8; Luke 3:1–18). A bit of historical background provides the context for John's ministry of immersion, important because of the later theological overlay and ecclesiastical divisions that have blurred its original nature and significance. Some in my audience may be familiar with the Fourth Gospel's distinctive material about the Baptist as well, especially John's denying that he is Elijah (John 1:19–28). Since the Synoptics present him as one like Elijah, the apparent contradiction must be explained.[6]

The accounts of John the Baptist's arrest, imprisonment, and death (Matt. 14:3–12; Mark 6:17–29; Luke 3:19–20) are seldom expounded, so

I want my congregation to become familiar with those events as well. Josephus, too, has an account of these incidents (*Antiquities* 18.116–19), so my next paragraph combines and selects material from these four sources. Preachers not as familiar with the full "database" of information we have about John should consult a good Bible dictionary or encyclopedia for help.[7]

The final paragraph on John in my message prepares the way for Jesus' remarks about John in the parable of the children in the marketplace. On the one hand, John was very popular for a while. Some listeners will know this, so it needs to be acknowledged. On the other hand, the official Jewish leadership clearly rejected him (cf. Luke 7:29–30); Jesus wants to affirm at least this much. So I reflect on some of the reasons behind John's popularity and rejection and pave the way for turning to Jesus by speaking of the messianic excitement that John's ministry spawned.

The larger portion of Eleazar's remarks deal with Jesus of Nazareth. By narrating them from a relatively sympathetic point of view, and yet from that of one who never became a follower of Jesus, I force my listeners to think as first-century non-Christian Jews. Most Gentile Christians today, in my experience, do not do this well and as a result retain numerous unwittingly inaccurate and even anti-Semitic stereotypes. They often think that any reasonably intelligent person who was an eyewitness to Jesus' ministry should have recognized who he really was, which is not at all supported by the historical facts of the matter. I want to generate a little tension in my audience by helping them to understand why many could not accept Jesus as Israel's Messiah. But I do not leave them mired there but give them a way forward at the end of the message.

Eleazar's comments about Jesus thus begin with the inevitable rumor mill that exists in every human culture. Because Eleazar was from Jerusalem, it is easy to imagine him not having firsthand exposure to Jesus for a while. At the same time, the oral tradition would have spread numerous reports around the entire country,[8] and I point out one consistent element that Eleazar would have likely believed—Jesus' frequent hobnobbing with the outcasts of society in a way that would increasingly anger the religious authorities and at the same time explain his initial popularity with the masses.[9]

Eleazar then has a chance meeting with Jesus as part of a Galilean crowd when he has reason to travel north. He learns of the context of Jesus' parable—which we can read in Matthew and Luke, but which will have to be told to Eleazar if he has just arrived on the scene. I have memorized the parable itself, both so that I can maintain eye contact with my audience throughout its reading and so that Eleazar can make the claim that Jesus' words have stuck in his mind ever since he first heard them. Unlike the other parables presented thus far, this one fits into the classic rabbinic model of *mashal* plus *nimshal*—two relatively short and fairly equally balanced sections of narrative plus interpretation.[10] So it is natural to imagine Eleazar as recognizing this much.

An issue in the parable that would have been more puzzling when Jesus first spoke it than after his death and resurrection is the reference to "this generation," exactly because his widespread rejection had not yet occurred. So Eleazar would have puzzled over it, but he, too, could recognize retrospectively what Jesus probably meant.[11] The two comments about playing a flute and singing a dirge would have led many in Jesus' original audience to think of the two most common occasions for such music: weddings and funerals, respectively. Hence, my paraphrases (and sermon title), "Let's play wedding" and "Let's play funeral." Because Jesus explicitly spelled out what each proposal corresponded to in the nonmetaphorical reality symbolized by the parable, and because of the background I have already provided to the larger ministries of John and Jesus, it doesn't take very long to unpack verses 18–19a. Verse 19b is a bit more puzzling, though, so I spend a little longer on it, appealing to the most important historical background—God personified as Lady Wisdom.[12]

Whereas there was nothing more to say about John after his death, a first-century Jew could hardly talk about Jesus (especially to a Christian audience!) without acknowledging the belief in his resurrection by his followers and the sect of Jesus worshippers that it produced. The key stumbling block, as Paul himself would stress in 1 Corinthians 1:18–2:5, was Christ's crucifixion—proof that he had been cursed by God (Deut. 21:23). Many Christians also know that Paul will explain how he overcame the contradiction of a crucified Messiah—by affirming that Christ was cursed not for his own sins but for the sins of the world. I will be happy to explain this to anyone who asks me about it after the message, but I don't want to alleviate the tension of reflecting a *non-Christian* Jewish perspective in this narrative, so I don't include an explanation in the sermon itself.

The sermon, in good inductive fashion, saves the big idea for near its end. I continue the tension by showing how unrealistic this idea would have seemed to many in Jesus' world. I play on the historical coincidence that we live about two thousand years after the time of Jesus, who himself lived about two thousand years after the time of Abraham. The conclusion of the sermon starkly poses the question of whether Jesus' followers could ever implement his big idea presented in this parable, with Eleazar promising to become a Christian if that could happen but also expressing his strong doubts that it ever could. I deliberately never give an explicit command or even an exhortation to the congregation—the implications of what they need to do emerge in an even more rhetorically powerful way by having Eleazar say merely what he does at the end of his talk. The final good-byes are deliberately abrupt, combining an ancient Hebrew greeting with a Hebraized American one. Listeners should go away with the big idea and its demands on Christians firmly in mind.

7

How Do You Hear?

Matthew 13:1–23

Y ou can't just divide humanity into two camps, Christian and non-Christian. That's so arrogant, as if to say that only one religion could possibly be right. There are endless gradations of good and evil, religion and irreligion, and varieties of world-views. Even among professing Christians one finds every shade and hue, from the thoroughly committed to the completely nominal."

How would Jesus respond to this collection of claims—he who more than anyone in the Bible taught extensively about heaven and hell, the only two destinies of humankind? At one level, I think he would have agreed. Every person has a unique life and a unique experience of God on Judgment Day. Jesus clearly recognized in his life more than two kinds of responses to his ministry.

In fact, four come to mind readily. First, there were his opponents, particularly many among the Jewish leaders who were hostile to Christ from the outset and never changed their tone. Second, there were the large crowds of superficial hangers-on, a broader group of those the Gospels sometimes call "disciples," who followed Jesus off and on, admired him for a time but then at one telltale juncture described toward the end of John fell away—when talk of Christ's death and his followers sharing his fate became too explicit. Third, there is the intriguing case of Judas, who was one of the inner circle of twelve who followed Jesus virtually all the way to the end of his life but who ultimately betrayed him, probably because he felt Jesus had betrayed the Jewish nationalistic cause. Fourth, and finally, there are the remaining eleven closest disciples, certainly not without their flaws. Peter denied Christ three times but later repented. All of the remaining ten fled from Jesus in the Garden of Gethsemane, but they too later returned and were recommissioned. It was this core of Jesus' initial followers that God through his Spirit after the resurrection mightily empowered that his church might be established and grow.

I believe Jesus had precisely these four groups of people in mind when he told the now familiar parable of the sower. It appears in all three of the Synoptic Gospels—Matthew, Mark, and Luke. We'll be reading it today in the version that appears in the Gospel of Matthew 13:1–9. Matthew writes,

> That same day Jesus went out of the house and sat by the lake. Such large crowds gathered around him that he got into a boat and sat in it, while all the people stood on the shore. Then he told them many things in parables, saying, "A farmer went out to sow his seed. As he was scattering the seed, some fell along the path, and the birds came and ate it up. Some fell on rocky places, where it did not have much soil. It sprang up quickly, because the soil was shallow. But when the sun came up, the plants were scorched, and they withered because they had no root. Other seed fell among thorns, which grew up and choked the plants. Still other seed fell on good soil, where it produced a crop—a hundred, sixty, or thirty times what was sown. Whoever has ears, let them hear."

The farmer's practice sounds strange to us. But in Jesus' world it seems to have reflected standard procedure for broadcast sowing. The farmer recognized that his seed would land in many different kinds of soil. But sowing often preceded plowing, and the farmer would simply walk up and down the rows of his field, tossing the seed out by hand; then, using a wooden plow drawn by oxen or donkeys, he would create furrows in the soil so that as many of the seeds as possible could take root. Jesus is telling a story based on the life experience that many in his audience would have had. What seems unusual to us was realistic to them, except perhaps for the harvest. A thirtyfold yield per seed was scarcely unprecedented, though certainly good. A sixtyfold yield was particularly welcome. A hundredfold yield would have been better than anyone could expect. Here is the one surprising or unrealistic part of Jesus' story by first-century standards.

This story not only proves fairly realistic by first-century standards but also seems to be one of the easiest of Jesus' parables to interpret. Out of the more than forty passages that are usually identified by commentators as parables, only two receive a detailed, point-by-point interpretation. One of them is the parable of the wheat and the weeds later in Matthew 13 (vv. 24–30, 36–43), and the other is our story of the sower. Verses 18–23 present Jesus' interpretation:

> Listen then to what the parable of the sower means: When people hear the message about the kingdom and do not understand it, the evil one comes and snatches away what was sown in their hearts. This is the seed sown along the path. The seed falling on rocky ground refers to people who hear the word and at once receive it with joy. But since they have no root, they last only a short time. When trouble or persecution comes because of the word, they quickly fall away. The seed falling among the thorns refers to people who hear the word, but the worries of this life and the deceitfulness of wealth choke the word, making it unfruitful. But seed falling on good soil refers to people who hear the word and understand it. They produce a crop, yielding a hundred, sixty or thirty times what was sown.

Again, some of the details may seem strange to us in the twenty-first century, for we are separated not only in time but in culture from the world of first-century Israel. But even without Jesus' explicit interpretation, his hearers probably would have surmised something similar, just from the story itself. Old Testament texts such as Isaiah 55:10–11 equate the preaching of God's word with one who sows seed and promise that God's word will never return void. So the equation of a sower or a farmer with the preacher of the word would have been natural for Jesus' first listeners. For some modern readers the most surprising portion of Jesus' interpretation is his equation of the birds with the devil. But we need to remember that birds in the Old Testament and in intertestamental Judaism often were harbingers of something evil. In 1 Kings 16:3–4, the Lord prophesied that he would judge the house of King Baasha, that dogs would eat the bodies of family members who died in the city while birds would feed on those who died in the countryside. More so than in our world, Jesus' audience could well have seen birds as an evil, even a diabolical, omen. Other than this one point of comparison that seems unnatural to us, the rest of the interpretation falls into place very naturally. If the seed is God's word sown, then the various kinds of soil most naturally refer to the kinds of people in which the seed does or doesn't take root, to how long it grows, and to whether or not it ultimately produces fruit.

In fact, the biggest controversy in the history of the interpretation of this parable is not about anything Jesus explicitly says but about what he doesn't say. How do the four different groups of soils correlate with Jesus' teaching elsewhere, if humanity divides itself into only two groups—those who are his followers and those who aren't? The first group, represented by the seed falling on the path so that it never takes root at all, clearly refers to non-Christians who never make any pretense of following Christ. The fourth and final group, those who are represented by the good soil and produce a good harvest of fruit, equally clearly refers to Christians, those who prove to be true followers of Jesus. The first group is obviously outside of God's kingdom. The last group is obviously inside. But what about the middle two groups and the seeds and kinds of soil used to depict them?

It's certainly understandable that many Christians throughout church history have wanted to identify these groups as "insiders." If we have any sensitivity or compassion, we will want there to be as few lost people in the world as possible. And we certainly know of all kinds of grada-tions of commitment among those we believe to be true Christians. So it is natural to try to make the second and third kinds of seed and soils in Jesus' parable correspond to less than fully mature believers. Or perhaps we may think of denominations or theological perspectives with less than what we would consider complete biblical truth. And if we believe in what is popularly called the doctrine of eternal security, we will avoid an interpretation of this parable that makes these two intermediate categories of seed represent people who were truly saved but then equally truly lost.

But I don't believe the imagery of our parable permits an interpretation that equates the second and third seeds with Christians of any kind. This is one of a large number of parables where two or more initial characters or episodes contrast with one climactic character and episode at the end of the passage. Think of the parables of the talents and the pounds where two good servants are first introduced as foils for the climactic, quite different wicked servant. Or consider the good Samaritan, in which both the priest and the Levite pass by an injured man on the road from Jerusalem to Jericho, with a Jewish audience naturally expecting them to be the heroes of the story and stop to offer aid, but instead, in striking contrast, it is the third passerby, the despised Samaritan, who turns out to be the true hero. Or we might think of the parables of the great sup-per or wedding banquet, in which initial groups of guests invited to the lavish feast ultimately reject the master's invitation, only to have Jesus conclude his story with a striking contrast by which outsiders—the poor, marginalized, and oppressed in Jesus' world—become the replacement guests who accept the master's invitation. It is natural, therefore, when we come to the parable of the sower and see four different categories of seed, building toward the one that produces the good harvest, to assume that the first three will be examples of the same kind and that the last category will reflect a contrasting climax. The very imagery of bearing fruit and harvesting a crop fits with all of these observations. Every farmer knows that it doesn't matter whether a seed produces a stem that pokes up through the ground, or leaves, or even a fair amount of other growth, if the particular crop for which that seed was planted never comes to maturity.

If we pay close attention to Jesus' interpretation, we will see that in fact these two intermediate categories of seeds are never described in language that must unambiguously be taken as referring to true disciples. The seed that falls on rocky ground refers to people, Jesus says, who hear the word and at once receive it with joy. Many people have heard the gospel message, have had some initial enthusiasm for it, but this certainly falls far short of true acceptance and commitment. The third category of seed is not even described as promisingly, but rather as referring to people who hear the word, but the worries of this life and the deceitfulness of wealth choke it out. Here there is not even any reference to initial reception with enthusiasm or joy. It is true that throughout Christian history—and particularly since the Protestant Reformation and the debate between the Reformers Calvin and Arminius—there are those who believe it possible to be a true Christian, repudiate one's faith, and lose one's salvation, just as there are those who believe that salvation cannot be lost or forfeited in any way. But what we often lose sight of in this debate, important though it may be, is that both Calvinists and Arminians agree that people can appear to be Christian, follow Jesus on some superficial level, even for a significant period of time, but then decisively turn their backs on him, entirely repudiate him, never repent, and wind up being lost for eternity. The only debate is about what is proven when that scenario unfolds. One side argues that such people were true Christians who lost their salvation; the other, that they were never true Christians at all.

I take my stand with the latter group, particularly because of John's description in his first epistle of false teachers who have left the Ephesian congregations he was pastoring. In 1 John 2:19 we read, "They went out from us, but they did not really belong to us. For if they had belonged to us, they would have remained with us; but their going showed that none of them belonged to us." This seems to be the clearest of all the various texts in the Bible that get quoted in this debate; it shows that those who commit apostasy demonstrate that they were never truly believers in the first place. But again, we can agree to disagree in that debate. The agreement that we must not lose sight of is that people who profess Christ, then repudiate their belief, and never change their minds are indeed lost, tragically, for all eternity. In our parable of the sower, then, it seems to me that the second and third seeds cannot be equated in any way with true believers. Although Jesus tells the story with four different possible responses, ultimately there are only two categories of people described here. There are only two categories of people in the world—those who are true believers and, therefore, by definition will bear fruit of some kind, and everyone else.

But there is another, perhaps even more difficult theological problem raised by material we've entirely (and deliberately) skipped over thus far. Why *do* people respond so differently to God's word, even if four different categories can ultimately be boiled down to two? Here is where the whole thorny issue of predestination comes in. Matthew 13:10–17 reads as follows:

> The disciples came to him and asked, "Why do you speak to the people in parables?"
> He replied, "The knowledge of the secrets of the kingdom of heaven has been given to you, but not to them. Those who have will be given more, and they will have an abundance. As for those who do not have, even what they have will be taken from them. This is why I speak to them in parables:
>> "Though seeing, they do not see;
>>> though hearing, they do not hear or understand.
>> In them is fulfilled the prophecy of Isaiah:
>> "'You will be ever hearing but never understanding;
>> you will be ever seeing but never perceiving.
>> For this people's heart has become calloused;
>>> they hardly hear with their ears,
>>> and they have closed their eyes.
>> Otherwise they might see with their eyes,
>>> hear with their ears,
>>> understand with their hearts
>>> and turn, and I would heal them.'
> But blessed are your eyes because they see, and your ears because they hear. Truly I tell you, many prophets and righteous people longed to see what you see but did not see it, and to hear what you hear but did not hear it."

The disciples begin by asking why Jesus speaks in a style of discourse that apparently is somewhat cryptic. His response, beginning in verse 11, distinguishes two categories of people, insiders and outsiders, in God's kingdom. In part, at least, parables are spoken to clarify a division that has already occurred among those who have heard Jesus throughout his ministry. Those who are willing to receive his message will learn more and receive more. Those who have not accepted what they have heard so far will lose even what they have heard. But all this, Jesus says, is a fulfillment of the prophecy of Isaiah. The pattern of Isaiah preaching to a stiff-necked and obdurate people in his generation is being repeated in Jesus' age. It seems, then, at first glance that Jesus is hinting at something like the strong Calvinist doctrine of double predestination—that God simply chooses in advance for some people to be saved and for some to be lost. And yet at the same time there are indications within this very text that Jesus recognizes humans have freedom to respond as they see fit. "Those who have" in the first half of verse 12 refers to those who have responded properly to the word thus far, and "those who do not have" in the second half of the verse refers to those who have not responded properly thus far. And whereas Isaiah records God's words to him in the form of a command—"Go and tell this people: Be ever hearing, but never understanding; be ever seeing, but never perceiving" (NIV)—Jesus rewords Isaiah's prophecy as a simple prediction, implying, this is how you will act, and this is how God will respond in return.

In fact, paradoxically, Scripture always balances talk of predestination with references to human free will. Reading Isaiah 6:9–10 in its larger context puts this into sharper perspective. The first five chapters of Isaiah have made it perfectly clear that God is calling his prophet to proclaim his coming judgment in response to the Israelites' clear, frequent, and repeated acts of sin and idolatry—of rebellion against their creator and redeemer. God is not acting out some deterministic agenda in which he has hardened his people's hearts from all eternity past. He is responding to their freely chosen hardening of their own hearts. The end of Isaiah 6 proves even more instructive, as God is confirming the current generation of Israelites in their disobedience, much as Romans 1 three times speaks of God giving over sinners to their depravity (vv. 24, 26, 28). Isaiah asks God how long this bleak situation will persist. The reply he receives concludes in the last half of Isaiah 6:13 with these words, "But as the terebinth and oak leave stumps when they are cut down, so the holy seed will be the stump in the land" (NIV). One day there will be a righteous remnant. God's hardening is not irrevocable. Those who repent will always be welcomed back. Those who do not God leaves and even confirms in their own devices. As C. S. Lewis once put it so memorably, "There are only two kinds of people in the end:—those who say to God, 'Thy will be done,' and those to whom God says . . . 'Thy will be done.'"[1] Those who demonstrate faithfulness to God by trusting in Christ show in so doing that they are his elect. Those who are not the elect God knows will never want him anyway. The danger comes when we attempt to play God and imagine we can identify who is and who is not among the elect. Because of our finite and fallen state, more often than not we are likely to guess wrong and damn those God intends one day to save and perhaps declare saved those who in fact may be lost. Because we cannot know unerringly who falls into either category, we, like the sower, must share the word with all people, however promising or unpromising the "soil" of their lives appears. Nor may we assume that their first reactions will match their final ones. And so we must continue sowing the word, at times throughout a lifetime, in relationships with people for whom we care dearly. Predestination is far better understood as a doctrine that helps us make sense of the responses we get to preaching the word after the fact rather than as a motive or guide for how to do ministry in advance.

So much for lofty theology! Irrespective of how others respond, what personal messages are there in this parable for you and me? Obviously, we need to be sure that we are like the seed in the good soil. This doesn't imply that all of us must be exceptional Christians. That's undoubtedly why Jesus spoke of the various yields, from reasonably ordinary amounts to seemingly spectacular ones. I assume that many here this morning have assurance that they are in this fourth category of good soil. It is possible that no one present here today is in the first category of those implacably opposed to Christ and clearly outside his kingdom. Those folks, more often than not, are wholly unwilling even to visit a church, though at times they will do so simply to be polite to a good friend who has invited them.

What concerns me most for contemporary application again is categories two and three. The seed falling on the rocky ground is described as those who, having inadequate roots, "when trouble or persecution comes because of the word . . . quickly fall away" (v. 21). We know very little of intense trouble and persecution because of the word in contemporary America, and what little we do know about, we often avoid by silence. Yet as we speak this morning, Christians are being martyred in Sudan, Iran, China, and various other countries around the world.[2] Children are being sold into slavery. Christians are meeting secretly for fear of imprisonment or execution. In certain Latin American countries those who speak out against totalitarian regimes simply disappear, presumably imprisoned and/or assassinated. In the twentieth century there were more martyrs for the Christian faith worldwide than in all nineteen previous centuries of church history combined. And as America becomes increasingly post-Christian, we will see more overt persecution. Those friends of mine who are active in sharing their faith and trying to take a stand for ethical behavior in secular companies—in the cutthroat, often unethical workplaces of multinational corporations—can attest to the attempts to silence them or the outright discrimination that they have often experienced. There is a time and a place to witness simply by good behavior and a Christian work ethic, and we don't always do that well either, but there also is a time and a place to take a stand unequivocally for what we believe to be right and true according to the gospel of Jesus Christ. Are we prepared to do that, and if not, what does it say about the genuineness of our Christian profession?

But I worry even more about the third category of soil. Jesus says, "the worries of this life and the deceitfulness of wealth choke" out the word in these people (v. 22). From one point of view, they may come even closer to being the real thing. Perhaps they would be prepared to maintain under fire that they were followers of Jesus and would think that they meant it. Judas stayed longer when other disciples had left. But what of the disillusionment that comes, as it did for Judas, when it is clear that Jesus doesn't deliver physical liberation in this life or its contemporary equivalent—the so-called health-wealth gospel? What are we to say when professing Christians in the United States on average give only between 2 and 3 percent of their annual income to all charitable giving put together, and when a full 20 percent give absolutely nothing, at least nothing that can be documented? It is far easier to sing hymns about surrendering all than to actually abandon a cherished affluence for the cause of Christ. The imagery of the parable teaches us to mistrust such professions of faith when they don't lead to substantive personal transformation.

How would Jesus answer the challenge of my opening salvo in this sermon? Ultimately, I'm convinced he would agree. There are only two kinds of people in the world: those who will delight in heaven and those who will suffer in hell. Our temptation is to endlessly multiply categories for the former. Jesus seems to expand the latter, and not just here. He elsewhere talks about the narrow way, the narrow gate, and the few who enter by them (Matt. 7:13–14). At any rate, the key for all of us is to make sure that we are in category four—true Christians, bearing fruit according to the ways God has gifted us and exhibiting the fruit of the Spirit: love, joy, peace, patience, kindness, goodness, gentleness, faithfulness, and self-control. Thus we commit our lives to serving God as best we understand his call to us in our little corners of the world, in our niches in his great kingdom activity. Which seed, in which kind of soil, are you? When the word is preached, how do you hear?

Commentary on "How Do You Hear?"

After the parables of the prodigal son and the good Samaritan, the parable of the sower may be the next best known of all of Jesus' stories. Because it is one of two parables for which Jesus gives point-by-point explanation, one wonders at first glance how much more the expositor can say. The parable clearly has a master figure—the sower—but can it be viewed as triangular when it has four contrasting subordinates—the various seeds in the various soils? It can if three of them can be grouped together as either variations of the good example or variations of the

bad. Determining the answer to this question thrusts the preacher right
into the thick of the passage's biggest interpretive controversy, and one
that troubles ordinary Christians as well. Do the two intermediate categories of seeds/soils belong with the clearly bad seed or with the clearly
good seed? Or are they truly separate categories? This issue will thus
command a significant portion of the sermon's attention and generate
the introduction as well.

The introduction catches attention and arouses interest by reflecting
the common perspective of today's pluralists, who believe in many ways
to God. But it also sets up the exposition of the parable, since the passage
itself contains four, rather than two, different kinds of seeds or soils. The
brief opening question is matched by an equally brief appeal to Jesus'
opinion. Tension is heightened here, since listeners will have expected
Jesus to refute the pluralist perspective rather than siding with it.

By focusing in the third paragraph on four kinds of responses to
Jesus, I bridge from the two introductory paragraphs to the reading of
the text. Scholars have plausibly suggested that Jesus (or the evangelists who recorded his parable) had precisely these four categories of
people in mind as corresponding to the four parts to the parable.[3] More
attention will be devoted to their contemporary equivalents, but I want
my listeners to recognize that in this case today's application closely
matches the originally intended application of the passage. Whenever
this happens, one can move from the ancient text to today's world most
readily, confident that one is applying God's word faithfully.[4]

The main points of the parable, and hence of any sermon on it, remain
unchanged from Matthew to Mark to Luke, though detailed nuancing
varies a little.[5] I chose Matthew's version in order to begin a three-part
series on the parables of Matthew 13 in a church in which I had been
invited to substitute for the senior pastor for three consecutive Sundays.
Only Matthew includes as many as eight parables consecutively in his
record of this juncture in Jesus' ministry (13:1–52), so his Gospel affords
a good opportunity to deal with a detailed and representative cross-section of Jesus' kingdom teaching. Because most liberal commentators
believe the parable itself is authentic but the interpretation is not, and
because one of the reasons they believe this involves the seemingly unnatural meanings the interpretation supplies,[6] I choose to comment on
the parable proper before reading the interpretation.

There are unusual features, of course, in the parable itself. As we
have discussed, the key to the symbolism of a passage usually resides
with what would have struck Jesus' audiences as unusual. That may or
may not be the same as what puzzles us, so I need to help my congregation distinguish between the two. Even though our contemporary
word "broadcast" came to be used for the dissemination(!) of words and

images over radio and television airwaves precisely because traditional cultures sowed their fields with seed in similar fashion, few people know that today.[7] Nor are they even aware of the history of agriculture per se.[8] So I must begin by explaining how that seemingly strange feature of the parable would *not* have surprised Jesus' audience. On the other hand, in our era of enormous yields from well-tended fields, one has to note how extravagant at least the hundredfold product of this sower's work would have been.[9]

The rest of the picture of the parable proper proves understandable for the majority of contemporary listeners, so I can now turn to the interpretation attributed to Jesus. By acknowledging how straightforward Jesus' remarks seem to many today, I let listeners who might be thinking the same thing know that I am not going to challenge a superficial, commonsense reading of the passage with anything too idiosyncratic. But I also whet the appetites of those who suspect that there is more to discover when one delves a little more deeply. I consciously skip over the intervening verses on why Jesus speaks in parables, both because I don't want to lose the connection between the parable and the interpretation and because I want to deal with Jesus' "parable theory" in some detail in a more climactic position later in the message.[10]

I likewise don't want to distract from the exposition of the parable and its interpretation by debating the authenticity of the latter.[11] But even for the evangelical audiences I typically address, the less obvious portions of the interpretation require justification—not because my listeners will jump to the conclusion that Jesus didn't say this but because they will wonder where he got it! I limit myself to key Old Testament references because I think they answer this question adequately,[12] and I don't have to explain how one can use intertestamental literature as key historical background without canonizing it. But it is worth pointing out that there are even closer parallels in the pseudepigrapha both to the imagery of the sower overall and to the use of birds as a cipher for the devil (see esp. 4 Ezra 8:41 and Jub. 11:5–24, respectively).[13] In my home church, where I have prepared people in past settings, or in a context in which people know me and my method well enough, I would probably add this information.

While wanting to deal with all the important exegetical issues raised by each portion of the text, I have not lost sight of the key question about the seeds that fell on the rocky ground or that were choked out by the thorns. I am aware of the huge divide between popular understanding and preaching, especially in more Calvinist circles, and scholarly understanding of this issue, so I begin with the approach many will have heard of and/or adopted but then go on to explain more carefully why I believe it can't withstand close scrutiny. The argument based on the structure of the parables does not depend on my somewhat unique structural classifications, though it fits perfectly with them. Rather, it flows from the standard form-critical observations that parables, like other jokes and short stories, often involve a series of parallel items that all set up and contrast with the final item, an item that is most emphasized by its climactic position.[14] Because most congregations are not familiar with form criticism, and would be suspicious of it if they were, I describe these principles in nontechnical language, backed up with noncontroversial illustrations from other parables and bolstered by an appeal to another more commonsense argument from farming: only what can be harvested counts.

The only remaining issue is then to demonstrate that Jesus' explicit interpretation does not necessarily contradict the view that sees all three of the first groups of seeds as less than full-fledged believers. Interestingly, even Calvin had a concept of "temporary faith" to which he appealed to explain such imagery, without denying his doctrine of the perseverance of the saints.[15] In any large evangelical congregation today, however, even within historically Calvinist denominations, there will probably be a smattering of people who wonder if eternal security is really true, not least because they will have watched people's behavior seemingly disprove the doctrine. Some may actually believe fairly strongly in the Arminian view that true Christians can lose their salvation through prolonged, unrepentant, and flagrant repudiation of their faith. I explain to them both why I do not take that position and why I believe they should feel free to do so, because there is a larger issue that Calvin and Arminius agreed on. Important and interesting as their differences are, we may permit them to remain as an intramural debate. What really counts is the fact that people can wind up in hell after at least appearing to be Christians, so all apparently Christian audiences should be regularly warned against this kind of apostasy. Not all Calvinists have followed Calvin on this point; many today take these kinds of passages as a mere loss of reward. Again, I don't want to get sidetracked from the main flow of the message by debating this point, but I know that anyone who holds that view, thinking that it in fact was Calvin's (as in my experience many do), will be challenged as he or she hears me refer to his real approach.[16]

Finally, I am ready for the even thornier issue of predestination that the verses in between Jesus' parable and his interpretation raise. If I were preaching only these verses, I would sketch out the three or four main approaches that have historically been taken to explain them.[17] But because this is only a small section of a much larger sermon, I simply sketch out the perspective that, after careful study, makes the most sense to me. It fits the contexts of both Matthew and Isaiah, from which Jesus' Old Testament quotation comes, and it is consistent with and follows naturally from the doctrine of the perseverance of the saints. But again, without getting into the larger debate that would take me to numerous other passages, I want to challenge Calvinists (and in this instance, it would seem, Calvin himself) on the issue of predestination to damnation. Without stating that I don't believe it is taught in any other text of Scripture (though I don't!), I provide enough explanation for why I don't believe it is taught here (and with this some Calvinist scholars would concur).[18] More importantly, I stress the freedom that Calvin agreed people have, and that I want to make sure my audience knows *they* have, to make choices for and against God in Christ and thus to urge on them the need for wholehearted discipleship that will endure and demonstrate true saving faith—hence, the C. S. Lewis quote.

This brings me directly to the contemporary application with which I conclude and thus most stress. I acknowledge that this sermon has been more overtly theological (and more theologically deep) than most, with the self-effacing remark, "So much for lofty theology!" I am trying to empathize with those who may feel they are in over their heads. I want to leave them with something easier to grasp, agree on, and act on. So I return to the two intermediate categories of seed and look for the most likely contemporary equivalents. The issues of bold witness, especially under threat of persecution, and the stranglehold of material possessions strike me as the two most urgent matters for most middle- or upper-class Western audiences. The economic themes may by now be tiring the reader of *this* book, but recall that this was the first in a short series of sermons at a church that hadn't recently read (or heard) several other messages including similar themes.

My conclusion comes full circle to where I began. While at one level Jesus would have acknowledged four (or even more) different ways people can respond to him and to his message, ultimately these responses boil down to only two options—for him or against him. Jesus has taken his stand against the pluralist after all, even if we have had to wait until the end of the message to hear him do it. We must move heaven and earth to ensure we are in the only acceptable category, that of the fruitful soil. I close with the central questions that this observation triggers and implicitly explain my choice of the sermon title in so doing.

8

Seeds, Weeds, and Explosive Growth

Matthew 13:24–43

In the mid-1990s, thanks to an unexpected opportunity to become friends with a professor of New Testament at Brigham Young University in Provo, Utah, I had the chance to coauthor with Stephen Robinson, a member of the Church of Jesus Christ of Latter Day Saints, a book, which we titled *How Wide the Divide? A Mormon and an Evangelical in Conversation.* In the book, we chose four central theological topics on which our two religious communities differ and went back and forth, taking turns writing sections, discussing why we believed what we believed and why we were not convinced by what the other community believed. One particular belief of the Mormon church that became clearer to me than ever before through those dialogues was the idea that there was a "great apostasy" after the last of the living apostles died off at the end of the first century, so that no true apostolic Christianity subsequently existed from roughly 100 A.D. until, as the Mormons believe, the prophet Joseph Smith in 1830 in the United States restored true apostolic Christianity. Of several problems with this belief, one very fundamental one is that Jesus, speaking to Simon Peter in Matthew 16:18, promised that he would build his church on the foundation of Peter's initial leadership of the community of Jesus' followers, and that not even the gates of hell—not even the strongest of demonic onslaughts—could prevail against it.

Of course, Matthew 16:18 also cuts against the grain of certain Protestant conceptions that have sometimes claimed that first Eastern Orthodoxy and then Roman Catholicism likewise erased all true

Christianity from the planet from fairly early on in the second century until at least the time of Martin Luther and the Reformation in 1517. Christ's words, however, don't mean that true Christianity in a given time or place throughout the history of the world might not become comparatively small. Jesus promised simply that his true church would never be utterly destroyed. Certainly there have been times and places throughout church history, and even in today's world at the beginning of the twenty-first century, when Christianity has seemed like a very beleaguered, tiny minority in certain places on our planet.

Almost certainly that's how Jesus' disciples would have felt as Jesus' ministry in the first century unfolded. By the time we reach what many consider to be the midpoint of that ministry, narrated in Matthew 13, resistance to Jesus' teaching and claims had grown to the point where the vast crowds that seemingly hung on his every word early in his public career began to give way to increasing hostility and opposition.

Matthew 13 begins with the parable of the sower, in which Jesus describes his true followers as good seed that bears a crop one hundred, sixty, or thirty times what was sown. But before this encouraging harvest, three unfruitful soils are described, suggesting that a considerable number of those to whom the gospel is preached will ultimately respond with something less than full-fledged discipleship.

The second section of Matthew 13 to a certain degree balances whatever negative portrait might have been created in the minds of Jesus' listeners by the depiction of the unfruitful soils in the parable of the sower. Three discrete sections mark off the central part of Matthew 13: the parable of the wheat and the weeds in verses 24–30; the twin parables of the mustard seed and the leaven in verses 31–35; and Jesus' explanation of the parable of the weeds in verses 36–43, when the disciples were with Jesus indoors after the public phase of his teaching on this occasion. The unifying theme that comes through these three passages is the very encouraging promise of first the survival and then the growth of seeds that are planted with very unpromising beginnings. Despite obstacles that might appear to threaten the entire destruction of the crop, these plants eventually produce a bountiful harvest.

Let's look at the first of these stories in Matthew 13:24–30, the parable of the wheat and the weeds:

> Jesus told them another parable: "The kingdom of heaven is like a man who sowed good seed in his field. But while everyone was sleeping, his enemy came and sowed weeds among the wheat, and went away. When the wheat sprouted and formed heads, then the weeds also appeared.
>
> "The owner's servants came to him and said, 'Sir, didn't you sow good seed in your field? Where then did the weeds come from?'

"'An enemy did this,' he replied.

"The servants asked him, 'Do you want us to go and pull them up?'

"'No,' he answered, 'because while you are pulling the weeds, you may root up the wheat with them. Let both grow together until the harvest. At that time I will tell the harvesters: First collect the weeds and tie them in bundles to be burned; then gather the wheat and bring it into my barn.'"

Verses 36–43 provide Jesus' very detailed interpretation of this parable, which we will read in a few moments. But even before reading it, we observe that the parable seems fairly transparent in its context. Jesus has just told the parable of the sower and explained it as well, and the seed there clearly stood for God's word, which was sown in varying kinds of soils. The different plants that grew in those soils stood for the different kinds of people in the world and the various ways in which they respond to God's word. Coming fresh from hearing that parable, we naturally assume that Jesus means something similar by the similar imagery in this passage. If Jesus, or even God himself, could be depicted as a sower earlier in the chapter, then it's natural to think of the farmer who sowed the good seed in this parable as a symbol for God as well. But God's enemy throughout Scripture is the devil, and clearly the devil is also at one level responsible for the wicked rejecting the gospel. So the wheat and the weeds naturally represent God's people and his opponents. Jesus often uses the image of a harvest as a symbol for Judgment Day, and many other parables that rabbis told in those days do likewise. Despite the claims of many critics who allege that the very allegorical or point-by-point interpretation of this parable in verses 36–43 could not be authentic—could not be what Jesus really taught—it's hard to see what else his story could have meant in an early first-century Jewish agricultural context. The parable and its interpretation both make good sense.

In fact, even at the literal level of the behavior of the farmer, this story makes more sense than we might realize. We actually have accounts from other ancient sources of what today would probably be called bioterrorism, even if at a very primitive level, in which an enemy of a powerful landowner clandestinely tried to destroy the landowner's crop during planting season by scattering the seeds of other plants in his field in the middle of the night.

But there is one item that would have seemed very unrealistic in a first-century story about farming. Even after Jesus' listeners recognized that this was a parable—a story with a symbolic, spiritual meaning—this detail would still have appeared somewhat puzzling, and that is the command from the farmer not to pull up the weeds. Every good farmer

weeded his fields to protect his crops. But in this case, premature weeding would destroy too much of the wheat as well, presumably because
the root systems had become intertwined. In addition, the Greek word
used here discloses that the weeds were "darnel," a plant that superficially appeared very much like wheat, especially when only the stems
and leaves of each had sprouted. Jesus says in essence, "Let them grow
together, and only at the time of the harvest will we separate the two
out." The unspoken assumption is that somehow the wheat will indeed
survive, despite the appearance of the weeds and the likelihood of their
choking out the wheat altogether.

It's interesting, isn't it, to reflect on ways in which Christians and
non-Christians likewise appear superficially similar. There's nothing
in our physical appearance that necessarily changes when we become
followers of Jesus to immediately set us off from the rest of humanity.
And both because Christians remain sinners throughout their lives and
because non-Christians often do many good things, it's often impossible
to single out Jesus' followers in a crowd even by observing their public
behavior. It's also interesting to reflect on ways in which Christians
perennially have longed for the premature destruction of evil people
in their world. Jesus' idea of letting good and evil coexist side by side,
even at times seemingly intertwined until his final judgment, doesn't
sit well with our desire to take God's justice into our own hands and be
his instruments of meting it out.

One obvious temptation throughout church history has been to try
to Christianize societies and cultures in the world in ways that have
often disenfranchised people of other religions or world-views. Much
of the Muslim terrorism that afflicts our world today is still, in Islamic
minds, exacting vengeance for the horrible slaughters committed by
the Crusaders a millennium ago throughout Europe and the Middle
East in the name of Christ. Still more of that terrorism is reinforced
and fueled because of the much more recent perception of American
political, economic, and cultural imperialism throughout the world,
and the belief, however misguided it may be, that America is a Christian nation. Thus, many Muslims think that typical American morals
reflect the essence of Christianity. Even in the United States, much of
the anti-Christian sentiment in the public sector, and particularly in the
media and the arts, reflects a swing of the pendulum away from an era
in which, rightly or wrongly, the perception was that Christian morals
dominated, at times in an unhealthy way, in American society. And the
resurgence of the religious Right and some of the most overtly political
attempts to reclaim Christian morality in the public sector, focusing on a
very narrow range of ethical issues, often perpetuates that perception.

But perhaps more dangerous today than the premature removal of "weeds" from our society is the reverse phenomenon, the premature removal of the "wheat." Fewer and fewer Americans in general and Christians in particular are actively involved in the political and democratic processes of our society. Without denying that every child's needs are different and that public schools, Christian schools, and home schooling all meet important needs of different children, we must acknowledge that if too many Christians withdraw from the public schools, whether as students or parents or teachers or simply community volunteers, the results could be very scary. Christians involved in the public schools have provided important checks and balances against the proliferation of too much blatant secularism and hedonism. Interestingly, I have a friend in news reporting and another in the filmmaking industry who are utterly convinced that it is basically ignorance rather than deliberate hostility on the part of most in the media that accounts for what seems like such an anti-Christian bias. Many public figures simply have no firsthand, up-close-and-personal awareness of a positive Christian presence in their industries. It has not always been so. As recently as the 1950s even a majority of the movies and musicals in this country primarily promoted a wholesome, moral message. In half a century, all that has changed, so that Christians today feel like Jesus' disciples in Matthew 13 must have felt—like a tiny, beleaguered minority.

When one is part of a small minority, it's easy to assume that one can have no impact on the large majority. Probably for that very reason, Jesus goes on to tell the next two parables that together form a unit in Matthew 13. Let's read the parables of the mustard seed and the leaven, and their aftermath, in verses 31–35:

> He told them another parable: "The kingdom of heaven is like a mustard seed, which a man took and planted in his field. Though it is the smallest of all seeds, yet when it grows, it is the largest of garden plants and becomes a tree, so that the birds come and perch in its branches."
>
> He told them still another parable: "The kingdom of heaven is like yeast that a woman took and mixed into about eighteen pounds of flour until it worked all through the dough."
>
> Jesus spoke all these things to the crowd in parables; he did not say anything to them without using a parable. So was fulfilled what was spoken through the prophet:
>
> "I will open my mouth in parables,
> I will utter things hidden since the creation of the world."

The mustard seed and the yeast, or leaven, together illustrate the potential of enormous growth resulting even from tiny, inauspicious beginnings. In a scientific age, it's sometimes pointed out that technically the mustard seed is not the smallest of all seeds. But it certainly was the smallest that Jews in the first century knew about and planted in any of their fields, which is all Jesus can be expected to mean. Seldom does a mustard plant grow to a height of over four or five feet. You can see them blossoming with bright yellow flowers in the spring on the hills surrounding the Sea of Galilee to this day. But every once in a while, one will grow large enough that you could think of it as a large bush or perhaps a very small tree. And that apparently is what happens to the mustard seed in this little story. The plant becomes a small tree, so big that "the birds come and perch in its branches." This last statement may well be an allusion to Ezekiel 17:23, in which another parabolic tree is said to shelter birds who come and perch in its branches. There the birds symbolize the Gentiles, all of the non-Jewish nations of the world coming to know about the God of Israel. Not surprisingly, however, in Ezekiel the tree is not a large mustard bush; it's a lofty cedar.

The parable of the yeast, or the leaven, moves from the world of farming to the world of baking, from what in Jesus' day would have been a typical man's occupation to a typical woman's occupation. Jesus may be consciously trying to relate to both genders in his audience. A small amount of leaven is mixed into a large batch of flour, a practice that people who bake bread from scratch still follow to this day. And the quantity of bread that is produced is enormous in comparison with the small lump of dough with which the cook begins. The amount of leaven described in this parable is computed to have been enough to feed over one hundred people.

The apostle Paul would later reuse this parabolic imagery in a negative context, warning Christians that a little yeast can leaven an entire lump, referring to the insidious spread and effect of evil (1 Cor. 5:6). There are commentators who have tried to read that kind of negative meaning into Jesus' words here, too. Then the parable of the mustard seed is taken to refer to the positive growth of the kingdom, while the parable of the yeast is said to teach about the equally large growth of opposition to the kingdom. But Jesus cannot be bound by what Paul would say later in a completely different context.

Other commentators point out that frequently in the Old Testament and in the Judaism of Jesus' day, leaven was something undesirable. One had to bake only unleavened bread at Passover and remove from one's house every trace of yeast. Jesus himself warns of the "yeast of the Pharisees and that of Herod" (Mark 8:15). But some sacrifices the Old Testament commands *do* involve leaven (e.g., Lev. 23:17). It is not always a negative symbol. And elsewhere, wherever Jesus tells a pair of closely parallel parables, and he does so several times in the Gospels, without exception these parables make basically the same point, rather than opposite points. So we should almost certainly allow the parable of the mustard seed to govern our interpretation of the parable of the leaven here as well. Despite the difference in imagery, perhaps appealing to the different genders in Christ's audience, both little stories nevertheless depict the positive growth of the kingdom, all out of proportion to its size at the beginning of the Jesus movement. And as Matthew, here and elsewhere, does at least twice as often as any other Gospel writer, he rounds off this section by highlighting how Jesus' behavior fulfills Scripture.

We don't even have to look to explicitly Christian contexts to see examples in our lifetime of this principle of great accomplishments from unpromising initiatives—Rosa Parks, the first black woman to refuse to sit at the back of the bus, whose action began the Civil Rights Movement in the 1950s; Mikhail Gorbachev, who broke from the strong anti-American rhetoric and positions of all his predecessors as Soviet premier and thereby initiated *glasnost* and *perestroika* and paved the way for the fall of the Iron Curtain in 1990; Bill Gates, the richest man in the world today, whose iconoclastic and unconventional computer breakthroughs catapulted him to international fame and wealth.

In explicitly Christian contexts we see even clearer examples of enormous growth from tiny beginnings—the proliferation of Christianity in China, even during the era of Chairman Mao; the explosive growth of the church in sub-Saharan Africa, despite decimation from famines, tribal warfare, and corrupt governments; the ongoing rapid growth of evangelicals in once almost exclusively Catholic Latin America, despite covert and overt persecution by very traditional Catholic authorities in many of those countries. Our money, resources, and technology in the United States give us the potential to do even more for Christ. But sadly we're often much more spiritually flabby and less committed than folks in very poor parts of the world, and so we don't see the results that we might. Yet even in recent American Christian history, we've seen how single individuals can found huge movements with tremendous impact—John Perkins, in impoverished rural Mississippi, beginning what would become the Christian Community Development Association; Bill and Vonette Bright, founding a college ministry at UCLA that would turn into Campus Crusade for Christ International; and Bill Hybels, planting a church in a suburban Chicago theater that would grow into Willow Creek and spawn an entire association of like-minded churches on every continent on the globe.

But there's another reason that we don't see the mustard seed and leaven factor reproduced in our little corner of the world as often as we might. And it's related to a faulty interpretation of the first of these two parables. It's time now, therefore, to read what we bypassed earlier—the explanation of the parable of the weeds in verses 36–43.

> Then [Jesus] left the crowd and went into the house. His disciples came to him and said, "Explain to us the parable of the weeds in the field."
> He answered, "The one who sowed the good seed is the Son of Man. The field is the world, and the good seed stands for the people of the kingdom. The weeds are the people of the evil one, and the enemy who sows them is the devil. The harvest is the end of the age, and the harvesters are angels.
> "As the weeds are pulled up and burned in the fire, so it will be at the end of the age. The Son of Man will send out his angels, and they will weed out of his kingdom everything that causes sin and all who do evil. They will throw them into the blazing furnace, where there will be weeping and gnashing of teeth. Then the righteous will shine like the sun in the kingdom of their Father. Whoever has ears, let him hear."

Did you notice the equation of the field with the world *and* with the kingdom as we read? Verse 38 states, "The field is the world," but then verse 41 declares, "they will weed out of his kingdom." That equation is often overlooked. A popular misinterpretation throughout church history, dating back as far as Augustine in the early fifth century, has understood Jesus to be talking about a mixed church of believers and unbelievers allowed to grow together within the professing community of Christ's followers, as if Jesus had said that the field equaled the church and that people were not to pull the weeds out of the *church*. That mistake was derived from another one Augustine made, one that many have followed ever since, which is to equate God's kingdom with the visible church. It's an error that made it into a very popular hit song of not too many years ago by the Christian artist Sandi Patty in a line that claimed, "Upon this rock, I'll build my kingdom." The song was alluding to Matthew 16:18, except that what Jesus actually said was "on this rock I will build my church." In the Bible, God's kingdom always refers to his dynamic reign or rule, not to a literal realm. It's his divine power, not a place. The kingdom, in other words, is always bigger than the church, but it includes true Christians as its subjects. God's vision of building his church is always but one part of the much larger cosmic task of advancing his kingdom—his righteous reign in the entire universe.

Advancing the kingdom creates an intra-Christian unity that comes from recognizing that God's purposes are much, much greater than what happens in my little corner of the world or in my local congregation or ministry. And that in turn generates the world-transforming power that Jesus prayed for in John 17:20–23, so that when unbelievers see

Christians throughout the world united, supporting a cause much bigger than themselves, then, Jesus says, the world may believe that God has sent him. As long as we focus only on our little circle of Christian activity or relationships, our in-house issues, our cozy fellowship, our preferred style of worship, and people of the same race, socioeconomic status, nationality, or age, we risk making our parochial interests the priority above God's kingdom interests, thereby quenching the power God wants to release through us. In essence, we come full circle, and we not only violate the warnings against prematurely separating the wheat from the weeds in our world but also separate the wheat from the wheat so that no one knows what an abundant and attractive crop might be harvested!

But we can take heart. God promises he will right all wrongs at the end of the age. He has not left himself without witness, even now. No era of church history has ever lacked true Christianity. Today more parts of the world have it than ever before, and the numbers and percentages of unreached peoples are smaller than ever in the history of the church, though there is still plenty of work to be done. Without attempting to legislate Christianity or coerce anyone into faith, with contemporary technology we stand at the threshold of an era in which we could do more good for God and more clearly communicate his gospel than ever in the history of the world.

But it will happen only when we trust God to do it through us, without attempting to manufacture it in our own strength—when we get ourselves and our pet agendas out of the way, when we realize God's kingdom interests are far broader than our personal interests, when we initiate cooperation with people very different from ourselves, and perhaps above all, when we see Christian activity as the single most important thing we do in our lives, more so than our secular jobs, more so than recreation with our families, more so than so many other things that gobble up enormous amounts of time and energy even as we claim Christ is number one in our lives! We don't have to remain feeling like, or at times even being, a beleaguered minority. God will preserve his church, but he wants to do far more than preserve it. He wants to grow it wherever it appears as a tiny influence into a powerful force for good in our world. Will you pray for God to show you what that might look like in your life, in your little niche in his grand scheme of things?

Commentary on "Seeds, Weeds, and Explosive Growth"

This is the second of the three messages in the series on Matthew 13:1–52. It would, of course, be possible to compose sermons simply on any one or two of the parables treated in this message. The shorter two, dealing with the mustard seed and the leaven, however, would require the inclusion of significant detail beyond mere exposition to occupy more than just a very short homily. Treating at least these three parables together makes good sense, therefore, while the sandwich pattern of the parable of the wheat and the weeds, two additional parables, and the interpretation of the wheat and the weeds suggests that Matthew composed verses 24–43 as a unit, at least on one level.[1] As the sermon unfolds, it becomes clear that a potential big idea unifies this material— the promised growth of God's kingdom despite its unpromising start.[2] Since one-point parables by definition do not lend themselves to subdivision, to be able to discern such a unifying theme is very helpful. Three subsections again lead to a three-part division of the message and of the reading of the text, which also proves rhetorically satisfying.

My own involvement in Evangelical-Mormon dialogue has made me very sensitive to the need to counter the historical myth of the so-called great apostasy, which orthodox Christians have often refuted by appealing not only to a more accurate reading of history but also to Matthew 16:18. But Protestants also have been guilty of exaggerating the "fall" from apostolic Christianity in early Orthodoxy and Catholicism; misuse of Matthew 16:16–19 in those circles does not justify abuse in the opposite direction on our part. So my sermon begins from a contemporary perspective, replying to two religious communities' use of a key verse in the Gospels that in many ways sums up the point of the parable of the wheat and the weeds. I can arouse interest, relate to a misuse of Scripture many in my congregations will have encountered, correct that abuse, and lead into the beginning of the passage for the day, all at the same time.[3]

The bridge to the reading of Scripture and the beginning of the body of the message note the immediate historical context of the parable and the immediate literary context (which also affords me a chance to review the previous week's message ever so briefly). I also overview the structure of the passage at hand as well as present the unifying theme found within it. After reading the parable of the wheat and the weeds, I need to explain why I am not jumping immediately to its interpretation: that comes only after intervening material in Matthew's Gospel. In the previous week's sermon, I jumped over intervening material to move to the interpretation of the sower because I wanted to save the intervening hard verses about Jesus' reasons for using parables for the climactic, final position in my message. Without such a rationale for rearrangement in this passage, I preserve the order of the text in my exposition.

The parable of the wheat and the weeds is the second (and only other one after the parable of the sower) to provide so detailed and point-by-point an explanation attributed to Jesus. Once again, however, the authenticity of that interpretation is almost universally rejected outside of explicitly evangelical circles, again to a large degree because of the unnatural allegorizing it seems to reflect. So I take the time to show how I think the interpretation is not that unnatural after all.[4] What will be most surprising to modern audiences is that the very action of sowing weeds in an enemy's field was by no means unknown in Jesus' world.[5] Even if modern bioterrorism is far more sophisticated, the comparison between modern and ancient "germ warfare" is timely and helps the story come alive, recreating some of its initial horror.

As we have noted before, there usually is at least one key place in each parable where the narrative becomes highly unrealistic, and this normally supplies a key to the symbolic or spiritual meaning of the account (see e.g., p. 39). So we need to spend some time reflecting on why the farmer doesn't want to make any attempt to weed his field, even after the crops mature. Any kind of plant could have caused the problem of intertwining roots, so the choice of a weed that was superficially indistinguishable from wheat must have been deliberate and meant to contribute to the symbolism of the passage.[6] The observations that the wheat and weeds must refer to those who are and aren't God's followers, respectively, and that the outward appearance of those groups often seems indistinguishable both reinforce this assumption.

If I were preaching just on this one parable, I would derive three points from it alone, corresponding to its triangular structure that highlights the farmer, the weeds, and the wheat: God's initial permission of the righteous and the wicked to exist together until the end of the age; the judgment ultimately awaiting the wicked; and the reward ultimately awaiting the righteous. Each of these in fact corresponds to one of three successive scenes in the passage: the apparent triumph of the enemy (vv. 24–28a); the survival of the wheat despite the subterfuge (vv. 28b–30a); and the final harvest with the destruction of the weeds and the preservation of the wheat (v. 30b).[7] In conjunction with the mustard seed and the leaven, however, I focus on what is not clearly repeated in those parables and stress what most links the three parables together. Clearly, Jesus' warning not to root out evil prematurely (another way of making the first of the three points) remains the most distinctive feature, and the mustard seed and the leaven reinforce the reason why this is possible—God will preserve his people and advance his kingdom mightily until the end. So that point will be my sole emphasis with respect to the parable of the wheat and the weeds in this message, especially since there are such timely and obvious applications in our pluralistic religious world—a world that is at the same time filled with religious zealots willing to destroy themselves and others in fighting against that pluralism. Because I focus on inappropriate weeding of both the weeds and the wheat, the parable's other two points about rewards and punishments come through at least implicitly as well.[8]

The feeling of being a part of an impotent minority provides the transition to the parables of the mustard seed and the leaven and to my reading of the second third of the passage. There are comparatively few exegetical points that need explanation here. Some listeners may be aware of the famous "error" concerning the size of the mustard seed, so a brief explanation is important. The NIV actually facilitated such an explanation with its rendering "the smallest of all your seeds," but critics correctly pointed out that "your" was not in the Greek text, and the TNIV has reinstated the more literal wording. So a word of explanation is again in order.[9] The bigger and better-known problem is how to think of the mustard bush as a tree. There may be a parody here of Ezekiel's lofty cedar; there is almost certainly an allusion to the birds perching in its branches.[10] The unusual again provides the key to the symbolism.

The biggest issue to address concerning the parable of the leaven is the well-known, old-line dispensationalist approach that saw the leaven as evil. Even within dispensationalist circles, scholars have almost entirely abandoned this view, but many people in local churches will have heard it and perhaps even adopted it. There are important contrasts between the mustard seed and the leaven, which I point out at the beginning and the end of my discussion of this short parable.[11] But the largest, intervening section explains why I follow the majority of commentators and see the leaven itself as a symbol for the positive power of God's reign.[12]

At the spiritual level, God's reign does not necessarily bypass human instruments for the outworking of his purposes. It certainly did not with the first group of Jesus' disciples. In my application, therefore, I focus on human examples of great accomplishments from very modest beginnings. Because God's kingly power operates both inside and outside the church, I don't limit my examples to Christians; indeed, I want to challenge believers to dream at least as big as many unbelievers did, people whose accomplishments led to the fulfillment of far more than their initial dreams. Thus I divide my examples into three groups of three—first looking outside explicitly Christian contexts, then turning to Christian models outside the United States, and finally coming closest to home with American evangelical illustrations. The sequence thus creates a climactic order, but to some listeners the examples closest to home will seem least dramatic. That potential perception provides the transition to the final third of the passage.

Although great growth occurs in all three parables, Jesus' focus is not on the period of growth in any of them as much as on the end of the process. Again, the principles hold true at the spiritual level. God may choose to do great things through one particular individual or group, but he may not, at least not as we typically define greatness. And wicked movements and institutions may likewise grow enormously. The only guaranteed justice comes on Judgment Day. That observation leads directly into the interpretation of the parable of the wheat and the weeds.

There are other details that must be examined here, too. The most famous is of course the mistaken equation of kingdom and church.[13] There is a subordinate sense in which various scholars have correctly stressed that God's kingdom in the teaching of Jesus can be seen as involving a realm as well as a reign,[14] but this kingdom is still not a literal piece of geography with national boundaries surrounding it. Thus I feel comfortable using the starker contrasts here. After all, the applications most needed among most evangelicals today involve a greater appreciation of how much bigger the kingdom is than the church.[15]

The final two paragraphs form the conclusion to the sermon and bring things full circle to the opening two paragraphs. Matthew 16:18 will be fulfilled not just throughout church history but in the glorious return of Christ at the end of history as we know it. We can contribute to the process, but God in his sovereignty entirely brings about the end. Hence, I close with the reminder that while we respond as best we can, ultimately all true progress depends on God.

9

The Kingdom of Heaven: Priceless

Matthew 13:44–52

In 1994 I had the chance to teach a New Testament survey class for one month at Saint Petersburg Christian University in Russia. One day after our lunch break, right at 1 P.M., when the students were normally all returning to class, I arrived about a minute later than usual to find most of them walking back out of the class again. When I asked my translator what was going on, she explained, "One of the students just learned that her mother has died. She lives a long train's ride away from here and doesn't have enough money even to pay for the trip home. Her classmates are all going back to their rooms to see if they can pool their resources to pay for the girl's train fare and to give her a little extra spending money as well." I knew that few, if any, of my thirty-some students had any money to spare. They were obviously making very sacrificial commitments to their classmate. I also learned that this is very typical among poor Christians in the former Soviet Union, partly because of their history of communal sharing that significantly predated Communism, but partly just because of their understanding of Christian commitment. Friends of mine who have traveled and ministered throughout Eastern Europe have shared similar stories on numerous occasions since.

In 1998 I had the chance to give a special lectureship at the evangelical seminary in Guatemala City. I had been to Latin America before on several occasions, but this was my first detailed exposure to a Latin American seminary. I learned of more than one full-time professor who also worked at least part-time on a local church staff, toiling long hours at both jobs to eke out a marginal salary, when he could have had a much better paying job in some other field for which he had trained at the university. I learned of several who could have accepted invitations to teach in a North American college or church and follow the path of many international students who have come to the United States, at first fully intending to return home and be of service to their poorer countries of origin but winding up contributing to the so-called brain drain and enjoying a far more comfortable standard of living in America. Interestingly, the dean of the seminary in Guatemala reported to me with some pride that they had never lost even one of their full-time faculty to this brain drain. Once again, I was struck up close and personal by genuine sacrifice made by people who followed what they understood to be God's call on their lives.

Far more close to home, every year at the seminary where I teach in Denver, a handful of very successful business people come to us as students, turning aside from their lucrative careers, in several instances selling homes or businesses in order to finance their education, moving with spouses and children into comparatively cramped campus apartments, and doing so willingly because of a profound sense of the call of God on their lives. Nor do they expect to return to their former standard of living after completing their seminary studies. Ministry for them implies considerable sacrifice, at least by American standards.

These are probably the closest real-life parallels that I've personally encountered to the characters in the parables of Matthew 13:44–46. There Matthew writes that Jesus declared,

> The kingdom of heaven is like treasure hidden in a field. When a man found it, he hid it again, and then in his joy went and sold all he had and bought that field. Again, the kingdom of heaven is like a merchant looking for fine pearls. When he found one of great value, he went away and sold everything he had and bought it.

The examples I've described are actually mild compared to numerous stories I have read or heard about the sacrifices Christians have made throughout church history and continue to make in many parts of our world today—be they missionaries who became seriously ill and/or died in an era before medicine, travel, and communication were what they are today, or believers persecuted or martyred for their faith, including many even as we speak in such difficult parts of the world as Sudan, Iran, China, North Korea, and elsewhere. But I can relate better to the people in the stories that I've told you because I've been to their communities.

I've seen and experienced firsthand their sacrifice. I've gotten to know them as genuine human beings and committed Christians.

We've been looking at the parables of Matthew 13 for the past two weeks. We've observed how they emerge at a key turning point in Jesus' ministry, as the larger crowds start to fall away and increasingly only Jesus' true followers linger close by. None of this has caught Jesus by surprise. He has talked about the varying receptions of the word by means of the parable of the sower. He has made the promise in the parables of the wheat and the tares, the mustard seed, and the leaven that God's kingdom will advance mightily, even through the tiny minority that now truly follow him, and despite the many obstacles that they will face. Now in this final third of Matthew 13, Jesus defines most pointedly what separates real disciples from the "wannabes" or hangers-on who don't really make the grade. Quite simply, *true disciples are those who recognize that God's kingdom is so valuable that it's worth sacrificing whatever it takes to be its citizens.* With his two illustrations of the man who accidentally stumbles across treasure hidden in a field and of the pearl merchant who regularly seeks precious oysters (vv. 44–46), Jesus covers the whole gamut of humanity—from those who are not spiritual seekers in any respect to those who look intensely over a long period of time.

The parables are that simple. We are not meant to complicate matters by asking about the ethics or the legality of finding a treasure, hiding it again, and then buying the field. Those details actually make the story realistic. There are other Jewish and Greco-Roman stories from ancient times with similar motifs. Today we say that possession is nine-tenths of the law. In first-century Israel it was virtually ten-tenths. Nor should we so press the details of either parable to make it seem as if we buy our way into God's favor—as if we purchase the kingdom. Jesus is speaking metaphorically, analogically, as in all his parables. Metaphors aren't meant to be pressed down to every last detail, and analogies all break down at some point. Most people, in fact, don't give up anywhere close to everything that they have in order to enter the kingdom. It's true that Jesus elsewhere tells the story of the rich young ruler whom he calls to do precisely that. But one of the Gospel accounts of that story appears in Luke 18, and in close proximity the first two stories of Luke 19 describe the conversion of Zacchaeus, who gives up only a little over half of his wealth, and the parable of the pounds, in which the good servants invest their master's money and make more. There is no uniform model that Jesus requires all believers to follow with respect to a quantity of money that they must give away.

But even with all those caveats, it's worth asking the question why we see so few examples, particularly in our American society, of people who obviously demonstrate sacrificial living—a commitment to Christ that truly costs them something significant, whether through downsizing their property and possessions, through changing jobs, or through radically different spending patterns. Why don't we see more who unambiguously demonstrate through an obvious, visible lifestyle that God's kingdom agenda is the highest priority for them, even to the point that life becomes noticeably less comfortable for them than it otherwise might be?

In fact, with rare exceptions we see precisely the opposite. Ours is a culture in which religious commitment, including Christian activity, functions as a kind of add-on to our real priorities. When convenient, we'll go to church or get involved in this or that program or small group. When not too much is at stake, we will witness or stand up for and model Christian integrity in the workplace. When we have a surplus, we'll give a little more to church or Christian causes, though probably nowhere close to a tithe, much less a graduated tithe, by which we increase the percentage of our giving as our earnings increase.

Why then are so many American Christians so shallow, so superficial in their commitment? At least one answer to that question, to which the next section of our passage for today points us, is because we really don't have a profound sense of how much *is* at stake. Jesus continues in verses 47–50,

> Once again, the kingdom of heaven is like a net that was let down into the lake and caught all kinds of fish. When it was full, the fishermen pulled it up on the shore. Then they sat down and collected the good fish in baskets, but threw the bad away. This is how it will be at the end of the age. The angels will come and separate the wicked from the righteous and throw them into the blazing furnace, where there will be weeping and gnashing of teeth.

This little parable of the net is a miniature version of the parable of the wheat and the weeds that we considered last week. It contains the identical sifting on Judgment Day but lacks a parallel to the potential obstacles that the wheat faced as it grew. After using an illustration from farming, Jesus shifts to imagery from fishing, to which many of his disciples could relate. Just as farmers look forward to the harvest, fishermen long for a great catch of fish. Both metaphors depict final judgment. But here Jesus speaks of catching "all kinds of fish." The word that Matthew uses in translating Jesus' expression would be a strange one, if all Jesus were talking about were fish. The word for "kinds" is the word from which we get our English "genus." It could also be translated "tribe." It was a common term for all kinds of people, but less natural for all kinds of fish. Yet that's precisely the point. Jesus is talking about the harvest of people. He wants his disciples to become fishers of men and women. On Judgment Day every kind of person, good and bad alike, will have to give an account before God.

Again, we mustn't press every detail to make the parable contradict the explicit teaching of Scripture elsewhere. This is not a depiction of salvation by works. If we were to flesh out the story, we would have to explain that fish, spiritually speaking, become good only because they have faith in Christ, and that the bad fish represent people who reject Christ. But the imagery of the passage probably does remind us, as the New Testament consistently teaches, that people of faith are transformed in various ways—hardly perfectly, with many reversals and setbacks throughout their lives—but nevertheless transformed in visible ways into obedient followers of Jesus who overall, from God's perspective, can be called good in ways that others can't. These people, then, who are thus labeled good at the end of the age will be separated out from the bad. At the end of the passage, Jesus abandons anything that literally applies to fish and speaks directly of hell. The unrighteous will be thrown into the blazing furnace, where there will be weeping and gnashing of teeth.

In other words, one of the reasons we don't sense the urgency to serve Christ sacrificially is because we don't really believe in hell as a danger for us. Various polls in recent decades consistently agree. About 84 percent of all Americans believe in some kind of life after death, and 82 percent believe in heaven. But only 69 percent believe in any kind of hell, a continuing conscious existence of punishment for the unrighteous, and almost no one believes he or she is personally going there.[1]

Now if we study church history, we'll recognize that writers and church leaders who are considered fully orthodox have varied in their views on certain details about hell. Simply saying that we believe in a place of conscious eternal punishment for the unregenerate does not commit us necessarily to believe in a literal fire or literal outer darkness. After all, either one of those pictures, if absolutized, would contradict the other. Believing in hell doesn't automatically satisfy the debate that orthodox Christians have had throughout the centuries as to the fate of those who have never heard the gospel. Belief in hell doesn't necessarily imply that any people ever remain separated from God against their will. C. S. Lewis, in his powerful novel *The Great Divorce,* describes the progression of the redeemed moving ever closer to God and the unredeemed moving ever further away and depicts in vivid and creative detail what creatures completely separated from everything bad or from everything good might look like. The result is that the redeemed may appear so glorious, from our current fallen perspective, that they might look like exalted beings we could be tempted to worship. The unredeemed, confirmed in their freely chosen rebellion against God and shorn of all the influence of his Spirit, of believers, and of everything good that mitigates evil in this world, might well look like the very devils whose place of torment they inhabit. Perhaps everyone who winds up in hell will never again want to be around things having to do with Jesus. As we noted two weeks ago, Lewis sums up much of his memorable portrait with an equally memorable slogan, "There are only two kinds of people in the end: those who say to God, 'Thy will be done,' and those to whom God says . . . 'Thy will be done.'"[2]

But the one option not permitted us by Scripture, and seldom accepted as orthodox throughout church history, is what today is increasingly being accepted—the belief in annihilationism. This concept holds that the lost simply die, cease conscious existence forever, and in that sense are eternally separated from God. But if that's all that hell amounts to, then it's hard to see why Jesus would say elsewhere that it would be better for such people if they had never been born (e.g., Mark 14:21). It's hard to understand why he pits the saved and the lost against each other in very parallel fashion in the parable of the sheep and the goats (Matt. 25:31–46), speaking of everlasting life, which is clearly conscious, eternal existence, as parallel to everlasting punishment, which thus must likewise be conscious, eternal existence (v. 46).

If only we understood and hence really believed all this so much more than we do! It's interesting that Jesus at this very juncture asks the disciples in Matthew 13:51, "Have you understood all these things?" They reply, "Yes." It's hard to know what to make of what might have been a very quick, glib affirmative, especially since as recently as verse 36, they were asking Jesus to explain one of the parables he had just told them. Nevertheless, Jesus apparently takes their reply at face value and proceeds to narrate the final little parable of this chapter in the last verse of our passage, verse 52: "He said to them, 'Therefore every teacher of the law who has been instructed about the kingdom of heaven is like the owner of a house who brings out of his storeroom new treasures as well as old.'"

This may be the most enigmatic parable in all of Matthew 13, not least because it's so brief. Yet given the repeated contrast between the old and the new in Jesus' ministry, his probable point is that the truth he articulates, like the era of history that he is inaugurating, has both clear points of continuity with all that has gone before in the Old Testament age and also clear points of discontinuity, especially as the new covenant is concerned with internalizing the Law and making God's will a matter of the heart.

After all, Jeremiah had prophesied,

"The days are coming," declares the Lord,
  "when I will make a new covenant
with the house of Israel
  and with the house of Judah.
It will not be like the covenant
  I made with their ancestors
when I took them by the hand
  to lead them out of Egypt,
because they did not remain faithful to my covenant,
  and I turned away from them,"
  declares the Lord.
"This is the covenant I will establish with the house of Israel
  after that time," declares the Lord.
"I will put my laws in their minds
  and write them on their hearts.
I will be their God,
  and they will be my people.
No longer will they teach their neighbors,
  or say to one another, 'Know the Lord,'
because they will all know me,
  from the least of them to the greatest.
For I will forgive their wickedness
  and will remember their sins no more."

This is the excerpt of Jeremiah 31:31–34 that Hebrews 8:8–12 quotes. Verse 13 then adds by way of commentary, "By calling this covenant 'new,' [God] has made the first one obsolete; and what is obsolete and outdated will soon disappear." Jeremiah's new covenant, which Jesus and all his first followers believed was fulfilled in the events surrounding Christ's coming and the establishment of his church, clearly talks about the same laws given to Moses as carrying over in some sense into this new age. And yet there is a permanence that contrasts with the transience of the old era. There is a security that contrasts with the insecurity of the Mosaic economy. There is a complete forgiveness that contrasts with the temporary forgiveness that animal sacrifices produced. The new arrangements of God with humanity are very much like a householder bringing out of his storeroom new treasures as well as old.

This is a fitting final reminder of how to take all of the teaching of Jesus' parables in Matthew 13. The person who hasn't really internalized the requirements of the Law, now defined in light of discipleship and following Jesus, will ask of the parable of the sower, "What is the minimal amount of fruit that I can produce and still be assured of remaining in the good soil?" The person who hasn't internalized a commitment to Jesus will grumble at the commands not to prematurely uproot the weeds, not to attack God's enemies in this life. The person who is not sold out for Christ will not really believe in the power of a tiny, highly committed minority, as Jesus illustrated with the parables of the mustard seed and the leaven. Such people will begrudge the kind of sacrifices described in the hidden treasure and the pearl of great price, and they will doubt the urgency that surrounds the parable of the net with its metaphor of impending judgment.

On the other hand, those who have internalized God's will, who recognize Jesus as the fulfillment of the Law, who recognize how he has both upped the ante in terms of commitment and also provided a greater power for obedience with his permanently indwelling Spirit, these people will ask how *much* fruit they can produce by fully yielding to Christ. They will not worry about the weeds—the evil people around them—but happily set out to be a positive model like the wheat. They will trust in God's ability to do great things with small resources, as with the mustard seed and the leaven. They will give up whatever it takes to acquire the kingdom, as in the hidden treasure and the pearl of great price, realizing, as in the parable of the net, that the eternal destiny of billions of people hangs in the balance.

Which group do you most naturally identify with? Be honest with yourself. My prayer is that all of us will say, "The group that has internalized discipleship—that is prepared to count the cost." Such people will be eagerly asking God what the next level of discipleship might look like for them and then will go out and joyfully seek it. Let's never forget what an immense sacrifice it was for the omnipotent God of the universe, in the person of his son Jesus Christ, to give up the uninterrupted privileges of divinity, to live within the constraints of a frail, mortal body, to experience rejection by his closest friends and a majority of his countrymen, and ultimately to be abused, mocked, flogged, and executed in one of the most excruciating and shameful deaths ever devised by human beings. He sacrificed all for us. How dare we shrink from recognizing the Christian life as one of sacrificing for him and for others in return?

Commentary on "The Kingdom of Heaven: Priceless"

This is the final sermon in the series of three on Matthew 13:1–52. With it, all eight parables in this chapter have been expounded. Like the message in chapter 8, this one treats several shorter parables in sequence. Again, it would be possible to compose a sermon on any one of them, but a lot of the detail would have to go beyond mere exposition. My message contains some theological expansion, but it still progresses through a reasonable chunk of text, explained section-by-section. There isn't an obvious unifying theme that sets verses 44–52 off from the rest of the passage; in a sense these verses are just what's left after the sections treated on the two previous Sundays. A big idea would thus have to be tripartite, enunciating the great value of the kingdom, in light of the rationale for this cost, followed by the resulting continuity and disconti-nuity of these claims with the Law. Instead of seeking some memorable way of combining these three ideas, I focus on each sequentially, with particular attention to my transitions that clarify the narrative flow.[3]

The simplest concepts appear in the first third of the passage, with the twin little parables of the hidden treasure and the pearl of great price. The hardest task here is not understanding Jesus' meaning but applying it. So I begin with three somewhat extended examples by way of intro-duction. As with the parable of the rich man and Lazarus, I begin with illustrations in which I have personally played a role. Especially when the preacher's theme involves some aspect of radical, countercultural living, it is too easy to cite an example from a different time or place that still leaves today's audience wondering, "But how could that hap-pen here and now?" or "Could *I* ever experience it?" On the other hand, in most large congregations, enough people have traveled to different parts of the world for a contemporary illustration in a quite different contemporary culture to be meaningful. I don't have any easy answers as to how one transfers the models of sacrificial Christian sharing in poor parts of the Second or the Third World to middle- or upper-class Western settings, but I wrestle with the issue and want my listeners to do so as well. But then I move increasingly closer to home with each successive illustration, so that people can't dismiss all my examples as irrelevant or impossible for them.

The similarities between the parables of the hidden treasure and the pearl of great price outweigh the differences, so I treat them together, much as I did the mustard seed and the leaven in the preceding message.[4] This also enables me to retain a three-part division to the passage—not that I don't sometimes have four or five subdivisions, but I try to have that many rarely because of the increased difficulty of audiences retain-ing each part. Once I have read the text, I make the point that even the most radical of my illustrations pales in comparison to what Christians, ancient and modern, have often sacrificed, a point that is important for modern Westerners to realize. But hopefully my less radical illustrations will help them bridge the gap between more extreme applications and the comparatively minor changes they might reasonably be expected to make in their lives in the short term.

Because this is the third message in a series, I then briefly review the ground covered in the preceding portions of Matthew 13 in the previ-ous two sermons. Because the two parables at hand each have only one main character, I believe, with the conventional wisdom of the day, that they make only one main point. I state that conviction and then explain what I think the significance of the differences between the two parables is. Jesus is creating a merismus—a figure of speech in which opposite ends of a spectrum are cited as shorthand for the whole spectrum. In other words, the kingdom is worth the ultimate sacrifice whether one is the most ardent of spiritual seekers, the most apathetic (or hostile) person imaginable, *or anything in between.*[5]

The necessary exegetical comments are then quite limited. The three misunderstandings that most commonly occur are the question of whether Jesus is promoting something illegal (or at least unethical) with the hiding of the treasure; if he is teaching that in some sense we purchase (or at least earn) the kingdom; and if he is calling all his followers to give up everything. The second of these questions has in fact led a small minority of commentators to suggest that Jesus is the treasure seeker here, who does indeed purchase salvation for us through his atoning death.[6] But while scholars discuss this interpretation, I have never run across it at the popular level, so I don't complicate factors by introducing this option. I address each of the three questions briefly. Additional comments that I would add if I were expounding fewer verses include the observation that the re-hiding of the treasure actually makes the story more realistic by ancient standards,[7] that a rabbinic parable likewise urges Israel to "purchase" the Promised Land without implying that the people merit it in any way,[8] and that "selling all" elsewhere can be a metaphor for renouncing claim to something without necessarily literally divesting oneself of it (see p. 185).

I don't want listeners to think the parables require more than they actually do—sacrifices that would truly be unrealizable for almost everyone—but neither do I want to lose the "sting in the tale." So I reflect some on American culture but then use the main reason that people do not take these texts seriously enough as the transition to the second third of the passage—the parable of the dragnet.

As with the parable of the wheat and the weeds in the previous week's message, were I preaching only this text I would want to demonstrate its tripartite structure, short though it is. As I point out, the parable really forms a miniature version of the wheat and the weeds without the emphasis on the period in which the plants grow together. "Verses 47–48a describe the action of the dragnet, which stands for God who will come to judge his people on the last day. Verse 48b describes the fate of the good fish, which stand for those God declares righteous, who are gathered together for further service and safekeeping. Verse 48c describes the fate of the rotten fish, which stand for the unredeemed, who are discarded as worthless."[9]

Given that I am dealing with more than just this parable, I limit myself primarily to the third and climactic point in this sequence. It is not really believing in the dangers of hell that creates the lack of urgency in applying the parables of the hidden treasure and the pearl of great price.

The picture of the fishermen and their dragnet is even more straightforward than that of the treasure seeker and the oyster hunter. The one unusual word in the Greek, and the key to the second or spiritual level of meaning in the passage, is the term *genos* ("kind" or "tribe").[10] Other details of the passage should not be pressed, especially with respect to how one becomes either a "good" or a "bad" fish. That much Jesus has already made clear, as recently as in the parable of the sower, with which Matthew 13 began.

Preaching on hell seems rare these days. When one expounds one of the New Testament texts that directly refers to it, one should take advantage of the chance and address related concerns. In much the same way they approach the controversial topic of the fate of the unevangelized, many preachers don't recognize either the breadth of orthodox interpretation throughout church history[11] or the lines that have been drawn to rule out certain views, biblically speaking. Many churchgoers hold views in the former category but don't know that they are orthodox and therefore don't talk about them. Conversely, many people today are increasingly drawn to annihilationism, without recognizing how few have considered it biblically acceptable over the centuries. And it is precisely when one recognizes the probable metaphorical nature of hell and the fact that God never overrules anyone's free will in choosing to rebel against him, now or in eternity, that one feels less of a pull toward annihilationism.[12] So I take some time to explore these matters. Although I cited C. S. Lewis only two weeks earlier, the quote bears repeating (see p. 111).

The final little parable of the scribe trained for the kingdom of heaven functions as a summary of Jesus' entire "discourse" in parables,[13] so the connection with the dragnet is less tight. Nevertheless, the dragnet reiterates what all the parables in Matthew 13 have demonstrated in one fashion or another, that, as we stressed in the first sermon of this series, there are ultimately only two kinds of people in the world, those on God's side and those not.[14] Because the diversity of humanity in the present world does not make such a simple division self-evident, it is natural for Jesus to ask if his disciples have understood all these things. In light of their responses and behavior elsewhere, it is equally natural to be a bit skeptical about how much they really do grasp. The logic of Jesus' using an illustration about the continuity and discontinuity between his teaching and the Torah at this point in his discourse resembles the logic of the Sermon on the Mount earlier in Matthew:

after radical beatitudes (Matt. 5:3–12) and challenging metaphors (vv. 13–16), Christ's audience could easily imagine that he was claiming to abolish the Law. There *are* radically new aspects to the kingdom age, but they involve the fulfillment rather than the abolition of Old Testament commands (vv. 17–20). By the end of Matthew, Jesus will be explicitly echoing the new covenant language of Jeremiah 31:31–34 (see Matt. 26:28), so it seems appropriate to introduce it here, too. And to help understand what is and isn't different, Hebrews 8, probably reflecting the same strand of early Jewish-Christian thought as Matthew, provides a helpful cross reference.

If the parable of the scribe sums up the whole chapter of parables, then a brief review of how each parable presents continuity and discontinuity with the Law is in order, particularly with respect to the central new feature of internalizing the Law. If there are ultimately only those who stand with Christ and those who stand against him, the conclusion of the sermon should raise the question as to which category each person in the audience represents. The theme of sacrifice for the sake of the costly kingdom has not recurred after the parables of the hidden treasure and the pearl of great price. But it is a good theme to which to return, both to bring the sermon full circle to its introduction and to remind listeners of what is involved in standing with Christ. I haven't explicitly commented on my sermon title, but some may recognize it as an allusion to TV commercials for credit cards, which can only pay for things that money can buy.

10

The Basement
of the Hard Rock Café

Matthew 7:13–27

If you've lived in Colorado long enough, you'll remember the tragedy of the Big Thompson Canyon flood in the mid-1970s. A typically dry gulch, in which many people camped, was swollen with days of heavy rains until a flash flood swept campers, tents, and gear to their deaths and destruction. Dozens were killed. I remember hearing the story as a college student in Illinois, because a significant number of Campus Crusade for Christ people were among those lost in the deluge, and I was in a Campus Crusade chapter at my college. It was a very unusual accident, much more freakish than the flooding of homes of people who build on the flood plain of a large river. This was an area that for almost every day out of the year, and at times for years on end, was perfectly safe. But then came unusual weather, a flash flood, and mass destruction.

The same occasionally occurs today in Israel, whose desert regions receive even less annual rainfall than the canyons of Colorado. Over there what we call a dry gulch, or what in Mexico is known as an arroyo, is termed a wadi. On two different trips to Israel, in 1986 and 1992, I got a chance to walk in and along a good portion of the Wadi Kelt, which runs downhill more or less in an easterly direction from Jerusalem toward Jericho and the Jordan River valley just beyond. In 1986 Israel had had one of its driest years on record, and all of its famous bodies of water were remarkably low. There was just a mere trickle of a stream at the bottom of the steep canyon that forms the Wadi Kelt, and in places one could jump across it. In 1992 the previous winter rains had been considerably better than average, and the place where we could leap across the stream six years earlier required careful wading for fifteen or twenty yards in waist-deep, swiftly flowing water to make it across. Interestingly, too, on both trips, we saw the fifteen-hundred-year-old Greek Orthodox monastery nestled in the side of the steep canyon walls, an enduring memento to the abilities of ancient construction workers. It was built quite literally into the rock and remained unaffected by either drought or flood.

It was imagery like that of the Big Thompson Canyon in Colorado or the Wadi Kelt in Israel that Jesus and his audience might well have had in mind when he told a very short and straightforward parable that's found at the end of Matthew 7 (and also Luke 6) as the climax of Jesus' great sermon. In Matthew we know it as the Sermon on the Mount, which occupies all of chapters 5 through 7 of that Gospel. Matthew's account of this parable begins in Matthew 7, spanning verses 24–27.

> Therefore everyone who hears these words of mine and puts them into practice is like a wise man who built his house on the rock. The rain came down, the streams rose, and the winds blew and beat against that house; yet it did not fall, because it had its foundation on the rock. But everyone who hears these words of mine and does not put them into practice is like a foolish man who built his house on sand. The rain came down, the streams rose, and the winds blew and beat against that house, and it fell with a great crash.

The imagery is vivid. It would have been readily understandable to Jesus' Jewish audience in Israel. The concepts are straightforward, two parallel pictures of storms deliberately described with the identical wording both times: "The rain came down, the streams rose, and the winds blew and beat against that house." But the two houses in view are built on diametrically opposite foundations—one a sturdy house built into rock, the other a house built on sand, a dry and stable enough surface most of the time, perhaps for a long time, but after a torrential rain unable to support the house erected on it. In Denver we might paint the picture in terms of people who build new homes on soil with bentonite under it—shifting, unreliable, mineral-laden soil that leaves huge cracks in newly poured concrete designed to provide a long-term, stable foundation for a new home. If a would-be homebuyer in the Denver area is wise, he or she will hire an inspector to confirm that a prospective piece of property does not have much bentonite in its soil.

Jesus, of course, was not giving literal advice for construction workers, sane as it is to apply his words in that industry. As with all his parables, he was using a familiar, common, everyday situation to illustrate spiritual truths. But unlike many of his parables, in which he waits until the end to explain his stories and even then leaves certain things cryptic, here Jesus makes plain right at the very beginning of his description of each of these two homebuilders what he is illustrating at the spiritual level. Verse 24: "Therefore everyone who hears these words of mine and puts them into practice is like a wise man who built his house on the rock." Verse 26: "But everyone who hears these words of mine and does not put them into practice is like a foolish man who built his house on sand." Both kinds of people have heard Jesus' words, but only one puts them into practice, and therefore only one is truly the wise builder.

Still, these seemingly straightforward spiritual lessons raise several important questions. First, is Jesus thus teaching good works as the means of salvation when he claims that those who do the things he has commanded will survive in the life to come? That conclusion, of course, would contradict much of biblical teaching, including Jesus' own repeated refrain elsewhere in the Gospels to various people that their faith has saved them (e.g., Mark 5:34 or Luke 7:50). It would contradict Jesus' regular practice of calling people to repentance and acceptance of his message and ministry, but then turning around and accepting and welcoming them and pronouncing them whole, free of sin, without waiting for some elaborate trial period to elapse during which they prove their mettle.

We need to observe the larger context of the Sermon on the Mount, of which this parable forms the conclusion. Jesus is speaking to crowds (Matt. 5:1) and has gone up into the Galilean hill country to sit down and teach them, but his most immediate audience is the Twelve—his disciples. The end of verse 1 and the first part of verse 2 read, "His disciples came to him, and he began to teach them, saying. . . ." The Sermon on the Mount is Jesus' manifesto of how those who have already committed themselves to him, already heard him welcome them as forgiven sinners, are to live out lives of discipleship. That's why the topics that Jesus pursues throughout Matthew 5–7 have to do with character traits that God will consider blessed, even though often they are the ones that the world ridicules (5:3–12). The sermon includes teaching for Jesus' followers on being the salt and the light of this world (5:13–16); on how the Old Testament Law applies in the kingdom age (5:17–48); on how they are not to parade their piety in public with their typical practices of almsgiving, prayer, and fasting (6:1–18); on how they are to store up heavenly rather than material treasures for themselves and not be anxious about God's provision in this life (6:19–34); and on how they are not to be overly judgmental of others, but to ask, seek, and knock on heaven's door for God's good gifts (7:1–11). And then in a verse that is widely understood as forming the conclusion to the body or major instructional portion of the Sermon on the Mount, we read in 7:12 what has come to be known as the Golden Rule: "So in everything, do to others what you would have them do to you, for this sums up the Law and the Prophets." All of this creates the collection of topics involved when Jesus in the parable of the wise and the foolish builder speaks of "these words of mine." Putting them into practice simply refers to living out a life of discipleship for those who have already trusted Christ and received his forgiveness.

A second question that exercises commentators involves the metaphor of the storm—the rain and winds and the flood that results from them. To what does this storm correspond in the spiritual realm? Some would argue that Christ is thinking of various crises in this life, whether a serious illness, the loss of a loved one, injury, joblessness, or whatever the greatest trauma one might experience turns out to be. Thus Jesus can be seen as teaching that the more mature a Christian has become—the further along he or she is on the path to perfection that is set before Christ's followers—the better he or she will be able to handle personal tragedy, persecution, or any other crisis. Undoubtedly, this interpretation reflects true theology. But regularly in Jesus' parables, a climactic moment of crisis turns out to be a metaphor for Judgment Day—the final harvest, the catch of fish, a day of reckoning, or, in this parable, the storm. Plus the fact that all the people of the world can be broken down into just two groups—those who, when God looks on their life globally, can be said to have put into practice Christ's words because they had committed themselves to him, and those who cannot—suggests that Jesus' primary purpose in the metaphor of the storm is to depict the last day of human history, the Day of Judgment, the Day of the Lord.

That brings up a third question. How many good works must one perform, how far along the path to maturity must one proceed, and to how many of the ideals of the Sermon on the Mount must one attain in order to be convinced that God's judgment on our lives will be that we indeed did put his words into practice? This question is probably wrongly framed from the outset. It misses entirely the logic of grace as consistently revealed in Scripture. The point of the entire Bible is that *all* true believers will experience tangible transformation in their behavior, better in some areas than in others, undoubtedly filled with ups and downs throughout one's life, perhaps with some issues remaining areas of lifelong struggle. And certainly each individual follower of Jesus experiences transformation and growth in unique ways that may not exactly mirror the experiences of any other fellow believer. But still, no matter the distinctives, each true Christian does experience change over time in his or her life that can be attributed only to the Spirit of

God. It can't be quantified as the question suggests, but it is greater than zero percent transformation and drastically less than the 100 percent transformation that we will experience only in the life to come in our resurrected and glorified bodies. Still, there is visible, tangible fruit; as Matthew 7:16 puts it, "By their fruit you will recognize them." Some will show by their fruit that they are healthy; others, that they are rotten (v. 17).

So we can dispense with the common theological questions that surround our short passage for today. But, as we have already observed, our parable is preceded by the very significant context of the entire sermon, and while we have surveyed the topics that make up the body of Jesus' message, we have deliberately not yet commented on 7:13–23. After the body of the message climaxes with the Golden Rule (7:12), Jesus gives no further ethical instruction. He in essence creates a conclusion to the message that simply says three times in three different ways that everyone has a choice: to either follow his teaching or to reject it. And the consequences of those two options prove to be diametrically opposite each other.

In verses 13–14 Jesus contrasts a narrow gate and a narrow road to which the gate opens, with a broad gate and a broad road. "Enter through the narrow gate," he says. "For wide is the gate and broad is the road that leads to destruction, and many enter through it. But small is the gate and narrow the road that leads to life, and only a few find it." In other words, Jesus is saying to follow the way of the faithful minority who persevere despite tribulation. The Christian life in general is not one of a certain level of promised comfort, at least not comfort as the world defines it. Crises of this life, like the difficulties of living on planet earth in general, do to a certain extent determine who is in or out of God's kingdom. Only a minority of the world calls itself Christian. Only a minority of professing Christians are evangelical, adhering to the historic, orthodox tenets of the Christian faith. And the superficial practice of even some who consider themselves evangelical suggests that not all who apply that label to themselves are truly born again, particularly in the United States. As Chuck Colson has often remarked, in America Christianity is three-thousand-miles wide and one-half inch deep.[1] The term that is translated "narrow" in these two verses could also be rendered "full of tribulation." Our faith may not be proven until hard times come. Jesus' parable of the sower speaks of tribulation and persecution as that which scandalizes some professing Christians, while the cares of the world and the deceit of wealth choke out others, causing both to fall by the wayside. Our advertising bombards us daily with countless messages in innumerable forms that claim we deserve health and wealth. So do certain fringe movements in charismatic Christianity—the so-called health-wealth or prosperity gospel. But people who would not outwardly identify with those movements nevertheless often considerably imbibe the idea that life, liberty, and the pursuit of happiness, ideals enshrined in the U.S. Constitution but not necessarily derived from biblical teaching, somehow really are their inalienable rights.

As I teach on the theme of giving in local churches, I often ask large adult Sunday school classes to write on note cards their response to the following scenario. Imagine that, for whatever reason, you realize that in the coming fiscal year you will have to live on 80 percent of your gross income from this year. In other words, you have 20 percent less to budget for all your financial obligations as well as your discretionary spending money. What will be the single biggest area you will have to cut back in? I've repeated that experiment four or five times in different suburban churches, and in every case without exception by far the most common answer has been, "We'd have to eat out less"—hardly the kind of thing that Scripture considers a sacrifice. But if that's the worst hit that many middle- and upper-class American Christians would take, why not voluntarily live on 80 percent of this year's income and give the remaining 20 percent to the Lord's work locally and worldwide? Until we've felt the pinch in some way, until we've sensed that we really are walking through a narrow gate, down a narrow road, until we've encountered some hostility or persecution because of our identity as Christians, we may not know entirely what we are truly made of or whether we're even truly one of God's redeemed.

But then Jesus introduces a second contrast in Matthew 7:15–20. He warns us to beware of false prophets masquerading as true ones. "They come to you in sheep's clothing, but inwardly they are ferocious wolves" (v. 15). Given the larger context of the Gospel of Matthew, Jesus probably has in mind certain key leaders of the Jewish religion, particularly among the Pharisees, scribes, and Sadducees. Elsewhere in Matthew, Jesus condemns their hypocrisy, describing them as loving outward adulation without truly caring for their people (see esp. chap. 23). One thinks of the theme that Jesus elaborates so helpfully in John 10, of a good shepherd who is willing even to lay down his life for his sheep rather than to dominate and domineer over them (vv. 1–21). When leaders become empire builders, beware. They may soon resemble ferocious wolves, attacking anyone inside or outside the church who disagrees with them, not merely on central tenets of the faith but even on minor personal preferences (cf. Acts 20:29–30). Congregations that have been blessed with servant leaders, who know little or nothing of this all too pervasive authoritarianism in conservative Christianity, should, on the one hand, be grateful but, on the other hand, be all the more vigilant, particularly when current, healthy leaders retire or go elsewhere, and especially if there has been no regular opportunity for vigorous but loving disagreement on issues among the church body. A church that doesn't know how to disagree in a healthy way is not going to be prepared when it has to disagree with a less than healthy leader.

It's also interesting to see how Jesus develops the rest of this short paragraph. Verses 16–20 are united by the theme of fruit bearing: "By their fruit you will recognize them" (v. 16a). And then Jesus expands by asking rhetorically if people pick grapes from thorn bushes or figs from thistles—good fruit from bad plants (v. 16b). Of course the answer is no, because a good tree bears good fruit and a bad tree bears bad fruit, and not the reverse (vv. 17–18). And with his eye on Judgment Day once again, Jesus adds in verse 19, "Every tree that does not bear good fruit is cut down and thrown into the fire." So beginning where he started, he concludes again, "Thus, by their fruit you will recognize them" (v. 20). Jesus never says what the fruit is, but in the context of the Sermon on the Mount it obviously refers to obedience to his various commands.

Of course, different people bear different kinds of fruit. Paul will develop the metaphor of the fruit of the Spirit in Galatians 5:22–23 and speak of those famous nine elements of love, joy, peace, patience, kindness, goodness, faithfulness, gentleness, and self-control. Fruit here appears in the context of discerning false from true prophets. That topic recurs in 1 Corinthians 14, where Paul explains that all alleged Christian prophecy must be tested or evaluated. Michael Green in his commentary on 1 Corinthians summarizes the full range of biblical teaching on criteria for identifying true prophecy—the true revelation of God by those who claim to proclaim his words—and lists seven helpful tests. Green suggests that the Christian congregation should ask first if a given message glorifies God or brings praise merely to the speaker. Second, is it in accord with Scripture? Third, does it build up the church rather than dividing it? Fourth, is it spoken in love? Fifth, is the speaker in obvious submission to the judgment and consensus of his or her Christian audience? Sixth, is the speaker in control of himself or herself? And seventh, is there a generally instructive nature or ethos to the message? There still will be times when we will not be entirely certain about a message, and we may simply need to wait and see what the ultimate outcome of someone's ministry is. But criteria like these can take us a long way toward becoming reliable fruit inspectors.

Third and finally, Jesus draws a contrast between those who do God's will and those who don't. Verses 21–23 read: "Not everyone who says to me, 'Lord, Lord,' will enter the kingdom of heaven, but only those who do the will of my Father who is in heaven. Many will say to me on that day, 'Lord, Lord, did we not prophesy in your name and in your name drive

out demons and in your name perform many miracles?' Then I will tell
them plainly, 'I never knew you. Away from me, you evildoers!'" Perhaps
the most striking feature of this little paragraph is that the illustrations of
those who are rejected by God are pictures of people apparently in positions of Christian leadership, of active Christian ministry—proclaiming
God's word, casting out demons, and working miracles in his name. Paul
might well call this the exercise of their spiritual gifts, especially the gift
of leadership, and especially some of the more so-called charismatic
gifts. Tragically, what Jesus is saying is that one can fake it in every one
of these areas while in fact working the kind of wickedness that would
lead God to label one an evildoer. It's not the up-front or the dramatic
that counts for all that much. That can easily turn into a masquerade.
What counts is what goes on behind the scenes, what goes on in one's
heart, in one's characteristic spirituality and behavior. Jesus is not saying
that true Christians don't blow it, even big-time, but for them at least
there is real substance behind whatever outward show for good or bad
may appear. It's interesting here, too, that nothing is said of anyone losing one's salvation. Instead Jesus declares to those who call out to him
as Lord but who have not done God's will, "I never knew you" (v. 23).
In other words, you were never the real thing in the first place. As your
church continues to seek to attract and retain godly, gifted leaders, look
for people who have proved themselves over time. Look for references
who can talk about what people are like behind the scenes in their private lives. Look for consistency and genuineness.

And so we've come full circle back to verses 24–27 again. Those who
hear God's word in Christ and put it into practice are like the wise man
who built his house on the rock. Those who turn their backs on obedience are like the man who built on sand, only to find what he has built
destroyed. Where are you building your house individually? Corporately
as a church body? In light of all the anti-Christian values pervasive in
our world and, sadly, in much of our church? In light of power rather
than service characterizing leadership in so much of our world and,
sadly, in much of the church? In light of our age of sound bites, video
clips, show over substance, in so much of the world and, increasingly,
in the church? Jesus is teaching in the three paragraphs leading up to
the parable of the wise and foolish builders that our faith may not be
proven until life gets hard, either through the difficulties of the fallen
world in general or through more explicit persecution for our Christian
faith in particular. He is teaching us that our faith is not proven except
over time and as all of the varied fruit our lives produce is considered as
a whole. He is teaching that our faith may not be demonstrated merely
by the visible but also by the invisible—our heart attitudes, our spirits,
our beliefs, our trust.

It is my prayer that each of you here today is building a deep and abiding faith in Jesus, trusting in the counter-cultural truths of the gospel in preparation for the storms and floods of this life, but above all for the final crisis of Judgment Day, when the true and the false will indeed be flawlessly distinguished by God's omniscience, despite all the apparent degrees of gradation within humanity in the present world.

I titled this message "The Basement of the Hard Rock Café." The Hard Rock Café, of course, is the logo that has become popular because of an international restaurant franchise by that name that advertises itself on T-shirts worn by many people throughout the world. Hard rock, of course, means something quite different for that franchise—a kind of music. But I've often thought of the parable of the wise builder when I've seen their logo. The basement of the hard rock café—if we can apply the language in a different context—is as solid as it gets. And that solid, firm, secure foundation is available only in Jesus and in putting his words into practice. Shall we pray for God to help us do just that?

Commentary on "The Basement of the Hard Rock Café"

All of the previous sermons have expounded three-point parables or have been parts of larger passages that at least contained a three-point parable. All but the last two of the remaining messages focus exclusively on two- or one-point parables. This one treats a two-point parable that may be diagrammed with a horizontal line. It presents a sharp contrast between two men, based on the contrast between the foundations on which each builds his home. The passage recurs at the end of the Sermon on the Plain in Luke's Gospel in slightly different form (Luke 6:46–49), but the two versions are probably variants of one original.[2] The central lessons clearly remain the same in Matthew and Luke, even if Luke may have contemporized the imagery by shifting the picture from a flash flood in an Israeli wadi to a storm that causes a river to overflow onto its flood plain, a common experience with the Orontes River in Syrian Antioch, where he may have been writing.[3]

One of my reasons for choosing Matthew's version is because Colorado, where I have most often preached this sermon, has dry gulches very similar to Israel's wadis. The portrait in Matthew's account thus remains very vivid and intelligible for audiences familiar with the Rocky Mountains. The most famous and most destructive flood in recent Colorado history is in fact the one in the illustration with which I begin the message—the Big Thompson Canyon disaster in 1976. Although Colorado has welcomed many new immigrants (and babies!) since then, so that only a minority of current residents actually remember the tragedy firsthand, the local media periodically retell the story, complete with vivid photographs, so that almost everyone in the area has heard of it.[4] And, again, though I was not living in Colorado at the time, my hearing of it through my involvement with Campus Crusade for Christ enables me to add a personal touch, as well as recounting for my listeners something with which they would be familiar.

The second half of the introduction transitions to a picture Jesus may have actually had in mind in composing the parable, again one with which I have firsthand experience. Slides of Israel, including the Wadi Kelt, are also common enough that one could project an image of the canyon on a screen at the outset of one's message if that technology is available. Photos of the closest local equivalents could be substituted by preachers without ready access to good pictures of Israel.

With these two partially parallel illustrations presented, I am ready to read the text. It is short enough that I see no great advantage in parceling it out bit by bit throughout the sermon as I often do with longer passages. If my purpose were to explore in detail first what the wise man looked like and then how the foolish man appeared, it would have been natural to cut the text in half and read verses 24–25 at the outset and verses 26–27 midway through the message. If one wanted to end on the more positive note of considering the wise man, one could reverse the sequence of the two parts. But just as I used the short parable of the children in the marketplace as an opportunity to teach about John the Baptist's and Jesus' ministries more generally (see chap. 6), I decided to use this short narrative to review key themes from the Sermon on the Mount more generally. Many Christians will be fairly familiar with individual parts of the Sermon, given its perennial popularity, but few will have surveyed the entire message all at once or recognized the integral connection of its concluding parable with the whole of what has preceded.

Having already sketched a picture of what Jesus might have been imagining in the parable proper, I next highlight the parallelism between the two halves of the passage, which makes the differences between the wise man and the foolish man that much more striking.[5] The contrast allows me to draw one further comparison with which virtually every homebuyer in the Denver area must deal—determining whether or not a given piece of property sits on bentonite. If some listeners still have not felt the force of the passage from my opening two illustrations, hopefully they will from this third one. Little else in the parable itself requires much explanation, although I don't take for granted that every last person recognizes this story is more than just sound advice for construction workers (or campers). So in reminding my audience that this is a parable with symbolic import, I also bridge to Jesus' explicit comparisons that introduce each half of the parable and at least partially explain the symbolism.

Nevertheless, as with several of the passages preached earlier in this book, even straightforward spiritual truths tend to spin off more controversial theological tangents that require some attention. The most obvious from the parable of the two builders is the question of works righteousness. Jesus could hardly be more explicit in saying the wise person puts his words into practice, so does this mean a certain level of obedience is required for salvation? The first and third of the theological questions I raise deal with this issue. The first shows works as the necessary outgrowth of faith in general; the third addresses the issue of quantifying them. Sandwiched between these two is the debate about the one key portion of the parable that Jesus does *not* explain, that is, what the storm represents. The three issues are intertwined, for if one argues that the storm refers solely to crises in this life, then one could take the foolish builder to stand simply for the Christian who loses a certain amount of heavenly reward. If the storm also (or exclusively) depicts Judgment Day, the contrast must be between believer and unbeliever, between the saved and the lost. So it makes sense to raise the question of works first, suggesting a coherent interpretation that doesn't make Jesus contradict his own teaching elsewhere,[6] next to examine the imagery of the storm to exclude the option that allows for only crises in this life to be in view,[7] and then to return to the question of how much transformation is necessary.[8] The sequence also creates a rhetorically satisfying *aba* structure.

An explanation of what it means to hear Jesus' words and put them into practice also requires defining which words Jesus has in mind. That allows the treatment of the first of the three theological issues to rehearse the contents of the entire Sermon as well. In the process, listeners acquire a feel for the whole that is often missing in analyses of small parts of the Sermon, and they also hear a great précis of Jesus' ethical mandates more generally, first in the choice of topics he included and then in his one-sentence summary that has come to be known as the Golden Rule.[9] The survey of the Sermon also clarifies what many readers have often missed—that this is Jesus' "kingdom manifesto" for how those already committed to him should live out a life of faith and discipleship. It does not present impossible entrance requirements designed to lead us to trust in grace rather than law, nor literal guidelines for political governments, nor the legislation for a future millennial kingdom, nor a host of other things that various interpreters over the centuries have tried to make it provide.[10]

It would not be realistic to use Jesus' concluding parable as a springboard for detailed exposition of the entire Sermon on the Mount in one message. But because the parable is as brief and clear as it is, time still remains to accomplish one more major task in this exposition: to explore in more detail the immediately preceding verses, which, with the parable, are regularly seen as forming the conclusion to Jesus' Sermon.[11] This conclusion is tripartite, with verses 13–14 contrasting the narrow and wide gates (and the paths that proceed from them), verses 15–23 comparing true and false prophets, and verses 24–27 highlighting the differences between wise and foolish builders. Because I have already dealt with verses 24–27, because verses 15–23 themselves subdivide naturally between verses 20 and 21, and because the second comparison is more than double the length of the first, I divide verses 13–23 into three parts, reading each part as I proceed, with commentary interspersed.

In this section Jesus employs metaphors that prove as transparent as his concluding parable. Not much explanation is needed, just incisive application. The Colson quotation sums up the American church's condition brilliantly and offers a geographical metaphor just as Jesus' gates and roads did. It also allows for numerous further applications that derive from this cultural analysis, including what readers by now will recognize as one of my favorite hobby horses—American spending habits. Discerning true from false leaders shifts gears and raises questions pastors probably deal with far too little, lest their own ministries come under uncomfortable scrutiny! (The same is true about the theme of spending, and the fact that my preaching ministry has been entirely of the interim or guest-substitute variety allows me to hammer on some themes that may be more difficult for regular pulpiteers to hit as hard.) Correctly understanding Jesus' call for "fruit inspection" is crucial in an era in which Mormonism is one of the world's fastest growing religions, and its apologetic regularly appeals to this text, combined with their good works, as a crucial reason for believing that they are the one true church of Jesus Christ in these "latter days."[12] A key part of an exegetically responsible reply to that apologetic is to point to the immediate context of verse 20: verses 21–23. There it is clear that a saving relationship with Jesus is the necessary foundation in order for good works to count for anything. Jesus' striking language, "I never knew you" (v. 23), rather than the expected, "I don't know you" (cf. Matt. 25:12; see p. 197), allows me to put in a plug for the Calvinist doctrine of the perseverance of the saints as well—which of course I accept because I believe it to be a *biblical* doctrine.[13]

As I do frequently in my preaching, I return in my conclusion to some aspect of my introduction, tying the message up in a bow, so to speak. The contrast between wise and foolish builders is simply a variation on the contrasts between narrow and broad gates and true and false prophets. I also frequently refer to the title of my sermons, if at all, only at the close of a message. Those who have paid attention to the titles printed in their bulletins may perhaps be wondering throughout the service how they apply. Perhaps I can build at least a little suspense by not offering an explanation until the end of the sermon. Of course, if the title is straightforwardly descriptive, I may not mention it at all. But surely some folks have been wondering about the meaning of "The Basement of the Hard Rock Café." Many will recognize the Hard Rock Café from its ubiquitous T-shirts (I saw them even in Saint Petersburg, Russia, less than four years after the fall of the Soviet Union, when I first composed this message). But a café is one kind of house, the parable clearly praises building a house on the solid rock, and modern Americans usually have basements as foundations for their homes. So, even if the title is a bit cornier than most, perhaps it will help some people to remember the key themes of the parable.

11

The Parable
of the Recovering Homosexual

Luke 18:9–14

I was helping to plan the twentieth-year class reunion for my college. A group of us who had been involved in a campus Christian organization wanted to have our own special reunion, just as we had done at ten years. We were able to contact a remarkable number of our old group, and a fairly high percentage told us that they would come. It was encouraging to hear how the last ten years had gone for so many, as God was clearly working great things in and through them. One close friend, however, I had lost touch with about twelve years earlier. The recently published alumni directory from my college listed his address in a large American city simply as "general delivery." It also gave a workplace and work phone number. In recounting this to my wife, she remarked that general delivery is the postal listing for people on skid row! I tried sending Mike a letter at this address, but I received no response. So after several weeks I called the work phone number, got a recorded voicemail, and left a message that I was a former college classmate of Mike's trying to reestablish contact with him. Again I heard nothing, until after a couple of weeks, I received a call one Saturday afternoon from his workplace. The employee I talked with explained that Mike had left his position with them a couple of years earlier, but he did have a home telephone number for him. He didn't know if it was current, but I was welcome to try it. With my curiosity piquing, I thanked the store employee and immediately called Mike at the number I'd just received.

To my surprise, after only one ring, Mike picked up the phone. I recognized his voice immediately. He was surprised to hear who it was on the other end of the line. I asked him how he was doing; he said, "Okay." I explained about the upcoming reunion and noticed a guarded, cautious tone of voice in each of Mike's fairly brief replies. I asked him what he was currently doing. He said he had been out of work for a little over a year. Finally after a long pause, he blurted out, "Craig, I have AIDS. Just about twelve years ago, I decided it was time to stop fighting the desires I had had all my life. I came out of the closet, moved in with a gay friend, and later became infected with the AIDS virus."

Mike's health had deteriorated to the point where he could not hold down a full-time job. He did work a few hours a week in a friend's store, but it paid very little. For the most part, he was living on welfare in low-cost community housing that had a number of AIDS sufferers in it. He still shared his small apartment with a male friend, but obviously he was living celibately, and this was not the man who had infected him.

I had heard stories about homosexuals, including those who had contracted AIDS, including some with whom I had had a passing acquaintance, but Mike was clearly the person closest to me, or who had once been very close to me, that I had ever known in this situation. Certain things that had been done and said years ago now made sense, in retrospect, but in those days I would never have guessed.

I quickly determined to do two things as our conversation continued. First, I wanted to assure Mike that I still cared for him, and that I was very concerned about his situation. I wasn't going to immediately pass judgment on him, certainly not without learning a whole lot more about the situation. Second, I very much wanted to find a tactful way to direct the conversation to spiritual things, to see if he professed any of the Christian faith that had once been so vibrant when we were in college together. As we talked, two more things also became clear. First, Mike harbored a lot of bitterness toward Christian friends and churches that had come to know about his situation and utterly rejected him, making blanket condemnations about homosexuals in general. The only real support from friends that he had experienced in the last decade was from the local gay community. Second, he spoke as if he still had a sincere hope that God had forgiven him, that God still loved him, and that his salvation was secure. As close to death as he said he had come a couple of times in recent years, it seemed to me unlikely that he was faking this confidence. After we had talked for a while and he had given me permission to share his situation with friends at the reunion, I told him I would keep in touch and hung up.

Several months later, we did indeed have a wonderfully encouraging college reunion, with an opportunity at a separate gathering for each person or couple from the Christian organization to share a little bit about what had been going on in their lives. Mike was obviously neither physically nor emotionally able to travel to this event, and we really had no idea how people would react to his news anyway. Mike, of course, was not the only person who had been close to us who was absent. Some simply couldn't come, a few we had lost touch with, and one or two replied to our invitations in a way that suggested they really didn't want our fellowship anymore, which, of course, made me wonder what things might have gone wrong in their lives. But overall it was a fantastic weekend, and when it was my turn to share a little bit about myself, I drastically abbreviated my own comments in order to have time to tell Mike's news and to encourage people to contact him, to show some love for him, and to pray for him.

When the sharing time was over, Bill came up to me. He was another man who had been a leader in our Christian group and every bit as close to Mike in his college years as I had been. In fact, he knew more about the years during which I'd lost touch with Mike, including the fact that he had molested several adolescent boys and spent some time in jail. "You know, he only got what he deserved," Bill declared emphatically. There didn't seem to be any love, any compassion, any sorrow, or any sense of obligation on Bill's part to try to restore contact with Mike. He added, "You shouldn't be surprised if most in our group don't rush to reach out to Mike. People aren't born gay. He made his free choices. Now he's paying the just penalty. We shouldn't be focusing our attention on Mike but on these wonderful friends who are here who have been faithful to Jesus." I went away from that conversation at least as troubled as I had been after that first phone call to Mike.

As I was reading through the Gospel of Luke recently, it dawned on me that there is a much briefer story that Jesus told that has some haunting similarities to my story about Mike and Bill. Today we know it as the parable of the Pharisee and the tax collector. It is found in Luke 18:9–14, and it reads as follows:

> To some who were confident of their own righteousness and looked down on everyone else, Jesus told this parable: "Two men went up to the temple to pray, one a Pharisee and the other a tax collector. The Pharisee stood by himself and prayed: 'God, I thank you that I'm not like the other people—robbers, evildoers, adulterers—or even like this tax collector. I fast twice a week and give a tenth of all I get.'
>
> "But the tax collector stood at a distance. He would not even look up to heaven, but beat his breast and said, 'God, have mercy on me, a sinner.'
>
> "I tell you that this man, rather than the other, went home justified before God. For all those who exalt themselves will be humbled, and those who humble themselves will be exalted."

Because of our familiarity with this story and because of the massive changes in modern culture, we scarcely feel its original force. Today a Pharisee is synonymous with a legalist or hypocrite, and tax collectors are at worst an annoyance. We need to remind ourselves of some crucial historical background.

In Jesus' world, the Pharisees were the most popular group of Jewish leaders. They were widely admired by the ordinary farmers and fishermen, the so-called people of the land. The Pharisees were descendants of a reform movement in Judaism from the mid-second century B.C. Their goal was to contextualize the laws of Moses, to bring them up to date and apply them to every area of modern life, so that God's people could know how to be obedient in every situation in which they found themselves, with as few gray areas as possible. The Pharisees believed that God's blessing, most noticeably ridding the land of the Romans, was contingent on their achieving a significant measure of obedience among themselves and among the populace as a whole. Although today we often think of them as legalistic, they did not believe so much in doing good works in order to "get saved"—they believed they already were saved by virtue of being born Jewish—as in minute obedience to their detailed laws in order to "stay saved," as we might phrase it today. After all, theirs was a world that had not yet encountered the notion of what we popularly call "eternal security." The Pharisees were also very nationalistic and fueled an intense hatred of Gentiles—people of other nationalities or religions. Perhaps the closest modern parallels to the Pharisees are found right within many very conservative evangelical circles, among those leaders who are on what we have come to call the "far Right," religiously or politically or both.

So, too, it was politics that made first-century Jewish tax collectors, on the other hand, so despised. The average Jew believed that tax collectors had sold out to the enemy by working for the occupying Roman forces, an empire that God had promised one day to destroy. In general, Judaism at the time tended to ostracize what we call the "down and out"—the poor, the sick (particularly lepers), as well as members of other ethnic groups like Samaritans and Gentiles. The tax collectors were the one fairly well-to-do category of Jewish people who were equally ostracized. You might call them the "up and out."

Who most corresponds to the tax collectors in our world? We have plenty of people who today suffer the stigma of being considered second-class citizens, even by some Christians—teenage moms; single or divorced parents of whatever age; the physically challenged; foreigners, particularly of Middle Eastern nationalities; the poor; the homeless; and so on. But most of these people are not well-to-do.

Neither are many who are infected with HIV. So why would AIDS sufferers particularly come to my mind as I read this parable? For three reasons, I think. First, because of the severity of the stigma. Combating abortion and fighting against gay rights have become the top two political issues for many in the conservative American Christian community. Second, like the sins of the abortionist, the sins of the practicing homosexual affect equally all socioeconomic brackets in our society, afflicting the "up-and-out" as well as the "down-and-out." Finally, leaving to one side debates about possible genetic influences and also the unfortunate plight of hemophiliacs who contract HIV through infected blood transfusions, most AIDS sufferers can trace their plight directly to specific, avoidable behavior. The same was true of tax collectors in Jesus' world. No one had to accept that illegitimate form of employment, working for the foreign empire as a traitor to one's country. In fact, in Jesus' world no other group was ever linked together with sinners in general. And yet on numerous occasions when one of the Gospel writers wants to talk about the people rejected by conventional Judaism at that time, he simply employs the expression "tax collectors and sinners." If that phrase sounds natural to you, you've been in church far too long! Imagine putting your occupation together with sinners: "plumbers and sinners," "computer technicians and sinners," or even "seminary professors and sinners!" The combinations are jarring, even shocking, but for the upstanding first-century Jewish leader, "tax collectors and sinners" came naturally to his lips as a logical combination.

In this kind of setting, then, Jesus tells the parable to those who literally "were continually in a state of confidence that they were righteous and continually despising the rest" (Luke 18:9 my translation). The tenses of the Greek verbs in this verse imply ongoing past action. Jesus' story proceeds to describe two characters. Both go to the temple at one of the six prescribed times for daily prayer (v. 10). These times of prayer were also times for offering sacrifices. So perhaps each man was bringing an animal to offer for the forgiveness of his sins. The Pharisee stands and prays "by himself," the rendering of the TNIV, which is a better translation than the original NIV ("about himself") or its footnote ("to himself"—v. 11). The Pharisee was concerned with ritual purity. He wanted to remain separate from the others and acted aloof from them as well. His prayer calls attention to himself and reflects a certain arrogance, as he thanks God that he is not like a variety of criminals and lawbreakers. One is reminded of the common Pharisaic prayer that Paul inverts in Galatians 3:28, in which the Jewish male thanked God that he was created a free man and not a slave, a Jew and not a Gentile, and a man and not a woman.

But this Pharisee in Jesus' story makes his prayer with specific reference to the throngs around him, including one notorious sinner whom he spies across the temple from where he is standing. The tax collector would have qualified as both a "robber" and an "evildoer," to use the Pharisee's categories. The Pharisee even reminds God of the extra meritorious duties that he performed. He fasted not merely once a year on the Day of Atonement, as the Hebrew Scriptures had commanded, but twice a week, as the Pharisees practiced. He gave not merely a tenth of the specified crops and produce that the Old Testament Law required—namely, grain, oil, and wine; rather, he tithed on all his property (v. 12). Though exaggerated, the portrait of the Pharisee is understandable enough in light of ancient Jewish developments.

Contrasting in virtually every respect with this Pharisee is the tax collector. He stands "at a distance" (v. 13). He recognizes his unworthiness to join the main group of Jewish worshipers. His posture is one of humility. He would not even look up to heaven, Jesus tells us, and his behavior is that which men in Jesus' world practiced only in times of acute distress—he beat on his chest. Normally this was an action reserved for women and one that men viewed as a sign of great weakness. In his prayer the tax collector asks for mercy. One could translate his pleas, "God be *propitiated* for me." In translating Jesus' words, Luke uses the same Greek verb that Paul will use in his letters for an "atoning sacrifice." The man's plea also echoes the first verse of David's classic penitential psalm, Psalm 51, which reads, "Have mercy on me, O God, according to your unfailing love; according to your great compassion blot out my transgressions" (NIV). In short, the man knows he has sinned grievously and wants to be forgiven. If the picture of the Pharisee is largely realistic, the portrait of the tax collector defies first-century expectations.

Clearly, Jesus is already preparing his hearers for a surprise ending. But still, he would have sent shock waves through the crowd as he delivered his conclusions. It was the tax collector who went home "justified"—again a key word that Paul uses in his letters for "acquittal" or "proper legal standing" before God. The Pharisee, on the other hand, despite all his appearances of religious devotion, was not forgiven. Put bluntly in our twenty-first-century Christian language, the tax collector was saved. He had become right with God. The Pharisee hadn't. The One who knows human hearts flawlessly recognized that years of conservative religious service, even involvement in a leadership role among God's people, still had not led this Pharisee to a genuine relationship with God himself. One commentator writes, "The parable reminds us that even the most religious person can miss the purpose, the goal of life. The text invites us to discover God as a living father and 'that tax collector,' whoever he or she may be as a brother or sister."[1]

In light of my conversations with both Mike and Bill, I can't help but ask a fairly terrifying question. Of those two good friends of mine from college days, could it be that God looks down today and recognizes Mike as saved and Bill as lost? The first of those ideas is easier for me to accept than the second, because I have other reasons for thinking Bill is a true believer. But it's worth asking how often our attitudes are indistinguishable from this Pharisee's when it comes to the notorious sinners in our world, especially when those attitudes match the Pharisees' condemning spirit here rather than Jesus' compassion. And it's not just this one story. The parable of the prodigal son makes a similar point in even greater detail. Throughout Jesus' ministry, especially in Luke's Gospel, sinners are given lavish welcomes at the slightest sign of genuine repentance, unlike the period of months and even years of penance that Jews typically required for grievous sins, only after which someone could be received back as a full member of the community. On the other hand, Jesus' harshest words throughout the Gospels, particularly in his woes to the Pharisees and scribes in Matthew 23, are reserved for the self-righteous, conservative religious leaders whose attitudes should have been quite different than they were. Paul adopts the same principles in his ministry, railing against the Judaizers—the legalistic insiders in the Jewish-Christian community—while bending over backwards to be "all things" to all unsaved people so that by all possible means he might save some (1 Cor. 9:19–23). He puts it even more concisely in 1 Corinthians 5:12–13, "What business is it of mine to judge those outside the church? Are you not to judge those inside? God will judge those outside." I wonder how often in contemporary, evangelical Christianity we completely invert these two principles, as we harshly judge outsiders, including outsiders who may have once been involved in church, while kowtowing to the stern, legalistic, compassionless, ultraconservative leaders in our midst.

Perhaps the issue of homosexuality is not one that has ever played a prominent role in your life or in the life of anyone you know well. Perhaps a better application today for you involves your discrimination against someone of another race or gender or marital status or ethnicity. Perhaps, on the other hand, you've been on the receiving end of ostracism and stigmatization because of your situation in life, and you still harbor grudges against those who mistreated you. I experienced the wrath and fury that some who call themselves evangelical Christians can unleash after I wrote a book several years ago with a Mormon friend, a New Testament professor at Brigham Young University. We took several key doctrinal issues that separate evangelicals and Latter Day Saints and took turns explaining why we believed what we believed and why neither of us was persuaded to change our minds. But we tried to do so in a respectful tone, trying to separate true statements about what our respective communities believed from stereotypes or false generalizations that we had frequently encountered. We committed to set forth in jointly authored sections of our chapters what things we agreed on and what things we disagreed on, so that we would force ourselves to agree on our lists of agreements and disagreements!

Despite frequently stressing that each of us still believed in evangelizing the other community and that our differences were still at least as deep as our agreements, I was regularly misrepresented, particularly within the community of countercult ministries, largely just for having adopted such a courteous format of dialogue. I was vilified by people who know only a combative and confrontational style of ministry. Oh, a majority of the letters, reviews, calls, and e-mails that I got were very positive, but a vocal minority persisted with a variety of objections to what I had done, with such a venomous spirit that, even if they were right in their charges, their tone fundamentally violated Paul's command to speak the truth in love (Eph. 4:15). Ironically, the rare occasions when Paul seems to break his own rule, or at least when his polemics suggest that he is exercising a kind of "tough love," are without exception when he is dealing with people within his churches who were overly legalistic, harsh, or censorious. The people who treated me so venomously are the very people who, biblically speaking, deserve harsh confrontation, rather than those against whom they unleash their invectives. The more that we're convinced that any Mormon or any homosexual or any other person quite different from us is lost and doesn't know Christ, the more we should bend over backwards in terms of loving that person into the kingdom. Latter Day Saints understand that principle and are beating us hands-down in winning converts, which makes it all the more acute for us to change our approach. The gay community understands that principle, too, and often takes care of its own better than most Christians do theirs. There is even an entire Christian denomination, the Metropolitan Community Church, that is otherwise evangelical in its theology but welcomes gays and lesbians, unfortunately without also doing justice to the biblical texts that clearly label homosexual intercourse as sinful.

Perhaps we could sum up Jesus' lesson with a hypothetical scenario. Suppose a polltaker randomly interviewed a representative sampling of non-Christians who know you, assuming you have enough non-Christian acquaintances for such a poll to be worthwhile. Though they would undoubtedly disagree with you on numerous theological, social, and political topics, would they be able to say, like the tax collectors and all the other outcasts who encountered Jesus, that at least they know you passionately care about them? Philip Yancey tells the story of asking numerous people whom he has sat next to on plane trips, before disclosing his own occupation or Christian commitment, what they think of when they hear the expression "evangelical Christian?" Yancey recounts that the two most common replies are those that refer to the pro-life movement and opposition to gay rights, or the like. Never once has anyone said a word about grace.[2] Now don't misunderstand me. I'm against abortion, and I oppose the sin of homosexual behavior, though I hope people would say that I love homosexuals and show grace to them. But what a tiny, narrow swath of Christian belief and practice is represented by those two issues! The heart of the gospel is about God's love for lost sinners, illustrated by Christian compassion. Yet that's not the way we've come to be perceived in our culture.

There are some pleasant exceptions. Exodus International is a thoroughly biblical, Christian ministry that is ministering tactfully and graciously to the homosexual community and seeing significant numbers of people come to the Lord and even change their sexual orientation. Others live celibate lives, refusing to give into the temptation of their sinful desires. But the Exodus staff often take a lot of flak because they do not take a more hard-line stance, as many Christians wish they would, and insist that every gay person change his or her orientation, as if that were realistically possible for all! Undoubtedly some of these attacks come from the same kind of folks who sent me hate mail.

The message of Jesus' parable, on the other hand, declares that God still loves tax collectors and all their contemporary equivalents, and he is willing to welcome them as saved people when they genuinely trust in him and repent of their sins, long before their lives are fully cleaned up. Besides, that's true for all of us, because none of us will clean up all of the sin in our lives this side of heaven. God still loves today's tax collectors, and he still hates the attitudes of the harsh Pharisees in our churches, who at the very least deserve stern rebuke for their loveless behavior, and in extreme cases, when they refuse to change, should receive the same kind of eviction from the church that Paul required for unrepentant Judaizers in Galatia (Gal. 4:30). As Jesus reminds us, back at the end of the parable with which we started, "For all those who exalt themselves will be humbled, and those who humble themselves will be exalted" (Luke 18:14).

Commentary on "The Parable of the Recovering Homosexual"

We turn to a second two-point parable that can be diagrammed with a horizontal line. As with many of the shorter rabbinic parables, it reflects a sharp contrast between two characters without any explicit master figure within the parable itself. In the rabbinic parallels, God (or a rabbi speaking in God's name) often judges between the two characters at the end of the narrative; here Jesus performs that function (Luke 18:14).[3] But his judgment does not add a third lesson to the story, since he merely spells out the surprising fates of each of the two characters within the story: the Pharisee, who is not justified and thus humbled, and the tax-collector, who is justified and thus exalted.

This passage may rank with the good Samaritan as one of the two most difficult parables for which to recreate the original shock value. Just as virtually everyone inside or outside the church "knows" that Samaritans are heroes (see chap. 3), so also contemporary Westerners "know" that Pharisees are "bad guys"—hypocrites even. Tax collectors are seldom individuals any more (but computer-generated notices), and those who are certainly don't work for a foreign, occupying nation. And again many people know that tax collectors in the Gospels frequently repent and become Jesus' followers. Two are even named—Levi/Matthew and Zacchaeus. So if I am going to shock people at all, I cannot allude to the parable in my title, nor can I print the text. I certainly cannot begin with the reading of the text.

Instead, I must look for a functional equivalent to the despised tax collector in today's world. Both from my own experience and from Philip Yancey's observations, which I cite midway through the message, the homosexual may be the closest I can come, at least within the more right-wing branch of American evangelicalism in which I am normally invited to preach. The fact that I had such a powerful and perplexing experience with my friend whom I'm calling Mike, and then struggled with Bill's reaction, makes it a natural jumping off point for the beginning of the sermon.

The parable of the Pharisee and the tax collector is comparatively short, and since I'm preaching it by itself, I can afford the time it takes to tell the story of Mike and Bill somewhat leisurely. My audience can relive some of my suspense as I tried to reestablish contact with Mike and then as I began my telephone conversation with him. Hopefully, they will empathize with me and not just move immediately to censure, as I describe how I tried to decide what to say in response to Mike's disclosures. I wish I could have described a situation I knew firsthand where there was clear and dramatic repentance, as with the tax collector in Jesus' parable. I am familiar with such stories but don't know any of their protagonists personally. Besides, repentance often is not instantaneous but gradual, motives remain mixed, and it is hard to be sure about someone else's spiritual state. So Mike's story may actually be the better example from those angles.

In any good case study, one not only disguises the characters by using different names for them but one changes or withholds enough of the details so that the people involved will not be readily identified.[4] I succeeded in doing that better with "Bill" than with "Mike"—Bill's comments are actually a composite of several individual friends' reactions to my conversation with Mike. As I explain later on in the sermon, I have separate reasons for thinking Bill is a true believer or, as I should now put it, that the several "Bills" are true believers. Again, I can't refer to people I personally know who as thoroughly fit the stereotypical response of the Pharisee as, say, Yancey can with his upbringing in the fundamentalism of the deep South in the 1950s.[5] But, again, stereotypical characters may be too easily written off. The "Pharisee" in my story has to show enough outward signs of being a true follower of God for Jesus' original shock to be replicated.

After narrating my encounters with Mike and Bill at some length, I am finally ready to bridge to the reading of the parable. I do that with a fairly short transition that recounts simply how I first made the connection between my experiences and this particular Scripture in the first place. As with the two builders, one could break this "contrast parable" in half and read the part about the Pharisee first and then discuss it, before turning to the part about the tax collector and its exposition. If one wanted further subdivision, as well as more suspense, one could read (and preach) verses 10–12 first, then verse 13, then Jesus' surprising verdict in verse 14, and only after that return to verse 9 as the bridge to looking for contemporary equivalents to people who are "confident of their own righteousness" or who look "down on everyone else." Neither Jesus nor the evangelists usually tell us *before* a given parable one of its central lessons or applications.[6] On the other hand, for that very reason, Luke may have deliberately put the information here to jar with the introduction of a "good guy"—a Pharisee—immediately afterward, in which case it may be important to preserve the sequence of the text. At any rate, I have kept verses 9–14 together, in order, for this sermon.

The most important features that my exposition must now clarify are how differently the Pharisees and tax collectors were viewed in Jesus' world as compared with today. Contemporary evangelical preaching, in my experience, consistently misses the mark when discussing the Pharisees and, at times, the Jewish leadership more broadly. We make numerous unwittingly anti-Semitic (and historically untrue) statements when we lump them altogether as legalists and hypocrites. Much scholarship has persuasively made this point for twenty-five years now, so the day is drawing near when preachers can no longer excuse themselves on the grounds that they haven't heard.[7] And even if one studies just the Gospels, one has to recognize that Nicodemus (John 3:1–5), Simon (Luke

7:36–50), another unnamed Pharisee who invites Jesus to dinner (Luke 14:1–6), and the unnamed Pharisees who warned Jesus about Herod (Luke 13:31) are all portrayed at least partially positively. One simply cannot tarnish every Pharisee with the same brush, even if some did merit Jesus' censure. And one certainly can't assume that most people in Jesus' original audience would have imagined the Pharisee to be the villain the minute he was introduced. Indeed, although they might recognize that Jesus' fictitious Pharisee was a bit pretentious, as soon as the tax collector appeared as the second character they would likely have reverted to the assumption that the Pharisee would be the hero and the tax collector, the whipping boy.[8]

Having clarified the roles that many Pharisees and tax collectors played in the first century, I draw my listeners back to the twenty-first century. How can I justify my use of homosexuals as a functional equivalent to tax collectors? They are not the closest parallel in terms of the actual sin associated with each. One is an occupation; the other, a lifestyle. But in terms of those who feel ostracized, in terms of those who often receive the harshest rebukes or wildest caricatures by more conservative evangelicals, in terms of an issue that cuts across society, affecting the richest as well as the poorest, they afford a good parallel. So I try to acknowledge that this is not the only application of the text or even necessarily the best, and I suggest several others. But then, with Yancey's help, I return to defend why I have chosen this group of people for *my* introductory "parable."

At long last I am ready to deal with several key exegetical details in the text. Commentators debate to what extent this Pharisee is meant to be a realistic portrait even of a minority of Jesus' contemporaries, or if it is merely a caricature.[9] I suspect it is some of each. Jesus wants to portray an extreme, jarring contrast between the two men. But there are enough other real people like these in the pages of the Gospels to suggest that at least some Pharisees and tax collectors in Jesus' world acted like these in the parable, making the need for Jesus' parable that much more acute. Much as a focus on the details of the prodigal son led to the sense that Jesus was depicting the depths of degradation, even though every detail was conceivable in its own right (see chap. 1), here, too, the various details of the Pharisee's behavior and speech combine to form at least a bit of an exaggeration.[10]

The same is true, on the other hand, for the tax collector. It is again Kenneth Bailey's wonderful cultural insights that highlight the extent of this man's distress.[11] The difference is that, apart from Jesus' own ministry of eliciting repentance from the outcasts of society, contrite tax collectors were unheard of, whereas hypocritical Pharisees were doubt-less at least as common as hypocritical people tend to be in any cross section of humanity. Nevertheless, as I point out in the message, despite these hints of a slightly exaggerated Pharisee and a very unusual tax collector, Jesus' audience probably remained unprepared for his conclusion, totally upending their expectation as to who would be justified in God's sight. At the very least, they would have expected the tax collector to undergo a period of penance to demonstrate the genuineness of his sudden outburst.[12] And even if the Pharisee's attitudes were somewhat inappropriate, the crowd could scarcely have expected Jesus to declare, in essence, that this man did not know God at all.

The stage is now set to return to my opening story. The terrifying possibility that I must consider reverses the spiritual states (and fates) of Mike and Bill (vs. conventional evangelical wisdom), just as Jesus did with the Pharisee and tax collector. But I need to generalize because many listeners in my congregation will not have "Pharisaic" attitudes toward homosexuals but may harbor inappropriate thoughts of malice and/or superiority toward other outcast people. I also recognize that some may largely have borne the brunt of such hostility by others, and I want them to know that I empathize. Hence, the example of the aftermath of *How Wide the Divide?* (on which, see chap. 8).[13] I've had folks accuse me of erecting a straw person when I've talked about evangelical hostility toward certain kinds of people, and it is true that the secular media often lump us all together as "fundamentalists" with some sweeping but inaccurate generalization about our attitudes to controversial social issues. So I wanted to include reference to the one situation in my life where I have experienced the greatest amount of that hostility firsthand, even if it was from a small minority of my book's reviewers and/or readers. It *does* exist. I know; I've felt it! I have no reason to doubt "Mike" when he tells me it was hardly just "Bill" who vilified and rejected him. This leads me back to Yancey one last time and one more pointed question about the image evangelicals in America have on the whole portrayed to a large number of unbelieving outsiders.

I want to end on a more positive note, however. Without condoning homosexual behavior, I stress how hard it may be to overcome, just as all of us may wrestle with other sins that can prove equally strong, damaging, or even addictive. I want to offer hope, hence, the reference to the ministry of Exodus International.[14] But I also want to offer realistic hope; hence, the recognition that healing may be a long, slow process. And God loves us through it all and wants us to spread that love to others.

12

Pray and Persevere

Luke 18:1–8

You will be appalled by the story I'm about to relate to you. Appalled, that is, if you have any kind of social conscience. The poor black, living on Chicago's South Side, sought to have her apartment properly heated during the frigid winter months. Despite city law in the matter, her unscrupulous landlord refused. The woman was a widow, desperately poor, and ignorant of the legal system; but she took the case to court on her own behalf. Justice, she declared, ought to be done. It was her ill fortune, however, to appear repeatedly before the same judge, who, as it turned out, was an atheist and a bigot. The only principle by which he abode was, as he put it, that "blacks should be kept in their place." The possibilities of a ruling favorable to the widow were, therefore, bleak. They became even bleaker as she realized she lacked the indispensable ingredient necessary for favorable rulings in cases like these—namely, a satisfactory bribe. Nevertheless, she persisted.

At first, the judge did not so much as even look up from reading the novel on his lap before dismissing her. But then he began to notice her, just another black, he thought, stupid enough to think she could get justice. Then her persistence made him self-conscious. This turned to guilt and anger. Finally, raging and embarrassed he granted her petition and enforced the law. Here was a massive victory over "the system"—at least as it functioned in his corrupted courtroom.[1]

The story I have just told you was written by David Wells, for many years now a professor of theology at Gordon-Conwell Seminary in Massachusetts. But in 1979 when he published this article in *Christianity Today*, he was still a professor at Trinity Evangelical Divinity School, where I was a young seminarian. Wells continues by stating what you may have already guessed: "In putting the matter like this I have not, of course, been quite honest. For this never really happened in Chicago (as far as I know)"—though I might add plenty of such things did happen a generation ago under the infamous machine of the senior Mayor Daley. Wells adds, however, "Nor is it even my 'story.' It is a parable told by Jesus (Luke 18:1–8) to illustrate the nature of petitionary prayer."

The story Wells has sought to update or contemporize originally appeared in Luke 18:1–8. Luke introduces the passage with the explanation, "Then Jesus told his disciples a parable to show them that they should always pray and not give up" (v. 1). Then he goes on to quote Jesus' words in verses 2–5:

> In a certain town there was a judge who neither feared God nor cared what people thought. And there was a widow in that town who kept coming to him with a plea, "Grant me justice against my adversary." For some time he refused. But finally he said to himself, "Even though I don't fear God or care what people think, yet because this widow keeps bothering me, I will see that she gets justice, so that she won't come and attack me!"

Jesus then applies this short parable, in verses 6–8:

> Listen to what the unjust judge says. And will not God bring about justice for his chosen ones, who cry out to him day and night? Will he keep putting them off? I tell you, he will see that they get justice, and quickly. However, when the Son of Man comes, will he find faith on the earth?

Oftentimes we have to update the parables, just as Dr. Wells did, in order for us to feel their original force or shock value. There is a key aspect of interpreting the parables that remains in dispute among the commentators. To what extent should they be considered allegories (point-by-point comparisons between literal and symbolic realities), or do they simply make one main point? It seems to me that in many cases a good compromise between these two extreme approaches is to read the parables through the eyes of each of the main characters and look for one lesson from each of these fictitious individuals.

This story obviously contains two explicit characters, the widow and the unjust judge. But there is a third character lurking in the background throughout this story as well, and that is God himself. He appears within the parable, when Jesus has the judge admit that he does not fear God. And he appears again, as Jesus applies the parable, as someone eager to dispense justice and bring about an age of complete righteousness when Christ himself, the Son of man, returns at the end of the age. It seems to me, then, that we can learn as many as three lessons from this passage by focusing, in turn, first on the widow, then on the judge, and finally on God himself.

The widow's circumstance in this story, particularly as portrayed in verse 3, creates a serious obstacle to her receiving justice. We're not given very many details about this woman except that she is described as a classic victim, a paradigm of helplessness in the ancient Middle Eastern world. Widows, like orphans, are presented throughout the Bible as poignant examples of the dispossessed. What little we are told about this particular woman suggests that she is destitute and has no male friend of any kind in a position to help her. Women, you see, went to court only if there was no man to plead their case. And we read here in verse 3 that this was a widow in a village who repeatedly kept coming to this judge with a plea, "Grant me justice against my adversary." She *does* have one advantage that men did not enjoy, precisely because she was in such a position of powerlessness. She could repeatedly return and even badger representatives of the judicial system, though in normal cases there was little chance of her receiving justice. A man, however, would quickly be evicted or perhaps even locked up if he behaved in such a way. But apart from these slender details, everything else about the woman's case is guesswork. Property disputes were commonly taken to local judges like this one, particularly disputes having to deal with inheritance. Maybe that's what the widow needed help with, especially if her husband had just recently died and there was a dispute over settling his estate. But whatever the specific situation, Jesus is clearly portraying a case of an individual who has all the odds stacked against her.

Somewhat uncharacteristically, Luke tells us one of the lessons of the parable right up front in verse 1, that Jesus intends to encourage his disciples always to pray and not to give up—*persevering prayer,* we might call it today. But immediately when we focus on the widow, we find someone whose position and circumstances seem to provide a great obstacle to such perseverance. They could easily have led to her being demoralized, giving up, and not continuing to come back and demand a fair shake.

If this parable is an illustration about persevering in prayer, then I would venture to say we need to pay careful attention. Persistence in prayer is not something contemporary Americans are very good at. All the recent studies suggest that American Christians today, even those in volunteer or paid ministry, often do not have regular times of daily prayer. Or if they do, they involve two, three, perhaps five minutes, hardly enough time to say much to God or hear much from him. From my own experience, as I have shared prayer requests with close friends, it often seems fairly obvious from subsequent conversations that they have not prayed for me, certainly not long enough for them to remember it. We take a significant portion of time praying for one another in our Sunday school class. But again, I'm afraid that, despite my repeated pleas, only a faithful minority of the class members actually take home and consistently pray for the things we've shared on Sundays. There are, however, antidotes to this malaise. There are cultures throughout the world that prove very faithful in public and private prayer. There are periods in church history when even Western Christians have distinguished themselves by this practice. For some folks today it may require setting aside a regular time each day, perhaps writing it on our calendars, telling other people, if there are conflicting appointments or pressures on our schedules, that we are already booked, which would be true. Perhaps it requires doing what I have found very helpful in the last couple of years, after a lifetime of hearing of others who have done so, and that is to make lists in different categories, one day praying for foreign missionaries that we know and support, another day for colleagues at the seminary, a third for a small collection of students whom I have committed to pray for, a fourth day for friends and events elsewhere in the United States, another day for the international scene, another day for church friends and events, and so on, with certain things such as family members being a priority almost every day. Perhaps for you it means simply writing down on a notepad or a Palm Pilot every time you promise to pray for someone and then going back and consulting those notes. Perhaps it means stopping for a few moments as you receive prayer requests by e-mail, as I often do, and just lifting those items up immediately to the Lord before you continue to type on your computer. It *is* possible, even in the frantic pace of contemporary American life, to make prayer a priority.

But what may be even harder is to persevere, to persist in prayer when no answer seems forthcoming. God hasn't granted our request, but he hasn't obviously closed the door either, and what we pray for certainly seems to us like a good thing that he would want to give us. The classic example is prayers for the salvation of a close friend or family member. Jesus' parable, with its audacious model of the persistent widow, suggests that we are simply to keep at it. It's interesting that while most people who make professions of faith do so as children or young adults, the second most common time people are particularly receptive to the gospel is during times of illness, especially in old age, as they realize they may be nearing death. I have several friends who have prayed for parents or other relatives throughout their whole lives and then rejoiced as those parents made commitments to Christ as very elderly people. We simply have to persevere and keep at it.

But persistence need not be limited to prayer. The woman's faithfulness in doing what she believed reflected God's just priorities encourages us to persevere in every aspect of Christian life and ethical living. In an age when commitment and loyalty seem to mean less and less in society as a whole, and at times even in Christian circles, there is a crying need for people to commit to staying in one community, in one church, in one ministry, even when opportunities may arise for them to go elsewhere, simply for the sake of providing continuity and stability in the lives of those around them when so much else is transient and changing. I watched my father turn down opportunities to leave the public school system in which he taught his entire career. And I watched the enormous doors of influence open up for him as he became very well known in a medium-size community in the state of Illinois, teaching the children and ultimately a few grandchildren of some of the first students he taught as a young man. I've been privileged to watch just the tail end of the life of a similar model, Dr. Vernon Grounds, the former president and current chancellor of Denver Seminary, who came as a young man in his thirties to be a professor, then became the academic dean, soon advanced to the presidency, and has now remained with one institution for more than fifty years, continuing a remarkably active ministry of counseling, teaching, and public speaking as an eighty-eight-year-old. He built a school and developed a reputation, along with a network of friends and influences, that would have required him in certain ways to start all over again had he jumped from one location to the next. I don't want to be so presumptuous as to say I know God is calling me to stay in Denver until and beyond my retirement. But the longer I'm here, going on seventeen years now, the easier it is for me to imagine doing so.

The widow's model of perseverance should challenge us in the area of faithfulness to our spouses, for those who are married, and to our wedding vows, even if marriage turns out to be less, perhaps even far less, than our youthful idealism once dreamed it might be. One of the statistics that profoundly affected me as I decided to commit my life to the Lord, as a teenager in the early 1970s, was that, of avowedly evangelical, born-again Christians, only one in fifty marriages ended in divorce,[2] whereas nearly one in three overall in the United States in the early seventies fell apart. Today the statistics are almost identical, one in three, or even a little bit more, for Christian and non-Christian alike. I know that the world has changed in thirty-two years, but it has not changed *that* much. People are simply reneging on their promises. That's why we need an organization like Promise Keepers to challenge us to faithfulness once again. The college Christian group that I was a part of has largely remained intact and kept in touch by a series of reunions for twenty-five years now, and, while we've lost touch with a few people, and while one or two marriages have fallen apart, more than 95 percent of our couples have stayed together, and most have even flourished. Faithfulness is possible, even at the beginning of the twenty-first century, if people are willing to be true to their commitments.

Finally, the most significant area in which we need without exception to be absolutely sure we remain faithful is that of our relationship to God, even when the Christian life seems harder than we ever imagined it could be, even when all those around us are calling us to abandon our standards and our values, even if our job is on the line because of our Christian faith, even when "everybody" is doing "it," including apparent Christians, but we know that whatever "it" is violates God's revealed will in Scripture.

It is interesting that the area this particular parable illustrates, however, was *perseverance in the arena of social justice,* and that leads us to the story's second character, a quite unjust figure—the judge.

We learn about him primarily in verses 2, 4, and 5. He is described as one who neither feared God nor cared what people thought. Whatever the widow's complaint was that required a court of law, it was highly ironic that the very place in which she should have found justice only compounded her problem. The judge is not concerned about what the Lord thinks or with the fact that one day he will have to stand accountable before him, nor does he seem to have any scruples about how the public looks upon him. This man is obviously involved in an elaborate system of bribery, as not a few officials throughout the Roman Empire were in the first century. People in numerous Third World countries today can often relate very closely to the corrupt system described here. Sadly, even in the United States, stories of corrupt officials in various walks of life are becoming more common.

In many ancient contexts community opinion would have shamed a public figure into right behavior, even if the threat of divine judgment wouldn't. But this man has steeled himself against public opinion. Nevertheless, the woman's perseverance eventually gets to him. Initially he simply refuses to hear her, as verse 4 states. But in time he recognizes, despite his wicked character, that he should dispense justice. The woman is getting very annoying. The widow keeps "bothering" him—the word that Jesus uses in verse 5. Thus, not because he is committed to providing justice for all but simply to be rid of her, he grants her request. The imagery of the last part of verse 5 reads literally "so that she won't come and give me a black eye." But the language is almost certainly metaphorical, just as today we might speak of somebody who "gives us a headache." That doesn't mean they've necessarily punched us in the face. But to be rid of this increasingly aggressive and annoying woman, despite his initial unwillingness, the judge will grant her justice.

I wonder how much of our praying, or of our Christian activity more generally, is directed against social injustice. Do we read the news, including Christian news, so that we can pray for world events, including religious developments? Are we outraged by the injustice in the Middle East? There's plenty to go around on all sides, though it's interesting that in all the overt hostility between Jews and Arabs, the Palestinians, whom many Americans don't even realize are a different ethnic group from Arabs, are caught in the middle. By the way, most Christians in Israel today are Palestinians. And those who are Christians are doubly harassed, both by the Jewish leaders and by fellow Palestinians who are Muslims and can't tolerate their profession of Christian faith. For almost our entire married life, Fran and I have been supporters of Bethlehem Bible College, the only Christian higher educational institution indigenous to the country of Israel. Most of its students and staff are Palestinians, but few Americans have ever heard of it, though the college is doing a great work.

Or what about those portions of the world, and there always are several, that teeter on the brink of famine? Today it's twelve million people in southern Africa, especially Zimbabwe and neighboring countries, where a food shortage is compounded by the economic policies of corrupt governments that have wrought havoc with once relatively stable farming economies. Are you aware of those issues? Do you pray for them? Do you give to help meet the needs? Or what about the daily murders and assaults and rapes in *our* streets in the United States, including the Denver metro area? Our country suffers an incredible number of murders because we have more ready access to guns and firearms than any developed country in the world. Oh yes, I know those wonderful slogans by the NRA and other folks that "guns don't kill, people do." But it's also true that people without guns kill far, far fewer people than those with guns. Isn't it fairly astonishing that five years after Columbine the Colorado State Legislature still has not been able to pass any significantly stiffer gun control laws? Isn't it time conservative Christians dramatically change their attitudes on these kinds of issues?

Would you consider choosing (or creating) a church, at least in part, on the basis of how much a priority it gave to addressing these issues of justice at home and abroad? Can we move beyond our typically narrow set of social issues—abortion and homosexuality, prayer in the schools, creation versus evolution, and so forth? Why don't we hear equally as much talk in our American evangelical congregations about the persecuted churches and peoples in the world, including persecuted Christians? Why don't we hear at least as much an appeal for Christians to eat out less, to waste less food and less gasoline, to stop going into such enormous debt with money that could be better spent? How much of our prayer time personally and in church focuses on the injustices of the world? In most cases the answer is precious little. But there's nothing preventing us from changing. And Jesus' parable demands that we do so.

The widow, then, is obviously a model of one of the most helpless categories of human beings in her world who needs justice. But the judge is by no means an obvious model of divine justice. In his case, Jesus' logic is what is called "from the lesser to the greater" or a "how much more logic." In other words, if a certain principle is true for fallible and even evil human beings, how much more must it be true with a perfect and good God? In this case, *God wants far more readily or quickly to grant his people justice* than the corrupt judge wanted to. And that leads us to the final character and to Jesus' concluding words in verses 6–8.

The Lord said, "Listen to what the unjust judge says. And will not God bring about justice for his chosen ones who cry out to him day and night?" The implied answer is, "of course." "Will he keep putting them off?" The implied answer is "of course not." "I tell you, he will see that they get justice, and quickly." And yet the ultimate dispensing of perfect justice will come only when Christ returns and human freedom to work evil and to choose to fight God's purposes is forever abolished. Thus the parable ends with the haunting question, "However, when the Son of Man comes, will he find faith on the earth?"

God is the ultimate standard or model of justice and righteousness, a major theme repeated throughout both the Old and New Testaments. The inadequacies of the helpless and the inequities of injustice among God's people will all be dealt with on Judgment Day. Some prayers, however worthy, will remain unanswered until then, but eventually all wrongs will be righted.

But can we really believe that promise, twenty centuries after Jesus spoke these words, and the world continues as corrupt as ever? This was a question that was raised even just one generation after Christ's death. And the most direct and the most encouraging answer found anywhere in Scripture to the problem of the delay of the end of the world as we know it appears in 2 Peter 3:8–9. There Peter writes, "But do not forget this one thing, dear friends: With the Lord a day is like a thousand years, and a thousand years are like a day. The Lord is not slow in keeping his promise, as some understand slowness. Instead he is patient with you, not wanting anyone to perish, but everyone to come to repentance." The reason God has not brought the end of the world and the righting of all wrongs more quickly is because, when he does, the door will forever be closed to even one more person responding and coming to him in faith.

The key issue is not if we can make sense of God's delay. We can. The key issue is the one Jesus poses in the last half of verse 8, which forms the conclusion and the climax of this passage. Even though from our perspective it seems like a long delay, will Christ, the Son of Man, find faith when he returns? That is to say, will he find his followers persisting in their faith, however long and arduous the wait is?

At least three lessons, then, emerge in this passage: First, pray perseveringly, work perseveringly, with optimism, confident that God much more gladly than the judge in this passage often does want in this life to grant us answers to our requests. Second, consider the helpless, and the injustice of this world that they experience, as a larger topic for your prayer life and for your actions, which often give those prayers feet. Finally, recognize that, even in those areas in which God does not in this age grant us our requests, he remains eager to grant justice but has good reasons for his delay.

Commentary on "Pray and Persevere"

We turn now from two parables that each presented two characters as contrasting subordinates without an explicit master figure to a two-pointed parable with a master and a single subordinate. Here the missing character, as compared with triangular parables, is the contrasting subordinate. In the parable of the two builders, the storm in part replaced the missing master figure. In the parable of the Pharisee and the tax collector, Jesus' closing verdict functioned similarly. Here there is nothing implicit, either in the parable itself or from its immediate context, to complete a triangle. Still, the closing verse of the passage refers to "the Son of Man" (v. 8b) and seems to make an additional point, by means of its rhetorical question, that the parable per se does not. Thus, while my book on interpreting the parables combines the lessons of the persistent widow and Jesus' closing question into a single point, so that I derive two lessons from the passage (one from the judge and one from the widow), it is possible to generate three points as well. For the sake of a fuller, richer, and, I hope, clearer sermon (not to mention my predilection for three points!), I have chosen a tripartite structure here, focusing in turn on the judge, the widow, and God.

My opening contemporization not only is personally meaningful, as I explain after I quote the story, but also continues, sadly, to be very "cutting edge." The conditions of our largest American slums and the systemic racism that often preserves them continue to afflict us twenty-five years after David Wells' story, even if progress has been made on some fronts.[3] The contemporization is also close enough in its imagery to that of Jesus' parable (reusing, e.g., the portraits of a corrupt judge and a poor widow) that astute listeners will recognize the similarities even while I am reading the story. No complicated bridge to the reading of Scripture is needed, so I turn immediately to the text.

The passage divides into three discrete sections: Luke's introduction (v. 1), the parable proper (vv. 2–5), and Jesus' appended remarks (vv. 6–8). One could, thus, parcel out the reading of the text throughout the sermon into these three segments, but I have chosen to keep them together, just as I chose to read the contemporization from David Wells all at once. I distinguish the three segments, however, by adding brief introductions to each as I read from Luke, rather than quoting the text without any explanatory interruptions as in most of my messages.

This is one of the few sermons in this book that I have preached only once, in a seminary chapel service to be specific. Because many in that audience would have already been introduced to the debates surrounding parable interpretation, I allude to the central hermeneutical issue and describe where I take my stand, at least briefly. I also explain why I think I can justify three points from a passage with two characters, and why I speak of a lesson to be derived from God rather than from Jesus, the Son of man, more directly.[4]

The parable proper does not neatly subdivide into two sections, one focusing on the widow and the other on the judge. Verse 2 introduces the judge; verse 3 presents the widow. Verses 4–5 recount the judge's soliloquy but refer to the widow three times within them. The judge's change of heart represents the climax of the short parable, so I end with that point. Thus, even though the judge is also the first of the two characters Luke introduces, I begin with the widow.

Once again, Kenneth Bailey provides important cultural background, demonstrating especially how the woman can get away with a kind of badgering that men, precisely because they more likely proved physical or political threats, could not have imitated.[5] Nothing, therefore, about her situation or her behavior appears terribly unrealistic. Describing her first also enables me to refer to Luke's introductory verse early on, even if I unpack the widow's plight before deriving the lesson from her behavior that Luke wants us to capture.

With this explicit command to persevere in prayer without losing heart, no further exegesis is necessary, and considerable time may be spent on contemporary application. For the very reason that current American Christians do not exhibit good track records with prayer in general, to say nothing of prolonged prayer, there is plenty of grist for the applicational mill.[6] Precisely because preachers often fall victim to the same malaise, those preparing to expound this text had better make sure they have applied the passage to themselves first and can share from their own experience ways of bucking the trend. Otherwise, at least some in the congregation will justifiably wonder if the expositor is indeed practicing what he or she preaches. Thus I go on to share some of the more successful strategies that have worked for me in this arena, as well as one example of a kind of persistent prayer that may pay rich dividends, even if only after decades of people's lives.[7]

Because the parable ends with Jesus' haunting question about whether or not faith in general will persist, if his return should be delayed, it seems legitimate to explore other important arenas of Christian persistence besides simply prayer.[8] I chose the three that are perhaps dearest to my heart and, arguably, the most central areas in which faithfulness to commitment proves crucial. I then deal with them in ascending, climactic order—faithfulness to ministry (especially in one location), faithfulness to one's spouse, and faithfulness to God.

An examination of the more intriguing picture of the judge comes next. He is merely the most dramatic example of several unscrupulous characters in Jesus' parables who in some sense are used in exemplary fashion—consider also the unjust steward or the thief in the night.[9] That the man is immune to the normal pressures of honor and shame in a culture so steeped in them proves striking. However, the verb *hypopiazō*, literally "to give a black eye," could also be rendered "slander" or "disgrace," so perhaps some element of potential shame finally does affect the judge.[10]

Before I leave the persistent widow too far behind, and now that I have explained the information about the judge necessary to understand him, I return to the issue David Wells goes on to discuss in his article that began with the poor black woman in Chicago—"Prayer: Rebelling against the Status Quo." One of the dramatic differences I consistently experience as I travel the world and minister in various countries is how much more concerned with praying for social injustice most Christians outside the United States are. They also typically find it incomprehensible why Americans (or at least American Christians) can't see the self-evident benefits of gun control that many of them have experienced. And the notion that Jews today somehow still have a divine right to the land of Israel flies in the face of New Testament theology on almost every page, as again most non-American Christians in the world recognize.[11] Far too many conservative evangelical churches, if they talk about social ethics at all, talk only about a very narrow cross section of the issues that trouble God on the pages of Scripture.

As a bridge to my third point, I need to explain the a fortiori (or "from the lesser to the greater") logic of Jesus' use of an unjust judge as a cipher for God. God is that much more eager to dispense justice even if he, like the judge in the parable, seems at times to delay a long time in granting it.[12] Jesus reassures the disciples that even when it seems like injustice is winning, God's sovereign purposes are being accomplished.

But he doesn't end with this insistence on the trustworthiness of God's promises. He throws back into his followers' laps the question of whether their (or anyone's) faith will endure.

In raising the perennial question of theodicy (the justice of God in the face of the problem of evil), the parable allows me to comment on what I believe is a Christian's most fundamental answer to why God allows suffering in this world—his desire that as many as possible be reconciled to him through Jesus Christ. Hence, the quotation of Psalm 90:4 in 2 Peter 3:8–9. Interestingly, this psalm formed a central text for pre-Christian Judaism to explain the apparent delay over centuries of the coming of the Day of the Lord that so many prophets had foretold. The issue of the perceived delay of the end was not a new theological problem for Christianity.[13]

Jesus can thus end, not by dwelling on God's inscrutable purposes, which we often cannot discern this side of the grave, but by challenging his followers to do that which they *can* do—persevere in faith. This includes prayer but moves on to actual involvement in putting "feet to their prayers," especially in the area of social justice. The conclusion of the sermon reviews the three themes and, because it already is a little longer than most, ends quickly.

13

The Cost of Discipleship

Luke 14:25–35

Large crowds were traveling with Jesus, and turning to them he said: "If anyone comes to me and does not hate father and mother, wife and children, brothers and sisters—yes, even life itself—such a person cannot be my disciple. And those who do not carry their cross and follow me cannot be my disciples.

"Suppose one of you wants to build a tower. Won't you first sit down and estimate the cost to see if you have any enough money to complete it? For if you lay the foundation and are not able to finish it, everyone who sees it will ridicule you, saying, 'This person began to build and wasn't able to finish.'

"Or suppose a king is about to go to war against another king. Won't he first sit down and consider whether he is able with ten thousand men to oppose the one coming against him with twenty thousand? If he is not able, he will send a delegation while the other is still a long way off and will ask for terms of peace. In the same way, those of you who do not give up everything you have cannot be my disciples.

"Salt is good, but if it loses its saltiness, how can it be made salty again? It is fit neither for the soil nor for the manure pile; it is thrown out.

"Whoever has ears to hear, let them hear."

Just this week, a mentally handicapped Christian worker in the Church of the Holy Nativity in Bethlehem unwisely ventured outside by himself and was murdered by Israeli troops. In late March terrorists threw hand grenades into a church in Islamabad, Pakistan, killing a dozen and wounding scores more. A missionary friend of mine would have been in attendance, except that he had to pick up a friend at the train station.

The opening months of 2002 have brought renewed imprisonment of Christians in China, while last year, in 2001, the world witnessed severe persecution and murder of Christians in Ambon, Indonesia. For several years, we've been aware of the tens of thousands of Sudanese Christians sold into slavery by Muslim leaders. In fact, the statisticians tell us that the number of Christian martyrdoms in the twentieth century surpassed the total of all previous centuries of church history put together.

How can we make sense of this biblically or theologically? Is all this persecution due to sin in believers' lives or to their lack of faith, as some in our world would claim? On the contrary, 2 Timothy 3:12 describes it as a normal part of the Christian life. There Paul writes that "everyone who wants to live a godly life in Christ Jesus will be persecuted." The question of the cost of discipleship is one Jesus discusses on several occasions but nowhere more famously than in our passage in Luke 14. In between introductory and concluding statements appear three sections, each reflecting on the topic, each containing a pair of statements or illustrations. Interestingly, as we analyze these closely, we discover that in each pair there is one item whose severity can easily be *overestimated* and one that can easily be *underestimated*. Every verse in the passage forms one of the so-called difficult or hard sayings of Jesus. Each can be readily misunderstood, so it is worth our time to take a careful look at this text, verse by verse or section by section.

Verse 25 forms the introduction to our passage and provides the setting for Jesus' teaching. We are in the middle of Luke's long travel narrative that occupies approximately nine chapters of the central portion of his Gospel. Jesus has been journeying toward Jerusalem since chapter 9, verse 51, and what Luke records of Jesus' itinerant ministry outside of Galilee is primarily teaching material, alternating between blocks of teaching addressed to the disciples in private and messages more directly addressing the crowds in public. In this verse we are explicitly told it is the crowds who are listening. That's a crucial observation, because in the history of the interpretation of this text, because of the demanding instruction that it contains, one dominant approach has been to reserve these principles for a special, elite class of disciples. In medieval Catholicism, these teachings of Jesus were regularly reserved for the clergy or members of monastic orders. Protestants have rightly rejected these distinctions but have often substituted the notion that Jesus' stringent demands here do not necessarily apply to all Christians but to a particularly mature class of believers called "disciples." A word study of the term translated "disciple," however, discloses that it simply means "follower," and Scripture offers no support anywhere for this kind of distinction between ordinary Christians who must obey only easy commands and specially mature believers who must follow everything

Jesus taught. Besides, Luke explicitly points out here in verse 25 that Jesus' words are addressed to everyone who is in any way interested in his movement.

The first pair of specific teachings on the cost of discipleship appears in verses 26–27. Verse 26 speaks of hating family members—a graphic, troubling declaration, especially for first-time readers of Luke's Gospel. Here, if ever, is a classic example of a hard saying of Jesus. Here, too, the danger is clearly one of *over*estimating the cost involved. Unlike our English words for "love" and "hate," Greek, particularly when influenced by Hebrew or Old Testament backgrounds as here, often used these words not to refer to an emotion but to a commitment, to speak of a person to whom one was more or less loyal. In other contexts, "love" and "hate" can mean "choose" and "not choose," as in the famous statement in Malachi 1:2–3 quoted by Paul in Romans that "Jacob I loved, but Esau I hated" (Rom. 9:13).

At any rate, that's how Matthew understands this teaching of Jesus, when in a different context, but making almost the identical declaration, Christ proclaims, "Anyone who loves their father or mother more than me is not worthy of me; anyone who loves a son or daughter more than me is not worthy of me" (Matt. 10:37). We can breathe a sigh of relief that we don't have to literally hate our own family members in the way in which that word is typically understood in English. But our text still poses challenging questions. If our love for God is to be so much greater than our love for our family that the latter seems like hate in comparison, is that how an outside observer of our lives would describe us? For example, are we parents far more concerned about providing generously for the Lord's work than with saving for our children's college education, important as that is? Are our young people more concerned to follow God's call on their lives, even if that might lead to the mission field, even when their parents are not enthusiastic about or even opposed to such a call? A recent study of Christian college graduates in the United States disclosed that the single most important reason young people stated that they did not consider full-time Christian work as a possible career was the objections of their *Christian* parents, who largely felt that their children wouldn't be earning enough money in such a career, including earning enough to pay back large educational debts.[1] Perhaps they should not have gone into so much debt, but the resistance to serving God in ministry is tragic.

Verse 27 offers a further caution against *under*estimating the cost of discipleship, as Jesus introduces his now-famous metaphor of carrying one's own cross. Unfortunately, such crosses are often trivialized, as in our jokes about in-laws who become the crosses we have to bear. We must recall that the cross was an instrument of public shame, torture, and execution for both slaves and criminals. Carrying the horizontal crossbeam was what the condemned person was required to do as he or she struggled to walk to the place of execution. The majority of Christians in any era of church history have not been called to literal martyrdom. But if it ever comes to that, we must be ready to accept it. The book of Hebrews is the one New Testament letter almost entirely about Christians facing growing persecution and possible martyrdom as a key test of the genuineness of their faith. One wonders how many untested, professing American Christians would pass.

Verses 28–32 introduce the second pair of somewhat parallel teachings. This time Jesus narrates two short parables. Verses 28–30 are often called the parable of the tower builder. Christ offers a timeless, commonsense illustration of the need to calculate the cost before embarking on a building program, so as not to leave the construction work unfinished and subject to public ridicule. A classic modern illustration of this greets visitors to Israel's West Bank, where the girders of what was to have been a palace for the now deceased King Hussein of Jordan are left standing, even though the work was incomplete when Jews overran that territory and evicted the Jordanians in 1967. Every Israeli government since has deliberately left that unfinished building stand as a dramatic reminder to other enemies of Israel of what could happen to them.

With this parable, the danger for the modern interpreter is one of *over*estimating the cost. Jesus is not saying that we must know everything God will ever ask of us throughout our entire lives and then agree to it in advance in order to become true believers. If that were his criterion, no one would ever qualify. Jesus is saying, however, that we must realize the amount that commitment could cost. If we are not at least in principle prepared to surrender every area of our lives throughout our entire lives, then we are not making Jesus our "Lord" or master above all human masters, including ourselves. In short, we are not becoming Christians. And surrendering every area means including the touchy areas of our lives that we don't do well talking about in Christian circles, perhaps most notably that famous triad of money, sex, and power.

The second parable in verses 31–32 concerns the king going to war. Again, the point of comparison is to count the cost, though here the stakes are clearly higher. In the parable of the tower builder the worst that could happen was public ridicule. Here bad judgment could lead to massive loss of life among soldiers who are substantially outnumbered by their enemy. The most easily misunderstood point here, however, is the phrase in verse 32 about sending a delegation and asking for terms of peace. To the modern ear, this sounds like negotiation, but in Jesus' world these were expressions for unconditional surrender. The danger in this parable, therefore, is that of *under*estimating Jesus' demands. The first parable asks if we can count the cost of discipleship. The second asks if we can afford to pay the price of refusing Jesus' call. The massive loss of life will include our own lives in hell, in an unending experience of separation from God and all things good. Who is most likely to be the rival master to Christ in your life? Your career or standard of living? Your house? Your car or cars? Sports? Recreation or travel? Perhaps even family? Whatever those things are, you must surrender them to Jesus today.

The third pair of teachings on the cost of discipleship spans verses 33–35a. Verse 33 speaks of giving up everything. Once again, the first danger is one of *over*estimating the harshness of Jesus' words. The straightforward interpretation of the command to "give up everything" sounds as if we must become totally impoverished. It may make us think of Jesus' command to the rich young ruler to sell all his possessions, give to the poor, and then follow Christ (Luke 18:22). But that passage actually gives us a clue to the correct interpretation of verse 33 here, because it's again Luke in his Gospel who juxtaposes to the story of the rich young ruler the conversion of Zacchaeus (19:1–10) and the parable of the pounds (19:11–27), in which very different models of dealing with money are depicted. Zacchaeus isn't commanded to give up anything, though he voluntarily gives up half. And the faithful servants in the parable of the pounds actually make more money, but they recognize that it all belongs to their master. The rich young ruler is in fact the only person in the entirety of the Scriptures who is called to give up everything. But every would-be Christian must give up whatever stands in the way of wholehearted discipleship.

In fact, the Greek verb rendered "give up" in Luke 14:33 is perhaps better translated "renounce," in the sense of "give up claim to." Jesus is telling his followers to recognize that everything belongs to the Lord. Do you have extra space in your home? Are you using it for the Lord's work, perhaps to house someone in need of a place to live at a lower price than he or she would be charged elsewhere? If you have extra money, are you generous in giving to others, including meeting those needs that can't always be met through a charitable gift and a tax write-off? Are you doing everything humanly possible to avoid going into debt, especially credit-card debt, with its outrageous interest charges, since spending what one doesn't have implies making a claim on future possessions rather than sitting lightly to present ones?

For the last time, in verses 34–35a, Jesus balances his previous set of remarks with a second that reminds us not to *under*estimate his claims on our lives. We are to stay "salty," lest we be discarded as worthless. On the one hand, it's probably significant that true salt can't lose its saltiness, and even in the first century people knew that. But what passed for salt was often an impure mixture of elements that could indeed lose its ability to give flavor or arrest corruption. To "lose saltiness" in this context is an expression that translates a Greek term that could also mean "to become corrupted" or "defiled." A true believer is not being threatened with loss of salvation here.

On the other hand, the one who loses his saltiness *is* described as being "thrown out," language that Jesus regularly uses elsewhere to refer to eternal punishment in hell. Here such a person isn't fit even for the manure pile that would be used to fertilize ground—the key indication that this bleak fate is in view here, too. While true Christians cannot lose their saltiness, people can claim to be Christians, can fool others, and perhaps even fool themselves for a time. But if they repudiate their faith, if they abandon their commitment at some point during their lives, they demonstrate they were never true believers in the first place. Little wonder, then, that Jesus rounds out this set of challenging teachings with a favorite call of his that those who have ears to hear should hear (v. 35b). Not all listen to his teaching with the same careful reflection that leads to obedience, but obedience is what is required.

Only God knows if you or I will face literal martyrdom at some point in our lives, as many Christians throughout church history have faced. In the immediate future, most of us, perhaps even all of us, will not. I have already given some examples of how this passage might apply to us in the United States, to us who still enjoy countless freedoms and amenities to make physical and spiritual life easier than it is for many elsewhere. I certainly don't pretend to be a stellar example of counting the cost. I know I have much to learn, but a passage like this certainly has affected my giving. Since early in our marriage, my wife and I have practiced the principle of a graduated tithe, which means that as our annual gross income increases above and beyond any simple cost of living increase, a percentage of our giving to the Lord's work goes up as well. We were challenged early in our marriage by two different pastors' models of giving 25 percent of their income back to their churches and to other Christian organizations they supported. In recent years our family has topped 40 percent in our level of giving, all without any huge sacrifices, though with a smaller house and car and entertainment center than most of our peers own and probably through eating out considerably less.

Because of a passage like this one, I have pursued a career teaching in a theological seminary rather than looking for one of many possible better-paying jobs that an undergraduate math major like myself might have been expected to seek. I realize that my choice has a huge financial impact on the amount of money I will be able to make in one lifetime. But early in my adult life, I became powerfully aware of God's call that I needed to be doing something full time that would affect people's lives for eternity. For me, a career in mathematics wouldn't have accomplished that.

Because of a passage like this one, I approach each new day with a certain sense of urgency. I don't presume to know how many years or months of life, or even of good health, remain. Unless it's part of a family activity, I watch very little television and then usually just a ballgame on the weekends while doing schoolwork or light reading on the side. Evenings, weekends, and summer vacation are crucial times for my research and writing, for ministry in places outside Denver and outside the United States. I don't look at those times as time off. Please don't mishear me. I'm not promoting workaholism. My family is a very good barometer, and I try to ask them regularly if I'm spending enough time with them. I just don't see any purpose in wasting time on activities that count for nothing in the long run.

Because of a passage like this one, I try to find ways to share my faith as tactfully as possible but recognize even then that rejection and ridicule will come. I've had people I've tried to talk to about the Lord swear at me, mock me, tell me flat out that I'm wrong. Because I teach in an overtly evangelical school, opportunities in the larger academy for writing, speaking, and influencing people pass me by, though they come to more liberal or unbelieving counterparts of mine at other colleges, seminaries, or universities. When people, even in the United States, say they experience no persecution whatever for being a Christian, I wonder how boldly and how frequently they tell others of their beliefs and principles. Sooner or later there will be some pretty harsh reactions. But there will also be some fantastically encouraging ones.

Counting the cost of discipleship may look very different for you from any of these examples I've given. I don't presume to know in detail your personal circumstances. But I do hope that you're at least asking the question, "What does it mean for me to count the cost, to put it all on the line for Jesus?" True disciples will ask that question. True disciples will then obey and ask for help in what seems to be too hard for them to do. True disciples will also fail, but they will then repent and return with renewed commitment as God forgives them. Are you willing to be a disciple? The alternative makes it far too scary to refuse. The ultimate, glorious reward makes it the most logical and compelling response to make.

Commentary on "The Cost of Discipleship"

Previous parables preached in this book have illustrated possible models for dealing with every category of three- and two-point parables that Jesus employed. Our sermons have also treated one-point parables as parts of a series of parables all dealt with in a single message. We have not yet illustrated, however, how one might deal with a text that contains *only* one-point parables. Interestingly, the six one-point parables of Jesus that are long enough to form actual narratives, however concise, and thus merit the label of "parable" in almost all works that study that literary form, all appear in pairs. The mustard seed and the leaven are paired in two of the three Gospels in which they appear (Matthew 13 and Luke 13; Mark 4 includes only the mustard seed); the hidden treasure and the pearl of great price appear together in Matthew 13. The tower builder and the king going to war are matched in this short segment of Luke 14. Thus while it would be possible to preach on just one of the members of each pair, it is natural to take them together. And because these two occupy only five verses, it is equally natural to link them together with surrounding verses that are usually understood to form a rhetorical and literary unit.[2]

A second unique feature of this sermon is that it is the first one in this volume so far in which I read the scriptural text at the very beginning of the message. In churches where the reading of Scripture is delegated to someone other than the preacher, I have to request for most of my messages that the text not be read in advance of the sermon. Or, if I sense that will be tampering with something perceived to be inviolable, then I simply read the text again at whatever junctures the sermon calls for it, though often something of the surprise value of my introduction is sacrificed in the process. For this message, I can happily let someone else read the text in advance if that is the church's custom.

This sermon was last revised and preached in April 2002 in a church that assigned me the theme of discipleship but left me free to select the text I wanted to expound. Because of my love of parables, this was the first one that came to mind. Because of recent internationally publicized events, it was easy for me to update my introduction, supplying fresh examples of the persecution and martyrdom Christians in our world have had to face. I worked backwards from the most recent illustrations to those a few years old and then generalized via a statistic I have used and documented earlier in this volume (see chap. 7). Given that most American Christians don't face overt persecution for their faith and very few ever face possible martyrdom, I wanted to remind people of contemporary realities elsewhere in the world that must be kept in mind to put Jesus' theme of "the cost of discipleship" in perspective.

The second paragraph after the reading of the Scripture adds a generalization from the New Testament that makes the experiences cited in the first paragraph seem the norm rather than the exception. It also raises pointedly the question that will dominate the rest of the message: Just how much hardship is a person signing up for when submitting to Christ as Lord? The observation that emerged inductively as I was studying this passage was that there were as many statements whose seriousness has been underestimated as there were statements whose severity has been overestimated. Because pairs of sayings seemed to alternate back and forth between these two ends of a spectrum, though not always in the same order, I utilized PowerPoint slides to present each pair, along with identifying the overemphases and understatements that often afflict them. These visual aids enabled people to follow readily (or so they told me!) what could otherwise have been an overly complex and/or confusing presentation.

Verse 25 does not fall into the paired-sayings format, which doesn't begin until verses 26–27. As I point out, it does form a crucial part of the passage—the introduction that indicates Jesus' audience—which is important to note to avoid the most common misinterpretation of this verse. Just as misinterpretations of parts of the Sermon on the Mount result when interpreters fail to observe that it was addressed to those who had already committed themselves to Jesus as followers (see chap. 10), so here failure to observe that these commandments are addressed to all would-be followers of Jesus leads to inappropriate attempts to narrow the audience to existing disciples or even certain elite categories of disciples.[3] The definition of "disciple" as any true follower of Christ is also important to note in this endeavor.[4]

My comments on verses 26–27 begin a pattern that will carry me all the way through the passage. With each pair of sayings, I identify which one is usually misinterpreted via underestimation and which one via overestimation of the cost Jesus calls us to count. In so doing, I explain what that misinterpretation usually involves, what the correct interpretation should be, and how I arrive at my conclusions in each instance.

In the case of verse 26, my explanation includes a combination of the background of the Greek terms used in Scripture for "love" and "hate," coupled with comparing Luke with a parallel saying of Jesus in a different context in Matthew.[5] For verse 27, it involves remembering how strong and powerful a metaphor, and often a literal reality, references to crosses and crucifixion were in Jesus' world.[6] Outside of the Gospel narratives, the book of Hebrews provides perhaps the most powerful and sustained cross reference.[7]

Verses 28–32 bring us to the pair of parables themselves. For the tower builder, my experience in Israel affords me a powerful modern visual parallel in the very land that Jesus was traveling when he spoke the parable. The misreading that overestimates Jesus' call here ties in directly with the notion that some people may accept Jesus as Savior before they are ready to acknowledge him as Lord. If I am going to challenge this notion, as I believe I must, based on other biblical grounds,[8] then I have to deal with the issue at this point.[9] Precisely because the two little parables are parallel in several respects, if I understand the first one correctly, the temptation is to assume that the second one is not saying anything stronger. Hence, here I need to point out the ways in which the parables are *not* entirely parallel and, indeed, are building to a climax that comes in verse 33 after the second parable is complete.[10]

At the same time, when verses 33–35a are taken together, the danger in reading about "giving up everything" is to assume that this is a literal call parallel to Jesus' command to the rich young ruler, even though Luke elsewhere provides the very different models needed to recognize that in the pages of the Gospels Jesus does not call anyone else to similar total material sacrifice.[11] One needs, therefore, to do a more careful study of the Greek word often translated "renounce."[12] On the other hand, the sting in Jesus' metaphor about saltiness (vv. 34–35a) is too easily assuaged by taking this verse and a half as referring merely to a believer's loss of reward. Ironically, the very doctrine that I want to affirm here—the perseverance of the saints—is often misused so that the real threat of someone masquerading as an entire unbeliever is not adequately felt. Pure salt cannot lose its saltiness, but much in Jesus' world that passed for salt was an impure mixture. And "being thrown out" (from the Greek *hexō ballō*) is never used elsewhere in the Bible for mere loss of reward.[13]

After a brief remark on Jesus' characteristic closing call to carefully heed his words,[14] I return to contemporary application. My introduction provided dramatic, current examples of Christians who have had to give up even their very lives for their faith. But what about the vast majority of Americans who may not be so called? As is frequently the case in these sermons, I could refer to more dramatic examples even closer to home, but I want my audiences to know that I have wrestled with every message I preach before ever "inflicting" it on them! Thus I have to be honest with how I have (or haven't) "counted the cost" myself. The examples of stewardship, career choice, time management, and evangelism are not the most radical illustrations even within American culture, but they are the ones I have most thought about and wrestled with. And virtually everyone in the kinds of congregations I normally address can wrestle with them, too, and can improve in some respect.

I deliberately repeat the introductory phrase "Because of a passage like this one" three times for rhetorical effect. I have discussed the concept of the graduated tithe previously (see chaps. 2, 5, and 9). Readers who wonder if I haven't committed "overkill" in returning to the theme of stewardship again and again must remember that these messages were not all preached in the same church in consecutive weeks as full-time senior pastors regularly do; they were addressed to different audiences in many different churches in Western (and non-Western) cultures where money still gets talked about far too little, at least in biblical ways, from the pulpit. But the other three arenas of application I address, for the most part, have not appeared in previous messages in this book.

Even after giving my listeners several examples that I hope many will be able to relate to, I need to acknowledge that I may not have "scratched" where everyone "itches." I also want to let them know I am aware that not all may equally apply to each person, given individual circumstances. I conclude by returning to the big idea of counting the cost, present already in my otherwise uncreative sermon title, to generalize and ask a question that every listener can raise for himself or herself. Like the parable of the prodigal son, I leave the message open-ended. It is up to each listener to decide what, if anything, to do. But my final comment reminds them that the stakes are infinitely high if they make the wrong choices![15]

14

How to Prepare for Christ's Return
Matthew 24:43–25:30

The story is told of Martin Luther that one day, while he was hoeing his garden, a friend came to visit and asked what he would do if he knew Christ was returning that very day. Luther is supposed to have answered, "I'd just keep on hoeing my garden." I've heard this story told by preachers several times to illustrate the point that, if we are constantly in the center of God's will, whatever we are doing is exactly appropriate for us to keep on doing, even if we knew the timing of the end of the world. I have to admit I'm not entirely convinced. I currently believe that study, writing, teaching, and occasionally preaching form a crucial portion of God's call on my life. But if I were diagnosed with a terminal illness and given only a few months to live, I'd certainly spend a whole lot more time putting in order personal relationships, including my relationship with God, as, in fact, I have watched dying Christians do from time to time. None of this would be because I think I'm deliberately avoiding problems now or postponing commitments that should be more urgent, but simply because one's priorities do change, depending on whether one is doing short- or long-range planning.

Still, I understand the point of the illustration about Luther, especially when it's used to play down apocalyptic enthusiasm. There isn't any aspect of our lives that we should be embarrassed about, or that we should be deliberately not confronting, because we presume to know that we have many years left in which to set our house in order. Ours is an age of great millennial interest, replete with those who set dates for the end of the world, those who write novels about imminent catastrophic events that will change the face of our planet, or even just those well-meaning Christian speakers who state solemnly that they are quite confident we're living in the last generation.

Jesus once gave a sermon to his disciples precisely to try to temper such confidence. We sometimes call it his Olivet Discourse, and it appears in its fullest form in Matthew 24–25. Its first main section comprises most of chapter 24 and concludes with a very unambiguous declaration: "But about that day or hour no one knows, not even the angels in heaven, nor the Son, but only the Father" (Matt. 24:36). Because we cannot know the timing of the end, we shouldn't spend our time trying to predict it. But Jesus goes on to stress in verse 42 that we are to keep watch precisely because we don't know when the end will come. Keeping watch, however, does not mean trying to correlate the daily newspaper with passages of Scripture; it *does* mean always being alert, always being prepared regardless of how soon or how distant the end turns out to be. The rest of Christ's sermon, which occupies the closing verses of chapter 24 and all of chapter 25, fleshes out this point. The part we want to look at today involves four in a series of five parables.

The first parable is the shortest. It occupies verses 43–44. "But understand this," Jesus says.

> If the owner of the house had known at what time of night the thief was coming, he would have kept watch and would not have let his house be broken into. So you also must be ready, because the Son of Man will come at an hour when you do not expect him.

This first and shortest parable in Jesus' series of five makes a simple point. It stresses the total unexpectedness of the timing of the end—of Christ's return. He will come just like a thief, like a burglar who breaks into someone's home, hoping to catch the residents entirely by surprise. And that, by the way, is the only point of the analogy. Don't worry about trying to figure out what Jesus, the thief, is coming to steal from us! The comparison is simply the unexpectedness of the timing: like that of a burglar, like the end of the world.

The second parable is a bit longer. Jesus continues, in verses 45–51:

> Who then is the faithful and wise servant, whom the master has put in charge of the servants in his household to give them their food at the proper time? It will be good for that servant whose master finds him doing so when he returns. Truly I tell you, he will put him in charge of all his possessions. But suppose that servant is wicked and says to himself, "My master is staying away a long time," and he then begins to beat his fellow servants and to eat and drink with drunkards. The master of that servant will come on a day when he does not expect him and at an hour he is not

aware of. He will cut him to pieces and assign him a place with the hypocrites, where there will be weeping and gnashing of teeth.

This second parable envisions two possible scenarios involving the
chief servant of an absentee master. The steward discovers his master
returning home sooner than he had expected him to. What will the
master find that servant doing—being a good steward or abusing his
freedom and shirking his responsibilities?

Many people, including Christians, postpone coming to grips with
God's call on their lives, assuming there's always a little more time. But
we never really know that. If Christ's return seems too unreal to consider,
surely the news of daily accidents, injuries, illness, natural disasters, and
even untimely deaths should keep us from presuming we will necessarily be alive tomorrow. Our situation is very much like the one described
by the ancient rabbi, Eliezer, who taught his disciples, "Repent one day
before your death." When asked how they were to know what day that
could be, he replied, "all the more reason" to "repent today, lest you die
tomorrow."

If you have never trusted in Jesus as your Lord, your sovereign master,
and accepted the free gift of salvation that comes with that faith, today
is the day for you to make that commitment. If you have unfinished
business with God, in terms of responding to his call on your life, even if
that might mean a change of vocation or standard of living, or if you're
in the right job from God's perspective but simply too preoccupied with
material things, or if there are relationships with someone, especially
family members, that aren't what they could be and you're refusing to
deal with your response to God's call or commands, then today is the
day for you to take steps to begin to obey.

I recently received a letter from a woman I'll call Alice, who, with her
husband and four children, had been good friends of our family more
than fifteen years ago. We had lost touch with them in recent years.
Alice wrote us and explained that her husband had left her for another
woman, that in fact he had illegally married the other woman before
the divorce proceedings were complete, and that he had said all kinds
of untrue things about his ex-wife in order to convince the Christian
ministry for which he worked to keep him in their good graces. Many
of you know of only slightly less bizarre tragedies. Alice's experience
hardly represented the first time something this sad has happened to
one of my friends. But I think it hit me harder than most other broken
homes I've known about, because there was a time when I told people
publicly that if they wanted to see the best living example I knew of a
godly, loving family with parents utterly committed to each other and
to their children, growing in the Lord and serving God, this would have

been the family to whom I would have pointed them. If Alice's family could unravel, anyone's can. I don't assume anyone here today is exempt from similar temptations. We have the enormous capacity to put on a good face in Christian circles and entirely mask deeply seated and unresolved problems.

As long as we remain alive, the possibilities exist for repentance, for restoration, for rehabilitation. But one day it will be too late, and that day could come sooner rather than later. And if reconciliation with God is the key issue we've been avoiding, then only the frightful prospect of eternal punishment awaits us. This little parable concludes with what is undoubtedly a metaphor, but the reality depicted there is frightening enough. "He will cut him to pieces and assign him a place with the hypocrites, where there will be weeping and gnashing of teeth" (v. 51).

The third parable about the ten bridesmaids in Matthew 25:1–13 reverses the scenario. This time the master figure, a bridegroom, stays away longer than was expected. Jesus continues his sermon in Matthew 25:1:

> At that time the kingdom of heaven will be like ten virgins who took their lamps and went out to meet the bridegroom. Five of them were foolish and five were wise. The foolish ones took their lamps but did not take any oil with them. The wise, however, took oil in jars along with their lamps. The bridegroom was a long time in coming, and they all became drowsy and fell asleep.
>
> At midnight the cry rang out: "Here is the bridegroom! Come out to meet him!"
>
> Then all the virgins woke up and trimmed their lamps. The foolish ones said to the wise, "Give us some of your oil; our lamps are going out."
>
> "No," they replied, "there may not be enough for both us and you. Instead, go to those who sell oil and buy some for yourselves."
>
> But while they were on their way to buy the oil, the bridegroom arrived. The virgins who were ready went in with him to the wedding banquet. And the door was shut.
>
> Later the others also came. "Sir! Sir!" they said. "Open the door for us!"
>
> But he replied, "Truly I tell you, I don't know you."
>
> Therefore keep watch, because you do not know the day or the hour.

This time the problem is not the surprisingly quick return of the master figure, but his surprising delay. Five of the ten bridesmaids in this parable are unprepared for the length of time they will have to wait for the bridegroom to emerge with his bride from the place of the wedding festivities and be escorted to the man's home, where the honeymoon night will be spent.

There are several points we could focus on if we were considering just this one parable alone. But the central point that emerges when considering the series of five parables stems from the shock when the five foolish bridesmaids finally do arrive and discover that they are forever excluded from the celebration. Even though life and the world may seem to go on forever, a day is coming when there will be no more second chances to get our lives right spiritually. Thus the last verse of this parable, Matthew 25:13, repeats the thoughts of 24:42, where we began: "Keep watch, because you do not know the day or the hour." There are those who are unprepared for lives prematurely cut short; there are others who are unprepared for the long haul. Perhaps they've received too glib or rosy a picture of the Christian life and can't cope with the crises and the suffering that often characterize life, even for believers, in this fallen world. Perhaps they're like the sprinter who tries to run a marathon—great initial enthusiasm, quickly leading to burnout and quitting the race. Perhaps there are folks who have been profoundly hurt by fellow Christians, and because their trust is in people more than in Christ, they can't separate the sinless, loving Lord from his often very sinful followers. Whatever the factors, Jesus' point remains that we must be prepared for the possibility of the prolonged delay of the end of this world as we know it or for this life to be harder than we had expected. This point again tempers any claims of knowing even in general the timetable of the end or that there are certain kinds of suffering or tribulation that God simply couldn't allow his people to endure.

If we review in reverse order the three parables we've thus far examined, I trust you'll agree that what we've seen are examples of Christ's return later than expected, Christ's return sooner than expected, and Christ's return coming simply at an unexpected time. I think that covers all logical possibilities and ought to put a stop to Christian guesswork about the timing of the end once and for all.

It's worth noting, too, that the man in the parable of the faithful and unfaithful servant in Matthew 24:45–51 is described as a servant both when he is doing bad as well as when he's doing good. In the first part of chapter 25, the wise and the foolish women are alike called bridesmaids, and in the next passage that we will come to—in the parable of the talents—we will see that all three individual men with whom the master has conversation are called servants. All of the subordinate characters in these parables are portrayed as if they were God's people. How can this be? The problem is that we too quickly Christianize Jesus' words and assume that in each case he is referring to true believers. But in Jesus' original context, as a Jewish teacher talking to Jewish disciples—often to large crowds, including his opponents as well as the uncommitted—we have to recognize that he uses the language of servants to refer to anyone who might consider themselves in some sense a child of God. In the Olivet Discourse, Jesus' audience is restricted to the Twelve, but that still includes Judas, who will shortly prove never to have been a true disciple in the first place. In other words, Jesus never takes for granted that everyone he is addressing, whether in a small gathering or in a large crowd, is truly his follower. But he uses imagery that suggests that outside observers of these people, and maybe even these people themselves, might *think* they are in a right relationship with God.

In a poll a few years ago, George Barna suggested that one in three contemporary churchgoers will one day give up church attendance for good.[1] At least some of these will be people in evangelical churches who have made explicit professions of faith in Christ. Of course some of these will be true Christians who have simply abandoned Christian fellowship in disobedience to Scripture (Heb. 10:25). But I doubt we can account for all of them that way. We can also debate the thorny question of eternal security or "once saved, always saved." I personally believe in that doctrine, and I find it interesting to compare Matthew 25:12, in which the bridegroom says, "Truly I tell you, I don't know you," with similar words of Jesus in the Sermon on the Mount in Matthew 7:21–23. There Jesus stresses that even people who have called him Lord, prophesied or exorcised or performed other miracles in his name, will not necessarily prove to be his true followers. Matthew 7:23 concludes his comments with the prediction, "Then I will tell them plainly, 'I never knew you. Away from me, you evildoers!'" In the parable of the ten bridesmaids, the wording is simply, "I don't know you." But I can't help wondering if Jesus' disciples weren't meant to recall his earlier words and interpret his comments here just the same as if he had said, "I never really knew you earlier."

Yet even as we raise the very important question of the security of the believer, let's not lose sight of what those who have believed in eternal security and those who have not still have in common. Both sides in the so-called Calvinist-Arminian debate agree that there are people who profess to be Christians, who decisively renounce their profession, never change their mind in this life, and are eternally lost. What the two sides disagree on is the theological interpretation of that behavior, with the Arminians arguing that it is possible to be a true Christian and renounce one's faith and the Calvinists arguing that such behavior demonstrates there was no true belief in the first place. That's an important debate, but not as important as the agreement in both camps that people who commit such apostasy face an eternity of only suffering and punishment; hence, the repeated strong warnings throughout Scripture against abandoning one's faith.

So how should we then live? If the end could come at any time, and we're not to try to predict it, what *are* we called to do? That question brings us to the familiar parable of the talents in Matthew 25:14–30, which reads,

> Again, it will be like a man going on a journey, who called his servants and entrusted his wealth to them. To one he gave five bags of gold, to another two bags, and to another one bag, each according to his ability. Then he went on his journey. The man who had received five bags of gold went at once and put his money to work and gained five bags more. So also, the one with two bags of gold gained two more. But the man who had received one bag went off, dug a hole in the ground and hid his master's money.
>
> After a long time the master of those servants returned and settled accounts with them. The man who had received five bags of gold brought the other five. "Master," he said, "you entrusted me with five bags of gold. See, I have gained five more."
>
> His master replied, "Well done, good and faithful servant! You have been faithful with a few things; I will put you in charge of many things. Come and share your master's happiness!"
>
> The man with two bags of gold also came. "Master," he said, "you entrusted me with two bags of gold; see, I have gained two more."
>
> His master replied, "Well done, good and faithful servant! You have been faithful with a few things; I will put you in charge of many things. Come and share your master's happiness!"
>
> Then the man who had received one bag of gold came. "Master," he said, "I knew that you are a hard man, harvesting where you have not sown and gathering where you have not scattered seed. So I was afraid and went out and hid your gold in the ground. See, here is what belongs to you."
>
> His master replied, "You wicked, lazy servant! So you knew that I harvest where I have not sown and gather where I have not scattered seed? Well then, you should have put my money on deposit with the bankers, so that when I returned I would have received it back with interest.
>
> "Take the bag of gold from him and give it to the one who has ten bags. For those who have will be given more, and they will have an abundance. As for those who do not have, even what they have will be taken from them. And throw that worthless servant outside, into the darkness, where there will be weeping and gnashing of teeth."

Again we have a parable with an absentee master. But in this case the timing of his return is not the issue. Rather it is the faithful stewardship of his servants. Different servants are given different numbers of talents, "each according to his ability" (v. 15). The first two go out and make different amounts of money in light of their differing abilities and the different quantities with which they have to work (vv. 16–17). Yet both are praised with identical language when the master returns to settle accounts (compare vv. 19–21 with 22–23). One servant, on the other hand, does nothing with his talent except bury it in the ground, which interestingly was one ancient form of safeguarding prize property. But he is eternally condemned with very harsh language when the master confronts him (compare v. 18 with 24–30).

Our English word "talent" actually comes from the use of the Greek term *talanton* in this passage. In the first-century Roman world a talent was the largest unit of currency, equivalent to twenty years of income at minimum wage. But Jesus is not teaching economic theory here, however much we might warm up to this model of apparent capitalist investment! Rather, as in all his parables, Jesus is using familiar imagery to symbolize spiritual truth. Everything God grants us—our possessions, abilities, opportunities, time, circumstances—he commands us to steward well. If it were Paul speaking, he would probably talk about our various spiritual gifts. Whether talents or gifts, the principle remains the same. What may not always be true in the economic realm is clearly true in the spiritual realm: "Use it or lose it!"

If we are good stewards of all God has granted us, then we will be prepared for Christ's return and the final judgment that it brings. And that's the topic of the fifth and final parable in this series, the so-called parable of the sheep and the goats (Matt. 25:31–46). This takes us beyond the portion of text that we're looking at today. It is already clear enough what our response should be to all the date-setters and to all the enormously popular but fantastic novels about what the end times might look like. Jesus' instruction is not to worry about the end, to stop guessing, stop being caught up in all the curiosity-seeking. Instead, we must simply get on with the business of being good stewards of all that he has given us, doing his work according to his unique call on our lives, to further his kingdom and the ministry of his church.

I don't know about you, but I actually have very mixed feelings about the prospect that the end could come soon. On the one hand, it's the most natural thing in the world to want suffering for ourselves and others to end, which it will when Christ returns. On the other hand, we also know that the second coming will put an end to the chance to repent for anyone who hasn't already done so. How wonderful that God in his sovereignty knows the perfect time for the end, and how wonderful that he hasn't left it up to us to figure it out!

So perhaps Luther was right after all. Hoeing my garden is one of many appropriate responses of the stewardship of God's creation to which he has called me, and if I knew Christ was returning the very day I was gardening, I should continue with my hoe. But we can't know that information and, after almost two thousand years and literally hundreds of attempts to predict the end throughout every era of Christian history, the one statement that we can accurately make is that to date 100 percent of those prophecies have proved false. When Christians make such predictions and they fail, all Christianity looks silly in the eyes of the world. We can't avoid all charges of silliness, but we can do our best to distance ourselves from those who would turn our faith into a pattern of contemporary trend watching in the belief that one can correlate current events with biblical prophecies. When other people are open to our perspectives, we can do our best to help them kick the habit as well. If we had perfectly executed all the far more ordinary responsibilities Christ has given us, maybe we might allow ourselves the luxury of just a little end-times speculation. Since we haven't come close to fulfilling all those responsibilities, let's take our cue from the faithful servants in these various parables and get busy doing the work we know he has commanded us to do. Then we can trust that, when the end does come, God will say to us as well, "Well done, good and faithful servant." That should be our prayer.

Commentary on "How to Prepare for Christ's Return"

We have now illustrated and commented on sermons based on every structure found among Christ's parables, with most of our examples presenting stand-alone stories but with a few treating two or more short parables in larger contexts. This next-to-the-last sermon illustrates how one may survey a comparatively long passage in a message of ordinary length. I was invited in late 1999 to address the topic of the end times in a series of three messages on consecutive Sundays. These were, of course, the months of intense speculation about Y2K—about what would happen to computers worldwide as the millennium changed on January 1, 2000. Many books, including Christian bestsellers, were trumpeting this moment as tying directly in with the events that would usher in the end of the age and Christ's return.[2] I chose as my texts Matthew 24–25 and treated them in three quite different-size chunks: Matthew 24:1–42, the heart of Jesus' eschatological discourse, which I titled "How Not to Prepare for Christ's Return"; Matthew 24:43–25:30, which is made up just of parables and includes all four true parables in this discourse; and Matthew 25:31–46, which comprises a "quasi-parable" and which is expounded in the last message in this volume.

Matthew 24:43–25:46 can be viewed as containing two overlapping sequences of passages. Chapter 24:43–25:13 presents a triad of parables that address the timing of Christ's return—Jesus comes unexpectedly (24:43–44), returns surprisingly early (24:45–51), or is unusually delayed

(25:1–13).[3] Chapter 25:1–46 reflects the chronological sequence in the life of a follower of Jesus, by enjoining proper preparation (vv. 1–13) and faithful service (vv. 14–30), in view of final judgment (vv. 31–46). By saving this final passage for a separate message, the structure of the current sermon winds up focusing on the three options for the timing of Christ's return, followed by the necessary stewardship all Jesus' disciples should practice, irrespective of that timing.

Structurally, the parable of the thief and the householder (Matt. 24:43–44), short though it is, has two characters and seems to make two points about (1) the necessary vigilance of believers, in light of (2) the possible coming of the end at any time.[4] The parable of the faithful and the unfaithful servant is a variant on the form of the monarchic or triangular model. Instead of a master with contrasting subordinates, we find a master with one subordinate considered in two diametrically opposite lights. But the upshot is the same as if we had read of separate servants, one good and one wicked. The three lessons here concern the possibility of the end coming sooner than expected, the reward for faithful service, and the judgment on the wicked.[5] The parable of wise and foolish bridesmaids adopts the classic triangular model, with five good and five wicked subordinates at each vertex at the base of the triangle. From the three main characters (or groups) we learn about the possible delay of the end; the need to be prepared for the end; and the time after which it will be too late to repent.[6] Finally, the parable of the talents reflects a complex monarchical model in which the two good subordinates are partly parallel and partly different. But there remains a foil, namely, the wicked servant, as well as an obvious master figure. Again we may identify three themes surrounding the master's call to stewardship and the good and bad examples of obedience to that call.[7]

A sermon covering all four of these passages, however, does not have time to develop all these points. So I largely restrict my focus to the points that surround the master in each case, the person who is the unifying figure in all but the first and shortest of these parables. And because of the juxtaposition of a surprisingly early with a surprisingly delayed arrival of that master in the second and third parables, I choose to focus only on the totally unexpected arrival of the corresponding figure, the thief, in the parable of the thief and the householder. At the end, I turn to the model of the servants in the parable of the talents as the proper response to this uncertainty of timing.

Because I haven't tried to track down the story attributed to Luther, I describe it in exactly those terms—as a common attribution. If he didn't say it, countless preachers have claimed it as his, and it is the story, not the attribution, that matters to me in this context. For those hearing the story for the first time, it can send powerful signals about how one should be living within God's will at all times. But as often as I've heard it, I imagine that many in my audiences will have heard it as well, so that my surprise will come in challenging its conventional wisdom. Since I will wind up directly opposing the view that one can know when the end is near, I want to empathize with one outgrowth of that perspective with which I agree—the greater urgency to be about Christ's work if the end is in fact at hand. I have used this message again after the millennium changed and no tragedy struck on New Year's Day 2000, so I have toned down some of the initial rhetoric about the ridiculous Y2K hype that afflicted us in 1999!

To review where the previous week's message ended and to reinforce the main theme that will emerge out of the first three parables in this week's passage, I cite the "unambiguous declaration" of Matthew 24:36. Verse 42 sets the stage for the fourth parable for today. As frequently in these sermons, I read each portion of the text as the message unfolds, in this case, taking one parable at a time and then commenting on it. As it turns out, each successive parable is longer than the previous one, and the extent of my commentary increases correspondingly, at least for the first three parables. The fourth parable is more straightforward and therefore doesn't require detailed exegesis, which helps prevent the message from becoming overly long.

The only clarification surrounding the parable of the thief and the householder that seems necessary is to limit the sense in which Jesus is likening himself to a burglar. We have another example of the picaresque and the logic of "from the lesser to the greater." Recall our comments about the parables of the unjust steward (Luke 16:1–13; see chap. 5) and the unjust judge (Luke 18:1–8; see chap. 12).

The parable of the faithful and the unfaithful servant doesn't require much additional explanation but demands considerably additional application. More so than with many of the parables, there is opportunity here for a direct, evangelistic appeal to listeners who may be postponing truly coming to grips with Christ's offer and demand on their lives. The rabbinic story that memorably illustrates this comes from the Babylonian Talmud (*Shabbat* 153a). But I want to make sure I address the needs of a predominantly Christian congregation. Thus I include the story about "Alice," which was fresh in my mind at the time I last revised this message.

The parable of the ten bridesmaids is the longest and most detailed thus far in this context, so I acknowledge that I am not focusing on everything that I might in this text, merely the most central lesson—that of the potentially prolonged (and seemingly arduous) nature of the Christian life. Here my applications take more the form of generalizations. I must be succinct if I am going to have time for everything I want to discuss.

A transitional paragraph reviews the three models with respect to the timing of the end. With proper, deliberate enunciation, I can usually draw a laugh when I say, "I think that covers all logical possibilities." Sometimes I add, "Let me know if you can think of one I've missed!" Before turning to the parable of the talents, however, I must take an important theological detour. I could have addressed it with the parable of the faithful and the unfaithful servant, but I wanted to make the point about the three possible timings of the end without distracting too much from that issue. Although I know of no bona fide biblical scholar who assumes the servants in Jesus' parables must all stand for his (true) followers, this is one of the simplest and most common conclusions lay Christians jump to.[8] Centuries of Christianization of the parables prevent us from hearing them as the stories of a Jewish teacher speaking to Jewish followers and not assuming all (or even many) in his audiences were necessarily right with God.[9] Once this is clarified, we can return to the twenty-first century with powerful applications for professing Christians in light of the distressing statistics about contemporary "fallout" from the Christian faith. But it will not be to threaten true Christians with loss of salvation. Rather, as elsewhere in these messages, texts that in fact promote the perseverance of the saints prove all the more threatening for those who may be masquerading as saints. I have heard preachers and lay teachers alike suggest that the place of weeping and gnashing of teeth in Matthew 24:51 is a compartment of heaven for believers who will be least rewarded! Talk about misunderstanding both the imagery of the parable and the kind of hope that the doctrine of the perseverance of the saints offers! True believers can look forward to nothing but bliss in the life to come; anyone experiencing weeping and gnashing of teeth is in hell, irrespective of what outward professions of faith he or she may have made in this life.[10]

The upshot of all this lofty theology is nevertheless eminently practical. Thus we come to the final parable in our four-part series, the parable of the talents. Again, a message focusing just on this parable would have to go into a lot more detail, but I give just enough of the structure and explanation to be able to turn to the big idea—the need for faithful stewardship. (On the monetary value of a talent, see chap. 4.) But just as the word "talent" has taken on more generalized meaning in English, so also must our application. This is, after all, still a metaphorical narrative, not (merely) a lesson in economics.[11] The only remaining tasks in the message are to retrace the fairly large area we have traversed, to bridge to the conclusion by reflecting one final time on those confident they can predict the nearness of the end,[12] and to return to the opening introduction. Despite my initial hesitation, Luther's illustration can prove useful. The most persuasive reason for not indulging in guessing about the timing of the end but in being ready for it to come at any time is the 100 percent failure rate of previous attempts.[13] A close second is the damage to our witness to a lost and skeptical world such predictions create when they fail. Of course, the primary reason believers should reject such an approach is because it is unbiblical, but, sadly, even in so-called Bible-believing circles, pure exegesis rarely generates the most persuasive reasons for *any* belief or behavior. So I have withheld these comments for the end. My final remarks leave my listeners with their biblically mandated task, however, and I enlist their allegiance by encouraging them to help others move in Bible-based directions as well.

15

Who Really Are the Sheep and the Goats?

Matthew 25:31–46

I don't know how well you can see the little baggie that I'm holding up in front of you, but I suspect many of you, if you could see it, would be surprised, because it is a Coca Cola bag. We're used to buying Coke in cans, and some of us can remember the days when it was typically sold in bottles, but this is Coke in a bag that one drinks through a small straw. I purchased this bag of Coke during a recent trip to Guatemala. In many parts of the Third World soft drinks are manufactured and sold in bags like this because they are cheaper than other containers, and the poor in those countries can thus afford to buy the drinks.

In fact, while I was in Guatemala, I taught at the evangelical seminary there, just blocks from a square-mile-large garbage dump where more than one thousand people live, combing through the daily additions to the dump to try to find small items that can be resold, the proceeds from which enable them to eke out a marginal existence. This was not my first such exposure to desperate poverty of this kind, but it remains no less touching and troubling. What should a Christian response be to such conditions? It's hard not to want to jump in and involve oneself in radical social action of some kind. One thinks of the often recurring debate about the nature of evangelism. Do believers simply preach an offer of spiritual salvation, or do we also render physical and material assistance to the needy? Or, if we're committed to both, what should be the balance between the two?

The text that enters into these conversations perhaps more than any other is today's parable. In Matthew 25:31–46, Jesus spoke the following words to his disciples, at the climax of his message to them on the Mount of Olives during the last week of his life:

> When the Son of Man comes in his glory, and all the angels with him, he will sit on his glorious throne. All the nations will be gathered before him, and he will separate the people one from another as a shepherd separates the sheep from the goats. He will put the sheep on his right and the goats on his left.
>
> Then the King will say to those on his right, "Come, you who are blessed by my Father; take your inheritance, the kingdom prepared for you since the creation of the world. For I was hungry and you gave me something to eat, I was thirsty and you gave me something to drink, I was a stranger and you invited me in, I needed clothes and you clothed me, I was sick and you looked after me, I was in prison and you came to visit me."
>
> Then the righteous will answer him, "Lord, when did we see you hungry and feed you, or thirsty and give you something to drink? When did we see you a stranger and invite you in, or needing clothes and clothe you? When did we see you sick or in prison and go to visit you?"
>
> The King will reply, "Truly I tell you, whatever you did for one of the least of these brothers and sisters of mine, you did for me."
>
> Then he will say to those on his left, "Depart from me, you who are cursed, into the eternal fire prepared for the devil and his angels. For I was hungry and you gave me nothing to eat, I was thirsty and you gave me nothing to drink, I was a stranger and you did not invite me in, I needed clothes and you did not clothe me, I was sick and in prison and you did not look after me."
>
> They also will answer, "Lord, when did we see you hungry or thirsty or a stranger or needing clothes or sick or in prison, and did not help you?"
>
> He will reply, "Truly I tell you, whatever you did not do for one of the least of these, you did not do for me."
>
> Then they will go away to eternal punishment, but the righteous to eternal life.

Strictly speaking, this text is not a parable. The likening of God's people to sheep and his enemies to goats are simply similes, straightforward comparisons at the beginning of the passage, and afterward their real identities are maintained. The passage is often treated in a study of Christ's parables, however, because of its similarity in structure, theme, and use of figures of speech to the other stories of Jesus that clearly fall into that category. The most common interpretation today, consistently in liberal Christian circles but increasingly often in evangelical ones, too, is that Jesus' story teaches that all the people of the world will be judged by their response to the poor, no matter who those poor people are. Some in more liberal circles would teach this text almost as if it promoted salvation by works. In evangelical circles, this kind of interpretation is presented in the context of the works that demonstrate Christian faith. But in either form, the key factor in this interpretation is that we have an obligation to some degree to every needy person in the world. Even more famous is the slogan made popular by Mother Teresa during her many years of ministry in the slums of Calcutta, that as we minister to the poor, whatever their religious background, we minister to Christ. Or, in the words she so often liked to use, "We see Jesus in the face of the poor."

Now, I don't want for one minute to deny that Scripture teaches some kind of responsibility to poor people of whatever background throughout the world. The good Samaritan clearly makes that point, as it offers a striking illustration of compassion for physical need across ethnic and religious boundaries (Luke 10:25–37). James 1:27 speaks of the outward manifestation of religion as epitomized by visiting orphans and widows in their distress as well as keeping oneself unstained from the world. In this summary, James includes no restrictions on the racial or religious backgrounds of the orphans and widows, the paradigm of the dispossessed in biblical cultures. Still, we also read in the New Testament texts, such as Galatians 6:10, that teach us to do good to all people but *especially* to those of the household of faith. And the strikingly communal, early Christian model of charity in Acts 2:44–45 is characterized first of all by care for the Christian needy. Moreover, people today often do not even realize that there are *two* main interpretations of the "parable" of the sheep and the goats throughout the history of the church, and that the one best known today is not the one that the majority of Christians throughout church history have adopted. I'd like, therefore, to sketch the other interpretation for us this morning and explain why I think it is the right one.

The key to this approach comes in verses 40 and 45 with the expression, "the least of these brothers and sisters of mine," and again, "the least of these." The TNIV rightly translates inclusively the Greek word that older translations typically rendered simply as "brothers." The word is common in Matthew's Gospel, and in every other instance refers either to biological siblings or to spiritual kin—a Jew speaking about a fellow Jew, or Jesus or one of the disciples speaking about another follower of Christ. The term in Matthew, therefore, does not refer to the brotherhood and sisterhood of all humanity but to those with whom one has significant spiritual commonality. The word "least" in verses 40 and 45 is what grammarians call the superlative form of the adjective "little"—little, less, least. And "little ones" is also a characteristic term for disciples in the Gospel of Matthew. In Jesus' message to the

Twelve in Matthew 18 he uses this expression several times. Consider verse 6: "If anyone causes one of these little ones—those who believe in me—to stumble, it would be better for them if a large millstone were hung around their neck and they were drowned in the depths of the sea." Or again in verse 10 we read: "See that you do not despise one of these little ones. For I tell you that their angels in heaven always see the face of my Father in heaven." Or finally, take verse 14: "In the same way your Father in heaven is not willing that any one of these little ones should perish." So unless major problems result in applying this understanding to the parable of the sheep and the goats, we should try to interpret the terms "brothers" and "least" as referring exclusively to Christians—true disciples of Jesus.

Does it make any sense, then, to say that all the people of the world on Judgment Day will be evaluated on the basis of how they have ministered to the *Christian* needy? Yes, I think it does, especially in light of another earlier passage in the Gospel of Matthew at the end of another sermon to the disciples. It appears in Matthew 10:40–42 at the end of Jesus' instructions to the Twelve when he sent them out on their first mission without him, designed to replicate his ministry of preaching, teaching, and healing. Jesus had commanded them to be dependent on the hospitality of the villagers in whose towns they ministered, even for such basic necessities as food, drink, money, and clothing. Matthew 10 then ends with a very close parallel to the language of our parable. Verses 40–42 read: "Anyone who welcomes you welcomes me, and anyone who welcomes me welcomes the one who sent me. Anyone who welcomes someone known to be a prophet will receive a prophet's reward, and anyone who welcomes someone known to be righteous will receive a righteous person's reward. And if anyone gives even a cup of cold water to one of these little ones who is known to be my disciple, truly I tell you, that person will certainly be rewarded." In the ancient world, one took someone into one's home as a sign of friendship, of intimacy, of support for what that person stood for. One can easily imagine, therefore, that Jesus is speaking of a welcome for messengers that reflects a welcome and an acceptance of their message. The parable of the sheep and the goats, then, makes very good sense as referring to final judgment based on how people have responded to needy, itinerant Christians, because in accepting these needy and ministering to them, they show that they have accepted the Christian message as well.

What difference does it make which of these two interpretations of this parable we adopt? At one level, perhaps not too much. I certainly don't feel compelled to go around trying to correct everyone I hear saying that this passage teaches that people will be judged on the basis of their ministry to the poor indiscriminately, except possibly at the seminary where I teach, because there we are trying to help people become as precise in their exegesis as possible. After all, in evangelical circles at least the people who adopt the newer, more popular approach to the sheep and the goats usually are those who already have strong social consciences and are ministering to whole persons, meeting needs of body and soul alike. These people are usually already acting counterculturally, recognizing the stewardship demands of Christ on their entire lives. Also, as I've already noted, I'm not urging that we help only the Christian poor. That would create the phenomenon of what have been called "rice Christians" in the history of Christian missions—folks who professed faith simply so that they could receive food (usually rice), whether or not they truly believed the Christian message.

But at another level the issue is important. Our resources as Christians in the United States, while enormous compared to those of many in the world, are nevertheless finite and cannot easily address all the massive needs of the entire planet. As individuals and as churches, we clearly have to make choices in our giving. I'm convinced that it is perfectly appropriate for us as believers to give to secular, charitable causes, but not if it prevents us from simultaneously being generous and giving to Christian causes, which we cannot necessarily expect non-Christians to support. And while the danger of creating "rice Christians" may still remain, such giving has a genuine evangelistic impact that Scripture describes, and that the church has experienced throughout her history, when the world sees how the church truly cares for her own. That's why Jesus prayed the last night of his life, in John 17:23, that we who came to faith because of the apostles' message might be brought to "complete unity," so that "the world will know," Jesus said to his Father, "that you sent me and have loved them even as you have loved me."

The late second-century apologist Tertullian has a remarkable passage in which he describes how this in fact played out in a good portion of the church in the Roman Empire in his day, describing what he calls "the peculiarities of the Christian society." He writes,

> We are a body knit together as such by a common religious profession, by unity of discipline, and by the bond of a common hope. We meet together as an assembly and congregation, that, offering a prayer to God as with united force, we may wrestle with Him in our supplications. . . . We pray, too, for the emperors, for their ministers and for all in authority, for the welfare of the world, for the prevalence of peace, for the delay of the final consummation. . . . On the monthly day, if he likes, each puts in a small donation; but only if it be his pleasure, and only if he is able: for there is no compulsion; all is voluntary. These gifts are, as it were, piety's deposit fund. For they are not taken thence and spent on feasts, and drinking-bouts, and eating-houses, but to support and bury poor people, to supply

the wants of boys and girls destitute of means and parents, and of old persons confined now to the house; such, too, as have suffered shipwreck; and if there happens to be any in the mines, or banished to the islands, or shut up in the prisons, for nothing but their fidelity to the cause of God's Church, they become the nurslings of their confessions. But it is mainly the deeds of a love so noble that lead many to put a brand upon us. *See,* they say, *how they love one another,* for themselves are animated by mutual hatred; how they are ready even to die for one another, for they themselves will sooner be put to death.[1]

And finally, Tertullian adds,

> One in mind and soul, we do not hesitate to share our earthly goods with one another. All things are common among us but our wives. We give up our community where it is practised alone by others, who not only take possession of the wives of their friends, but most tolerantly also accommodate their friends with theirs.[2]

In our age, too, the two fastest growing religions for the last decade or so have alternately been Mormonism and charismatic Christianity. Both have grown at significant rates, especially outside the United States. Both religions, in the places where they're growing, are characterized by great concern for fellowship, love, compassion, and meeting the physical and spiritual needs of their members. And there is a demonstrable correlation between this caring and their growth, even to the extent that doctrine takes a back seat, certainly in the case of Mormonism and at times in the case of more extreme forms of charismatic Christianity. People aren't so concerned that certain unbiblical teachings are promoted when they are being loved and cared for so consistently. Would that evangelicalism would be so concerned to model similar care while retaining sound doctrine!

So how do we do it? One group, the charismatic community, often does it with a strong commitment to small groups; the other, the Latter Day Saints, by an elaborate denominational infrastructure. Both models can be abused, but both can provide good examples for us to imitate, at least in part. Depending on the denomination, evangelical Protestants may not want a large organizational superstructure. But there's certainly no reason that shepherding within the local church couldn't be far better organized and carried out in every denomination as well as in nondenominational settings.

There is also the question of who *are* the neediest fellow Christians. Usually they're not found in our suburban, North American churches but rather in our inner cities, and usually the most destitute remain in the major cities and countryside of the Third World. When was the last time you helped out locally with a ministry to the poorest in your community? How much do you and your church know about and respond to the even more desperate needs of fellow believers around the world? In talking with Christians in Guatemala, when I had established enough of a relationship to get the local Christian leaders to be honest (and North American missionaries were even blunter), the recurring theme that emerged was their amazement at how much money we spend on ourselves, not merely as a country but as churches, and how little we share with the rest of the world, especially with fellow Christians, especially with those in some of the poorest places in the world, like the neighborhoods near the seminary in Guatemala City. Organizations like World Vision, Compassion International, Food for the Hungry, TEAR Fund, and others make it so incredibly easy for American Christians to make all the difference in the world in the lives of needy children, with child sponsorship programs for roughly twenty-five dollars a month—less than one dollar a day. Children who otherwise wouldn't have access to secular or Christian education or the basic decencies of life needed to promote their physical health can have their living situation transformed, and a substantial majority of them come to faith in Christ if they are not already believers. My wife and I personally sponsor four such children, three girls in Latin America, because we can exchange letters with them in Spanish, and an African boy in Uganda. There's no reason that most middle- or upper-class American Christians couldn't easily sponsor several children a month. Churches could sponsor dozens. One Chinese Christian church here in the Denver area just a few years ago had barely more than one hundred members. Yet it sponsored a dozen needy children around the world and had their pictures prominently displayed on the windows that separated the auditorium from the lobby. Imagine what churches of several hundred or a thousand or more members could do if they made similar commitments.

And what about the percentage of church budgets committed to missions and to holistic missions that care for people's bodies as well as souls? Not too long ago one study showed that the average American congregation spent no more than about 7 percent of its annual budget on anything apart from ministry within its four walls to its own people. Of that 7 percent, slightly less than half ever left the United States; and, of that half, only about one-third actually went to meeting people's physical as well as spiritual needs.[3] Put another way, roughly one penny on every dollar of American Christian giving to the local church winds up directly implementing Jesus' vision articulated here in the parable of the sheep and the goats across national boundaries. We could do so much better if we were willing! The first two churches my wife and I joined after we were married, one in the United States and one in the

United Kingdom, gave approximately 50 percent of their annual budgets to missions, with an emphasis on holistic mission work abroad. The considerably larger church, with a large staff and facility to fund, to which we now belong still manages to give 20 percent to missions as a whole and is continually trying to spend more on unreached peoples and on the poor. It can be done, but one has to consciously decide to do it and forego various other kinds of spending.

What's at stake in applying the parable of the sheep and the goats? Ultimately the eternal destiny of all humanity. These are indeed the works that demonstrate true saving faith. Jesus is clear. Everyone must respond to his message but then have a priority concern for everyone else who is likewise committed to that same message, especially the desperately poor. Then, as that famous song from the 1960s put it, "they will know that we are Christians by our love." Then the vision of John 17 will be fulfilled. That fulfillment, more than any discussion about programs of outreach, strategies for church growth, building projects, and the like, will have an enormous evangelistic impact and greatly glorify our God. Who really are the sheep and the goats? Which are you? Will you trust your life to Jesus and demonstrate by your compassion for fellow Christians, especially suffering ones, that your commitment to following Jesus is genuine? Can you think of any ways of increasing that commitment today? This week? In the immediate future? Shall we pray?

Commentary on "Who Really Are the Sheep and the Goats?"

The final sermon in this book deals with a passage that is not, strictly speaking, a parable. As a result, I did not consider it in my book on interpreting the parables. The passage begins with metaphorical imagery as if it is going to be a triangular, monarchic parable—with a king and contrasting subordinates, the sheep and the goats. But these metaphors are abandoned as the narrative continues, and the straightforward identification of each metaphor is substituted—Jesus as the Son of man, his followers (or "brothers"), and his opponents. Nevertheless, it is popularly labeled "the parable of the sheep and the goats" and is treated from time to time in more general studies of the parables.[4] Whatever its precise form, it is a highly influential passage that merits preaching and commentary. So I have chosen to include it as our last example in this volume. This message also comprises the sequel to the previous sermon on Matthew 24:43–25:30.

The pervasive issue in this message is my concern to correct what I believe is a common misinterpretation of the passage. So the message also illustrates one way of dealing with sensitive texts that one believes have often been mishandled. A full history of interpretation of the passage appears in a monograph by Sherman Gray, who demonstrates that the view I endorse is in fact the majority view of church history, even though he adopts the more popular twentieth-century perspective.[5] Numerous other studies, however, well defend the older, majority view.[6]

The first time I preached this sermon I had just returned from speaking as a guest lecturer at the Seminario Teológico Centroamericano in Guatemala City. I brought the Coca Cola baggie back as a souvenir, and it struck me that this would be a good visual aid to use at the start of a sermon on this passage. That, plus a description of the garbage dump not far from the seminary, would raise in pointed fashion the kinds of questions that usually lead to the "social action" interpretation of our text. With that lead-in, I then proceeded to read the text in its entirety fairly early in my message. Had the sermon been structured to focus more on the contrast between the "sheep" and the "goats" than between the two major interpretations of the passage overall, it would have been natural to read only verses 31–40 first and then use verses 41–46 to introduce the second half of the message.

As I mentioned earlier, I also initially preached this sermon as the third and final one in a series on Matthew 24–25. My congregation had therefore just heard my message on the four preceding parables, so it made sense to comment a little on the form of this passage and why it was not, technically, a parable. But my main concern, to which I move almost immediately, is the interpretation. I begin with the approach that I know a majority will be most familiar with. Before contesting that approach, I need to guard against the misinterpretation that I am against helping as many needy people as possible, Christian or non-Christian. As Greg Beale has so memorably phrased it, we often teach "the right doctrine from the wrong texts"![7] Because the interpretation of the sheep and the goats that I defend is both new and strange for many, I also stress that this is the majority view. Not that this makes it right, but I need to predispose the audience to consider an alternative. Letting them know of its long and storied pedigree in circles that are by definition "conservative" will better gain it a hearing.

The key exegetical support is actually overwhelming. Not often can one make the sweeping claims one can here about *every* other use of a common word in a Gospel being uniform in its meaning. Here we can do it twice! But there are times in the New Testament where certain words mean something consistently in every other appearance of the word, but a given context simply precludes that meaning there. The Greek word *kosmos* occurs 185 times in the New Testament. In 184 instances, the English "world" is a reliable translation. But in 1 Peter 3:3 ("your beauty should not come from outward *kosmos*, such as elaborate hairstyles and the wearing of gold jewelry and fine clothes"), this rendering makes no sense. One must return to an older meaning of the word and translate *kosmos* as "adornment." (The earth, as the one planet known to have life, was originally viewed as the adornment of the universe.) Immediate context can always trump consistent usage elsewhere.[8] But if an author's frequent and consistent usage of a word *does* make good sense in a given context, it is precarious to the extreme to suggest another meaning for the term never found in the works of that particular writer anywhere else.[9]

The key to understanding how the interpretation that takes "the least of these my brothers" to refer to needy Christians can make sense of this parable is the concept of "receiving" or "welcoming" someone. I cross-reference Matthew 10:40–42, where closely parallel language occurs. But the larger context of Matthew 10 is Jesus sending out the Twelve without him to minister in the villages of Israel and to be dependent on welcoming people for "bed and board." In the ancient world, to take people into one's home and provide sustenance for them over a prolonged period of time normally meant that they were relatives or other people with whom one had close ideological bonds. Table fellowship, in particular, was normally not thrown open to all indiscriminately. Thus, to welcome a messenger, as I phrase it, truly was to welcome the message.[10] Applying this principle to the imagery of the sheep and the goats, Jesus is teaching that people typically minister to needy Christians when they themselves have embraced the Christian message.

Because this interpretation will be new to many of my listeners, I have to add several caveats after I have articulated it. The most important one is that I don't believe the more common, recent interpretation is in any way harmful or unorthodox. If I were to try to "correct" what I believe are orthodox misinterpretations of texts by preachers (i.e., the right doctrine from the wrong texts) every time I hear them, there would be few sermons I would ever listen to that would not force me to respond in this way, and it would be very difficult for me to worship and hear God's word to me through the generally solid parts of most messages to which I listen! But at the seminary, we aim to teach students greater exegetical and homiletical precision, so I will (gently, I trust) challenge such interpretations there. And when other preachers in other contexts invite response, I will try to make a few constructive suggestions. In this particular instance, because the social ethic that is often proclaimed from this "parable" is in fact a central but often underemphasized theme of Scripture elsewhere,[11] I am even more cautious about trying to correct expositions. By including thoughts along these lines in the message myself I hope to alleviate the concerns of those who may still be convinced by the other approach to the text.

At the same time, I *have* decided to preach this particular passage and to present the approach I believe to be correct. So I don't want to take all the sting out of the tale. The practical issue of wise allocation of scarce resources and the extent of biblical teaching elsewhere of providing first of all for fellow believers drives me to stress that certain, important issues are at stake in the interpretation of the text. The extensive quotation from Tertullian focuses what the church should be like in response to this interpretation as powerfully as any description I know. The fact that the kind of community that Tertullian describes, however stylized or idealistic it may be, at times more closely mirrors faith communities that are *not* my own and are not the circles that I am invited to address heightens the urgency to challenge typical evangelical congregations to greater obedience to Christ's vision for what we could create even in this fallen world. So I try to separate the biblical ethics that characterize those communities from the unorthodox doctrine that, to varying degrees, may also afflict them.[12]

The twin realities that the needs are often far greater in the Third World than in the United States and that a majority of American Christian giving, even to missions per se, never leaves America, drive my comments on the international situation. I am also coming full circle to my introduction regarding the poor in Guatemala and providing numerous practical examples of comparatively minor changes that most middle- and upper-class First-World Christians could make in their lifestyles and actually make a significant difference in the lives of many in other, poorer contexts.[13]

The application of the parable of the sheep and the goats that does make all the difference in eternity is, of course, the question of into which group of people one will ultimately fall. Within evangelicalism, both the "social ethic" interpretation and the approach that sees Jesus talking about ministering to Christian messengers agree that the behavior described is the outgrowth of one's belief in Jesus.[14] Neither interpretation espouses salvation by works. As so centrally for James, these are works that demonstrate one's faith (cf. esp. James 2:14–26). Therefore, I end the message with that point of agreement and raise the question of salvation for any in the congregation who might not be believers. Preachers who at least periodically end services with evangelistic appeals could move naturally to explicit invitations to receive Christ following the closing prayer.

Conclusion

As I remarked in the introduction, I do not expect my collection of sermons to win any awards for all-star homiletics or rhetoric. Plenty of preachers exist who excel in these areas. It *is* my hope, however, that such people can glean useful material from the principles of interpretation illustrated here, along with the outlines and structures of my talks, the examples of contemporization and application, and the commentary sections on each sermon. Hopefully good communicators can then introduce their own superior rhetoric and delivery and produce even better messages. If I have at least encouraged those who might have steered clear of the parables to consider them afresh for serious preaching and teaching, a significant objective of this work will have been fulfilled.

As I reread my messages, I am struck not only by the issues of interpretation, structure, and application but also by the parables' recurring themes. It is impossible to expound any significant cross section of Jesus' teaching in parables without having to come to grips repeatedly with money matters—Christian stewardship, to be more precise. I have noted several times in the commentary material that had I been preaching all these passages sequentially on consecutive Sundays at the same church, I would have toned down my emphasis on financial issues a little, lest the recurring refrains prove counterproductive and "turn off" those whom I wanted to prod on to whatever the next level of stewardship for them might look like. On the other hand, stewardship does remain the single most recurring theme in this corpus of literature. So perhaps the moral of the story is that one should not attempt too long a series just on parables. After all, no single Gospel groups them all together, so that sequential exposition of any of the Synoptics does not require treatments of parables every week (though Luke's central section—9:51–18:34—and chapters 14–16 in particular do present a fairly intense flurry of them).

Other recurring themes clamor for attention as well, however. While only fifteen parables have been expounded in this volume, I am not aware of any major motif from any of the parables of Jesus that has not appeared in at least one of the texts and corresponding messages presented here. In fact, we may use the triangular structure that reflects a majority of Jesus' parables as a template for arranging the theological emphases of these texts. The gospel message, after all, is essentially triangular in nature—a master figure (God, through Christ's atoning death) seeks to redeem lost humanity, but some rebel and refuse his offer of salvation (the wicked subordinates), while others accept his grace-based offer and respond by becoming Jesus' disciples (the good subordinates). As in the parables, we are often surprised by who falls into each category.

Thus, a focus on the master figures in Jesus' parables teaches us repeatedly about God's magnificent grace, classically in the parable of the prodigal son but also at the outset of the unforgiving servant and at the close of the Pharisee and the tax collector. God is equally a God of justice, though. A day of judgment is coming when it will be too late to respond to his gracious offers, and unbelievers will be condemned to eternal punishment. We have seen that theme repeatedly, in the rich man and Lazarus, the unforgiving servant, the wheat and the weeds, the dragnet, the two builders, and the entire sequence of eschatological parables in Matthew 24–25. Yet God is gracious in delaying this punishment as long as possible (the bridegroom, the talents) and promises to preserve his people even when that delay seems to call into question his faithfulness (the wheat and the weeds, the persistent widow). God shows extra special concern for the disenfranchised of this world (the prodigal, Lazarus, the tax collector, and the unjust judge), especially in Christian circles (the sheep and the goats). Perhaps above all, God is sovereign, still in control of the universe, even when and where it seems most out of control (the wheat and the weeds, the mustard seed, the leaven, the unjust judge).

Those who would truly be God's people are called to accept the completely free gift of forgiveness (the prodigal, the good Samaritan), yet at the same time to count the cost of discipleship, which might prove more arduous than they expect, even, in extreme cases, to the point of martyrdom (the tower builder, the warring king). The best harmonization of these apparently opposite statements that I've ever heard, appropriately in a sermon rather than in a scholarly tome, is "Salvation is absolutely free, but it will cost you your life."[1] Being a subject of God's kingdom is worth whatever it costs for each given individual (the hidden treasure, the pearl of great price). The life of discipleship reflects to progressively greater degrees the communicable attributes of God, including concern for society's oppressed and afflicted (the good Samaritan, the rich man and Lazarus), avoiding the idolatry that comes with a needless accumulation of possessions (the rich man and Lazarus, the unjust steward, the talents), not allowing religion to get in the way of caring (the good Samaritan, the Pharisee and the tax collector), forgiving others as one has been forgiven (the unforgiving servant), responding with the right combination of joy and repentance to the messages of God's spokespersons (the children in the marketplace), obeying more and more of Jesus' commands (the two builders), and bearing fruit of many different kinds (the various seed parables). Prayer plays an important role in believers' lives (the persistent widow), and salvation is guaranteed contingent on perseverance (the unforgiving servant, the bridesmaids). "Eternal security" is not the promise of automatic salvation to all who ever make a profession of faith. Rather, as suggested by the Reformation-era nomenclature, the doctrine of "the perseverance of the saints" means that all true believers do persevere. But the way we determine who these people are is to watch and see who, in fact, remains (or in Elizabethan English, "abides").

Those who are not God's people may thus masquerade as believers for a time (many of the servant parables). But eventually their true colors will emerge as they abandon their professions of faith and do not demonstrate throughout their entire lives the "fruit befitting repentance" (the sower, the two builders). Positions, even of leadership, in organized religion do not necessarily correlate with the presence of true faith (the good Samaritan, the Pharisee and the tax collector). Now is the day of salvation, while Christ delays his return (parables of judgment). No sin or state of rebellion or unbelief is so vile that the truly repentant will not be welcomed home by God (the prodigal).

Ultimately all of humanity will fall into one of two camps, those who spend an eternity with God in unspeakable bliss and those who spend an eternity separated from God and everything good. We would be remiss not to address the readers of this book directly with this final query: After working your way through the parables and these messages on them, do you have the assurance that you are a true disciple of Jesus Christ, so that you can look forward with confidence (but not complacency) to eternal life in perfect happiness in the company of the Triune God and the redeemed of every era of human history? If not, please take this opportunity to make your peace with God by submitting to the lordship of Christ and accepting his free offer of forgiveness of sins that nothing you could ever do could ever merit. If you have done this, my next prayer is that this book will enable you to move to a deeper walk with Jesus in discipleship, a walk that includes helping others come to him and grow in him as well. And may God receive all the glory!

Notes

Preface

1. For documentation see my *"Today's New International Version:* The Untold Story of a Good Translation" (paper presented at the Denver Institute of Contextualized Biblical Studies Conference, Denver Seminary, 2003). The essay is accessible on Denver Seminary's website (www.denverseminary.edu/dialogue/translation.php), as of February 2004, and elsewhere.

Introduction

1. Thomas O. Long, *Preaching the Literary Forms of the Bible* (Philadelphia: Fortress, 1989), 87.

2. A detailed history of the interpretation of parables is included in my earlier work, *Interpreting the Parables* (Downers Grove, Ill.: InterVarsity Press, 1990), 13–167.

3. Adolf Jülicher, *Die Gleichnisreden Jesu,* 2 vols. (Freiburg: Mohr, 1899).

4. Craig Blomberg, "The Tradition History of the Parables Peculiar to Luke's Central Section" (Ph.D. diss., University of Aberdeen, 1982).

5. Craig Blomberg, "New Horizons in Parable Research," *TrinJ* 3 (1982): 3–17; idem, "Midrash, Chiasmus, and the Outline of Luke's Central Section," in *Gospel Perspectives*, vol. 3, ed. R. T. France and David Wenham (Sheffield: JSOT, 1983), 217–61; idem, "When Is a Parallel Really a Parallel? A Test Case—The Lucan Parables," *WTJ* 46 (1984): 78–103; and idem, "Interpreting the Parables: Where Do We Go from Here?" *CBQ* 53 (1991): 50–78.

6. Craig Blomberg, "The Parables of Jesus: Current Trends in Needs and Research," in *Studying the Historical Jesus,* ed. Bruce Chilton and Craig A. Evans (Leiden: Brill, 1994), 231–54; and idem, "Poetic Fiction, Subversive Speech, and Proportional Analogy in the Parables," *HBT* 18 (1996): 115–32.

7. Craig Blomberg, "Preaching the Parables: Preserving Three Main Points," *PRS* 11 (1984): 31–41.

8. See, e.g., the reviews by David J. Graham in *EQ* 64 (1992): 274; Daniel B. Clendenin in *JETS* 35 (1992): 254–56; David L. Turner in *CTR* 6 (1992): 141–42; and David E. Garland in *RevExp* 90 (1993): 429–30.

9. E.g., Warren W. Wiersbe, ed., *Classic Sermons on the Parables of Jesus* (Grand Rapids: Kregel, 1997); idem, *Classic Sermons on the Prodigal Son* (Grand Rapids: Kregel, 1990).

10. E.g., C. H. Spurgeon, *Sermons on Our Lord's Parables* (Nashville: Cokesbury, 1933); Emil Brunner, *Sowing and Reaping: The Parables of Jesus* (Philadelphia: Fortress, 1972).

11. David A. Hubbard, *Parables Jesus Told* (Downers Grove, Ill.: InterVarsity Press, 1981); Earl F. Palmer, *Laughter in Heaven* (Waco, Tex.: Word, 1987); D. Stuart Briscoe, *Patterns for Power* (Ventura, Calif.: Regal, 1979).

12. James M. Boice, *The Parables of Jesus* (Chicago: Moody, 1983); J. Dwight Pentecost, *The Parables of Jesus* (Grand Rapids: Zondervan, 1982); Robert C. McQuilkin, *Our Lord's Parables* (Grand Rapids: Zondervan, 1980).

13. John C. Purdy, *Parables at Work* (Philadelphia: Westminster, 1985).

14. J. Ellsworth Kalas, *Parables from the Back Side* (Nashville: Abingdon, 1992); Megan McKenna, *Parables: The Arrows of God* (Maryknoll, N.Y.: Orbis, 1994).

15. E.g., Morris L. Venden, *Parables of the Kingdom* (Boise: Pacific Press, 1986); Brian A. Nelson, *Hustle Won't Bring the Kingdom of God* (St. Louis: Bethany, 1978); Douglas Beyer, *Parables for Christian Living* (Valley Forge, Penn.: Judson, 1985).

16. Neal F. Fisher, *The Parables of Jesus: Glimpses of God's Reign* (New York: Crossroad, 1990).

17. Robert F. Capon, *The Parables of the Kingdom* (Grand Rapids: Zondervan, 1985); idem, *The Parables of God's Grace* (Grand Rapids: Eerdmans, 1988); idem, *The Parables of Judgment* (Grand Rapids: Eerdmans, 1989).

18. W. A. Poovey, *Banquets and Beggars: Dramas and Meditations on Six Parables* (Minneapolis: Augsburg, 1974).

19. John Killinger, *Parables for Christmas* (Nashville: Abingdon, 1985).

20. John T. Carroll and James R. Carroll, *Preaching the Hard Sayings of Jesus* (Peabody, Mass.: Hendrickson, 1996).

21. Keith F. Nickle, *Preaching the Gospel of Luke: Proclaiming God's Royal Rule* (Louisville: Westminster John Knox, 2000).

22. Blomberg, *Parables*, 78–94.

23. D. Moody Smith, *Interpreting the Gospels for Preaching* (Philadelphia: Fortress, 1980).

24. George R. Beasley-Murray, *Preaching the Gospel from the Gospels* (Philadelphia: Judson, 1956), in a chapter promisingly titled "The Gospel in the Parables of Jesus," 102–25.

25. Sidney Greidanus, *The Modern Preacher and the Ancient Text* (Grand Rapids: Eerdmans, 1988).

26. Roy Clements, *A Sting in the Tale* (Leicester: InterVarsity Press, 1995).

27. Clements acknowledged to me in private conversation his reliance on my work.

28. David M. Granskou, *Preaching on the Parables* (Philadelphia: Fortress, 1972), 56–57.

29. Lloyd J. Ogilvie, *Autobiography of God* (Ventura, Calif.: Regal, 1979).

30. Richard L. Eslinger, "Preaching the Parables and the Main Idea," *Perkins Journal* 37 (1) (1983): 24–32, quotation from p. 32.

31. Eduard Schweizer, "Preaching on the Parables," in *Biblical Preaching: An Expositor's Treasure*, ed. James W. Cox (Philadelphia: Westminster, 1983), 249, 252.

32. Robert G. Hughes, "Preaching the Parables," in *The Promise and Practice of Biblical Theology*, ed. John Reumann (Minneapolis: Fortress, 1991), 157–70.

33. Peter R. Jones, "Preaching on the Parable Genre," *RevExp* 94 (1977): 231.

34. Ibid., 236, 238–40.

35. Mark Thomsen, "A Parabolic Theology for Preaching," *Dialog* 19 (3) (1980): 199–209.

36. Bernard B. Scott, *Hear Then the Parable* (Minneapolis: Fortress, 1989).

37. Mark Trotter, *What Are You Waiting For? Sermons on the Parables of Jesus* (Nashville: Abingdon, 1992); Thomas Keating, *The Kingdom of God Is Like . . .* (New York: Crossroad, 1993).

38. Bernard B. Scott, "On Having Ears: From Text to Sermon," *LexThQ* 16 (1981): 103.

39. Eric Osborn, "Parable and Exposition," *ABR* 22 (1974): 11–22; Timothy R. Sensing, "Imitating the Genre of Parable in Today's Pulpit," *RestQ* 33 (1991): 193–207.

40. Eugene L. Lowry, *How to Preach a Parable: Designs for Narrative Sermons* (Nashville: Abingdon, 1989), 25.

41. Ibid., 104.

42. Ibid., 135.

43. David G. Buttrick, *Speaking Parables: A Homiletic Guide* (Louisville: Westminster John Knox, 2000), xiii.

44. Ibid., 39–57.

45. See esp. Haddon W. Robinson, *Biblical Preaching* (Grand Rapids: Baker, 1980).

46. Barbara Reid, *Parables for Preachers* (Collegeville, Minn.: Liturgical, 1999), 18.

47. I owe this big idea to Professor Elodie Emig.

48. See esp. John W. Sider, "The Meaning of *Parabolē* in the Usage of the Synoptic Evangelists," *Bib* 62 (1981): 453–70; cf. Joachim Jeremias, *The Parables of Jesus*, 3d ed. (Philadelphia: Westminster, 1972), 20.

49. Of many good works, see esp. George R. Beasley-Murray, *Jesus and the Kingdom of God* (Grand Rapids: Eerdmans, 1986); cf. Bruce Chilton, *Pure Kingdom: Jesus' Vision of God* (Grand Rapids: Eerdmans, 1996).

50. Blomberg, *Parables*, 296–313.

51. For parable-by-parable analysis and defense of the material in this paragraph, see ibid., 171–288.

52. Ibid., 13–167.

53. Thus T. F. Torrance ("A Study in New Testament Communication," *SJT* 3 [1950]: 304–5) explains, "The Kingdom of God comes into the midst and throws a man into the crisis of decision, and yet by its veiled form the Word of the Kingdom holds man at arm's length away in order to give him room and time for personal decision." Again, "Jesus deliberately concealed the Word in parable lest men against their will should be forced to acknowledge the Kingdom, and yet He allowed them enough light to convict them and to convince them."

54. I have made a beginning in my "Interpreting the Synoptic Gospels for Preaching," *Faith and Mission* 12 (1994): 22–43.

55. "Le père et ses deux fils: Luc XV, 11–32," *RB* 84 (1977): 321–48, 538–65.

56. Cf. Simon Kistemaker, *The Parables of Jesus,* 2d ed. (Grand Rapids: Baker, 2002), 40: "The Word of God is proclaimed and causes a division among those who hear; God's people receive the Word, understand it, and obediently fulfill it. Others fail to listen because of a hardened heart, a basic superficiality, or a vested interest in riches and possessions." This summary, however, does not form "one particular truth."

57. Robinson, *Preaching,* 20.

58. Walter C. Kaiser, Jr., *Toward an Exegetical Theology* (Grand Rapids: Baker, 1981); Gordon D. Fee, *New Testament Exegesis,* rev. ed. (Louisville: Westminster John Knox, 2002).

59. Steven D. Mathewson, *The Art of Preaching Old Testament Narrative* (Grand Rapids: Baker, 2002).

60. Wayne B. Robinson, ed., *Journeys toward Narrative Preaching* (New York: Pilgrim, 1990).

61. Raymond Bailey, ed., *Hermeneutics for Preaching* (Nashville: Broadman, 1992).

62. In addition to literature already cited, see esp. John R. W. Stott, *I Believe in Preaching* (London: Hodder & Stoughton, 1982); Walter L. Liefeld, *New Testament Exposition* (Grand Rapids: Zondervan, 1984); and Keith Willhite, *Preaching with Relevance* (Grand Rapids: Kregel, 2001).

Chapter 1: The Parable of the Prodigal Sons and Their Father

1. For the use of the plural, cf. Colin Brown, "The Parable of the Rebellious Son(s)," *SJT* 51 (1998): 391–405.

2. The close parallelism between these two segments of the parable has been demonstrated in detail by Mary A. Tolbert, *Perspectives on the Parables* (Philadelphia: Fortress, 1979), 98–100.

3. Cf. Arland J. Hultgren, *The Parables of Jesus: A Commentary* (Grand Rapids: Eerdmans, 2000), 73.

4. Cf. Helmut Thielicke's classic exposition, *The Waiting Father* (New York: Harper, 1959), 17–40.

5. See originally Kenneth E. Bailey, *Poet and Peasant: A Literary-Cultural Approach to the Parables in Luke* (Grand Rapids: Eerdmans, 1976), 158–206; with important supplementary material in idem, *Finding the Lost: Cultural Keys to*

Luke 15 (St. Louis: Concordia, 1992), 109–93; and idem, *Jacob and the Prodigal: How Jesus Retold Israel's Story* (Downers Grove, Ill.: InterVarsity Press, 2003). For a complementary comparison of the parable with relevant Greco-Roman background, see David A. Holgate, *Prodigality, Liberality and Meanness: The Prodigal Son in Greco-Roman Perspective* (Sheffield: Sheffield Academic Press, 1999).

6. The theme of repentance ties in well with Luke's distinctive emphasis on this topic. Cf. esp. Greg Forbes, "Repentance and Conflict in the Parable of the Lost Son (Luke 15:11–32)," *JETS* 42 (1999): 211–29.

7. Thus, classically, Joachim Jeremias, *Parables*, 128–32.

8. Brad H. Young (*The Parables: Jewish Tradition and Christian Interpretation* [Peabody, Mass.: Hendrickson, 1998], 132) observes that "seldom has the significance of the elder brother been carefully considered."

9. On the probable implied contrast between the father's behavior and other villagers' reactions, see Richard L. Rohrbaugh, "A Dysfunctional Family and Its Neighbors (Luke 15:11b–32)," in *Jesus and His Parables: Interpreting the Parables of Jesus Today*, ed. V. George Shillington (Edinburgh: T & T Clark, 1997), 141–64.

10. This pattern obtains consistently throughout Jesus' parables. See esp. Norman A. Huffman, "Atypical Features in the Parables of Jesus," *JBL* 97 (1978): 207–20.

11. This is one of the reasons some today would at times prefer to call God "mother" as well as or even instead of "father." Interestingly, the generally authoritarian behavior of fathers in the Roman world considerably exceeded that of the typical contemporary father in its cruelty. Yet the first Christians insisted on calling God their Father, so I believe that we should do so too, even while helping people understand what is and isn't meant by that metaphor.

12. Full details of both ceremonies appear in Karl H. Rengstorf, *Die Re-Investitur des verlorenen Sohnes in der Gleichniserzählung Jesu: Luk. 15, 11–32* (Köln: Westdeutscher Verlag, 1967).

13. Cf. Darrell L. Bock, *Luke*, vol. 2 (Grand Rapids: Baker, 1996), 1320.

Chapter 2: Can I Be Saved without Stewardship?

1. My source is John L. Ronsvalle and Sylvia Ronsvalle, *The Poor Have Faces: Loving Your Neighbor in the 21st Century* (Grand Rapids: Baker, 1992), 45. These statistics are now a bit dated, but the Ronsvalles regularly update them. Most recently, see their book *The State of Church Giving through 2000*, 12th ed. (Champaign, Ill.: empty tomb, inc., 2002).

2. Ronsvalle and Ronsvalle, *Poor Have Faces*, 53–54.

3. The reason for these conventional expectations is the Old Testament covenant with Israel in which God promised to bless it as a nation when it, and especially its leaders, demonstrated sufficient obedience, and to punish it when they didn't. But the OT clearly presents this model corporately, as how God treats Israel as a whole, not as a guarantee of "health and wealth" for all pious individuals. Indeed, the Hebrew wisdom literature presents many examples in

which the wicked prosper and the pious suffer. See further Craig L. Blomberg, *Neither Poverty nor Riches: A Biblical Theology of Material Possessions* (Leicester, England: InterVarsity Press, 1999), 57–69.

4. Cf. further Blomberg, *Parables*, 203–8.

5. Cf. Darrell L. Bock, "The Parable of the Rich Man and Lazarus and the Ethics of Jesus," *SWJT* 40 (1997): 63–72.

6. For the first two approaches, along with intermediate options, cf. Robert G. Clouse, ed., *Wealth and Poverty: Four Christian Views of Economics* (Downers Grove, Ill.: InterVarsity Press, 1984).

7. Most importantly, by noting the shifts from narrative discourse (vv. 19–23) to direct discourse (vv. 24–31). Cf. Eugene H. Wehrli, "Luke 16:19–31," *Int* 31 (1977): 279–80. Bock (*Luke*, vol. 2, 1365–77) offers a variation of this approach by labeling vv. 19–21, "The Rich Man and Lazarus in This Life"; vv. 22–23, "The Rich Man and Lazarus in the Next Life"; and vv. 24–31, "The Rich Man's Pleas to Abraham." Less distinctively, a majority of commentators divide the passage simply into vv. 19–26 and 27–31, because of the Egyptian and Jewish parallels to the first of these segments, on which see esp. Richard Bauckham, "The Rich Man and Lazarus: The Parable and the Parallels," *NTS* 37 (1991): 225–46.

8. Particularly helpful in summarizing the economic stratification of the first-century Roman world is William R. Herzog II, *Parables as Subversive Speech: Jesus as Pedagogue of the Oppressed* (Louisville: Westminster John Knox, 1994), 53–73.

9. To borrow a widely used label. See, e.g., Allan Verhey, *The Great Reversal: Ethics and the New Testament* (Grand Rapids: Eerdmans, 1984).

10. For a balanced critique, see Bruce Barron, *The Health and Wealth Gospel* (Downers Grove, Ill.: InterVarsity Press, 1987).

11. This is a major objective of the biblical theology movement. An outstanding resource for preachers (and others!) that helps us recognize the dominant and distinctive theology of each part of Scripture is now T. Desmond Alexander and Brian S. Rosner, eds., *New Dictionary of Biblical Theology* (Downers Grove, Ill.: InterVarsity Press, 2000). See specifically my chapter on "The Unity and Diversity of Scripture," 64–72.

12. A helpful exploration of this dynamic appears in Stephen T. Wright, "Parables of Poverty and Riches (Luke 12:13–21; 16:1–13; 16:19–31)," in *The Challenge of Jesus' Parables*, ed. Richard N. Longenecker (Grand Rapids: Eerdmans, 2000), 230–31. Wright notes the power of the parable in its restraint as well as both its prophetic and practical message, closely equivalent to the two points just noted.

13. As Thomas E. Schmidt ("Burden, Barrier, Blasphemy: Wealth in Matt. 6:33, Luke 14:33, and Luke 16:15," *TrinJ* 9 [1988]: 188) puts it so poignantly, "To stand still because the end is so far away is to miss the point of discipleship as a journey. Most of us could travel a considerable distance on that road before anyone suspected us of extreme obedience."

14. The principle of the graduated tithe is succinctly presented in Ronald J. Sider, *Rich Christians in an Age of Hunger*, 4th ed. (Dallas: Word, 1997), 193–96.

Chapter 3: Who Is My Most Important Neighbor?

1. David Prior, *The Message of 1 Corinthians: Life in the Local Church* (Leicester, England: InterVarsity Press, 1985), 83 (originally commenting on 1 Cor. 5:9–13).

2. For an up-to-date assessment of the Samaritans in Jesus' world, see Ingrid Hjelm, *The Samaritans and Early Judaism: A Literary Analysis* (Sheffield: Sheffield Academic Press, 2000). For the enmity with Jews in particular and the role of the parable in countering that enmity, see Philip F. Esler, "Jesus and the Reduction of Intergroup Conflict: The Parable of the Good Samaritan in the Light of Social Identity Theory," *BI* 6 (2000): 325–57.

3. For the details as presented in the local media, see Michael BeDan, "Good Samaritan Is Eulogized," *Rocky Mountain News*, July 27, 2002.

4. For full details, see John M. Darley and C. Daniel Batson, "From Jerusalem to Jericho: A Study of Situational and Dispositional Variables in Helping Behavior," *Journal of Personal and Social Psychology* 27 (1973): 100–108.

5. I owe this information to my colleague, the chair of Denver Seminary's Counseling Division, Dr. James R. Beck, in personal conversation.

6. All of vv. 25–37 hangs together as a tightly structured unity, despite frequent claims to the contrary. See esp. E. Earle Ellis, "How the New Testament Uses the Old," in *New Testament Introduction*, ed. I. Howard Marshall (Grand Rapids: Eerdmans, 1976), 205–6. More recently, cf. J. J. Kilgallen, "The Plan of the 'NOMIKOΣ' (Luke 10.25–37)," *NTS* 42 (1996): 615–19.

7. E.g., Gordon D. Fee and Douglas Stuart, *How to Read the Bible for All Its Worth*, 2d ed. (Grand Rapids: Zondervan, 1993), 147.

8. For a helpful, recent, and representative treatment, see J. Ian H. MacDonald, "Alien Grace (Luke 10:30–36)," in *Jesus and His Parables*, ed. V. George Shillington (Edinburgh: T & T Clark, 1997), 35–51. On the legal issues in particular, see esp. Richard Bauckham, "The Scrupulous Priest and the Good Samaritan: Jesus' Parabolic Interpretation of the Law of Moses," *NTS* 44 (1998): 475–89.

9. See esp. Robert W. Funk, "The Good Samaritan as Metaphor," in his *Parables and Presence* (Philadelphia: Fortress, 1982), 29–34; Young, *Parables*, 101–18.

10. Young, *Parables*, 116.

11. See, e.g., Michel Gourgues, "The Priest, the Levite, and the Samaritan Revisited: A Critical Note on Luke 10:31–35," *JBL* 117 (1998): 709–13.

12. See, e.g., Robert H. Stein, *Luke* (Nashville: Broadman, 1992), 317–18.

13. Kenneth E. Bailey, *Through Peasant Eyes: More Lucan Parables* (Grand Rapids: Eerdmans, 1980), 48.

14. Still defended by a handful of modern scholars—e.g., Birger Gerhardsson, *The Good Samaritan—The Good Shepherd?* (Lund: Gleerup, 1958); S. Willis, "The Good Samaritan: Another View," *ExpT* 112 (2000): 92.

Chapter 4: Can I Be Saved If I Refuse to Forgive Others?

1. D. A. Carson, "Matthew," in *Expositor's Bible Commentary*, ed. Frank E. Gaebelein, vol. 8 (Grand Rapids: Zondervan, 1984): 407.

2. H. N. Ridderbos, *Matthew* (Grand Rapids: Zondervan, 1987), 346.

3. Or somewhat more precisely, vv. 24–27, 28–31, and 32–34, with vv. 23 and 35 forming the introduction and conclusion to the parable, respectively.

4. The TNIV's renderings are better than the NIV's, even when it was first published, but they still noticeably underestimate the amount represented by one hundred denarii. For the value of weights and measures in the New Testament, including these, see Lewis A. Foster, "The Metrology of the New Testament," in *Expositor's Bible Commentary*, vol. 1 (1979), 609–13. On the meaning of "myriad," cf. "μύριοι," in Walter Bauer, *A Greek-English Lexicon of the New Testament and Other Early Christian Literature*, rev. and ed. Frederick W. Danker, 3d ed. (Chicago: University of Chicago Press, 2000), 661: "in our lit. used hyperbolically, as in Engl. informal usage 'zillion', of an extremely large or incalculable number."

5. Cf. W. D. Davies and Dale C. Allison Jr., *A Critical and Exegetical Commentary on the Gospel according to Saint Matthew*, vol. 2 (Edinburgh: T & T Clark, 1991), 794.

6. See, e.g., Craig S. Keener, *A Commentary on the Gospel of Matthew* (Grand Rapids: Eerdmans, 1999), 457–61.

7. Cf. Donald A. Hagner, *Matthew 14–28* (Dallas: Word, 1995), 539.

8. Even recent Catholic commentary increasingly agrees with my interpretation. Cf. Rudolf Schnackenburg, *The Gospel of Matthew* (Grand Rapids: Eerdmans, 2002), 181: "Naturally the refunding of the entire debt is illusory. Its expression indicates everlasting punishment."

9. Likewise, D. A. Carson, *The Farewell Discourse and Final Prayer of Jesus: An Exposition of John 14–17* (Grand Rapids: Baker, 1980), 98, in the context of commenting on John 15:2.

10. Cf. further my *Matthew* (Nashville: Broadman, 1992), 277–85; Troy Martin, "The Christian's Obligation Not to Forgive," *ExpT* 108 (1997): 360–62. For more details on applying the biblical texts on church discipline, see my *1 Corinthians* (Grand Rapids: Zondervan, 1994), 107–15, under the treatment of 1 Cor. 5:1–13.

11. For unpacking, see Myrla Seibold, "When the Wounding Runs Deep," in *Care for the Soul: Exploring the Intersection of Psychology and Theology*, ed. Mark R. McMinn and Timothy R. Phillips (Downers Grove, Ill.: InterVarsity Press, 2001), 294–308; Dan B. Allender, *The Wounded Heart* (Colorado Springs: NavPress, 1990), 219–40. I owe these references to my Denver Seminary colleague, counseling professor Dr. Joan Winfrey.

12. Cf. Hultgren, *Parables*, 29–30.

Chapter 5: Shrewd Stewards

1. I obtained this information from a *Denver Post* article that appeared in early 2000 but have been unable to retrieve the exact reference.

2. The statistics and anecdotes cited here are documented in my *Neither Poverty nor Riches*, 17–18 and 251–52.

3. Jean Pirot (*Jesus et la richesse: Parabole de l'intendant astucieux [Luc XVI, 1–15]* [Marseille: Imprimerie Marsellaise, 1944], 17–31) plausibly sees vv. 1–8a as teaching about the behavior of the sons of darkness and vv. 9–13 as teaching

about the behavior of the sons of light, with v. 8b providing the bridge between the two sections.

4. On extraordinary elements in Jesus' parables in general, see Frederick H. Borsch, *Many Things in Parables: Extravagant Stories of New Community* (Philadelphia: Fortress, 1988).

5. For similar recent scandals, cf. Matt Kelley, "Online Markup," http://abcnews.go.com/sections/scitech/DailyNews/Pentagon_spending010322.html on April 8, 2003.

6. For full details, see my *Neither Poverty nor Riches*, 111–46. For the point about one-fifth of Jesus' teaching being on money, see David P. Seccombe, *The King of God's Kingdom* (Waynesboro, Ga.: Paternoster, 2002), 265.

7. C. H. Dodd, *The Parables of the Kingdom* (London: Nisbet, 1935), 30.

8. Beginning, classically, with Jülicher, *Die Gleichnisreden Jesu*, and alluded to in virtually every introductory hermeneutics text.

9. See esp. J. Duncan M. Derrett, *Law in the New Testament* (London: Darton, Longman & Todd, 1970), 48–77.

10. Thus Bailey, *Poet and Peasant*, 86–110. Cf., with variations, Hans J. B. Combrink, "A Social-Scientific Perspective on the Parable of the 'Unjust' Steward (Lk. 16:1–8a)," *Neot* 30 (1996): 281–306; Justin S. Ukpong, "The Parable of the Shrewd Manager (Luke 16:1–13): An Essay in Inculturation Biblical Hermeneutic," *Semeia* 73 (1996): 189–210.

11. For full details of the history of interpretation, see Dennis J. Ireland, *Stewardship and Kingdom of God: An Historical, Exegetical, and Contextual Study of the Parable of the Unjust Steward in Luke 16:1–13* (Leiden: Brill, 1992). Cf. also Dave L. Mathewson, "The Parable of the Unjust Steward (Luke 16:1–13): A Reexamination of the Traditional View in Light of Recent Challenges," *JETS* 38 (1995): 29–39.

12. Markus Barth ("The Dishonest Steward and His Lord: Reflections on Luke 16:1–13," in *From Faith to Faith*, ed. Dikran Y. Hadidian [Pittsburgh: Pickwick, 1979], 65) sees vv. 1–8a illustrating the teaching "be as shrewd as serpents" and vv. 10–13 illustrating "be innocent as doves" (with vv. 8b–9 as the hinge between the two sections).

13. The book that resulted from my dialogue, coauthored by Stephen E. Robinson, was *How Wide the Divide? A Mormon and an Evangelical in Conversation* (Downers Grove, Ill.: InterVarsity Press, 1997).

14. See, e.g., Robert A. J. Gagnon, "A Second Look at Two Lukan Parables: Reflections on the Unjust Steward and the Good Samaritan," *HBT* 20 (1998): 2–5, 9.

15. For a good model, see Ronald J. Sider, *Completely Pro-Life* (Downers Grove, Ill.: InterVarsity Press, 1987).

16. See esp. John and Sylvia Ronsvalle, *Behind the Stained Glass Windows: Money Dynamics in the Church* (Grand Rapids: Baker, 1996).

17. Patterns of generational giving, described in this third application of my second main point, can be found already in Tom Sine, *Wild Hope* (Dallas: Word, 1991), 143–64.

18. On this expression, see esp. Hans Kosmala, "The Parable of the Unjust Steward in the Light of Qumran," *ASTI* 3 (1964): 114–15.

19. Cf. esp. 2 Cor. 8:13–15, on which see, e.g., Linda L. Belleville, *2 Corinthians* (Downers Grove, Ill.: InterVarsity Press, 1996), 220.

Chapter 6: Let's Play Wedding, Let's Play Funeral

1. The two fullest recent conservative treatments of John are Robert L. Webb, *John the Baptizer and Prophet* (Sheffield: JSOT, 1991); and Joan E. Taylor, *The Immerser: John the Baptist within Second Temple Judaism* (Grand Rapids: Eerdmans, 1997).

2. The only significant difference is Luke's use of "children" rather than "wisdom" in the closing verse of the parable, but the two amount to nearly the same thing. See the consecutive analyses in Hultgren, *Parables,* 206–11.

3. This is the structure I have opted for in my *Interpreting the Parables,* 208.

4. This leads some to think that Jesus means that the Jewish leaders tried to temper John's stern message with greater levity and Jesus' "permissiveness" with stricter legalism only to find both men uncooperative. See, e.g., I. Howard Marshall, *The Gospel of Luke* (Grand Rapids: Eerdmans, 1978), 300–301.

5. See, e.g., Joseph Fitzmyer, *The Gospel according to Luke I–IX* (Garden City, N.Y.: Doubleday, 1981), 678–79.

6. See further Craig L. Blomberg, *The Historical Reliability of John's Gospel: Issues and Commentary* (Downers Grove, Ill.: InterVarsity Press, 2001), 76.

7. The best, detailed, evangelical example is *The International Standard Bible Encyclopedia, Revised,* 4 vols., ed. Edgar W. Smith Jr. (Grand Rapids: Eerdmans, 1979–86).

8. On this process, see esp. Kenneth E. Bailey, "Informal Controlled Oral Tradition and the Synoptic Gospels," *Asia Journal of Theology* 5 (1991): 34–54.

9. A key element that even the otherwise highly skeptical but highly influential portrait of the historical Jesus by J. Dominic Crossan (*The Historical Jesus: The Life of a Mediterranean Jewish Peasant* [San Francisco: HarperSanFrancisco, 1991], 332–53) accepts as authentic and central to Jesus' ministry.

10. Cf. esp. David Stern, *Parables in Midrash* (Cambridge, Mass.: Harvard University Press, 1991), 8–9.

11. Cf. Olof Linton, "The Parable of the Children's Game," *NTS* 22 (1976): 159–79. On "Jesus: A Glutton and a Drunkard," more specifically, cf. Howard C. Kee, in an article so titled in *NTS* 42 (1996): 374–93.

12. Harald Sahlin, "Traditionskritische Bemerkungen zu zwei Evangelienperikopen," *ST* 33 (1979): 84. For a variant of this, which denies a direct connection between wisdom and John/Jesus, see Colleen Shantz, "The Use of Folk Proverbs in Q7:31–35," *TJT* 17 (2001): 249–62.

Chapter 7: How Do You Hear?

1. C. S. Lewis, *The Great Divorce* (London: Geoffrey Bles, 1946), 66–67.

2. On the numbers of martyrs for the Christian faith, see the various publications of Voice of the Martyrs. On the twentieth century in particular, see

esp. *By Their Blood: Christian Martyrs of the Twentieth Century* (Grand Rapids, Baker, 1996).

3. See esp. Mary A. Tolbert, *Mark's Gospel: Sowing the Word in Literary-Historical Perspective* (Minneapolis: Fortress, 1989).

4. See further Craig L. Blomberg, *Making Sense of the New Testament: Three Crucial Questions* (Grand Rapids: Baker, 2004), chapter 3.

5. Cf. Hultgren, *Parables,* 190–99.

6. The classic treatment appears in Jeremias, *Parables,* 77–79.

7. Seccombe, *King,* 329.

8. Thus it has been disputed that sowing would have preceded plowing. But see Philip B. Payne, "The Order of Sowing and Ploughing in the Parable of the Sower," *NTS* 25 (1979): 123–29.

9. See esp. Robert K. McIver, "One Hundred-Fold Yield—Miraculous or Mundane? Matthew 13.8,23; Mark 4.8,20; Luke 8.8," *NTS* 40 (1994): 606–8.

10. Inductive expository preaching permits this kind of rearrangement so long as one keeps self-contained units together, precisely because contemporary rhetorical strategies may have to vary from ancient ones in order to be faithful to the text's original purposes. See, e.g., Paul Borden, "Is There Really One Big Idea in That Story?" in *The Big Idea of Biblical Preaching,* ed. Keith Willhite and Scott M. Gibson (Grand Rapids: Baker, 1998), 67–80, esp. p. 79.

11. The best defense remains Philip B. Payne, "The Authenticity of the Parable of the Sower and Its Interpretation," in *Gospel Perspectives,* vol. 1, ed. R. T. France and David Wenham (Sheffield: JSOT, 1980), 163–207.

12. See esp. Craig A. Evans, "On the Isaianic Background of the Sower Parable," *CBQ* 47 (1985): 464–68.

13. On 4 Ezra 8:41, see John Drury, *The Parables in the Gospels* (London: SPCK, 1985), 26–28; on Jub. 11:5–24, see Michael P. Knowles, "Abram and the Birds in Jubilees 11: A Subtext for the Parable of the Sower?" *NTS* 41 (1995): 145–51.

14. For these laws of threes and end stress, and related patterns, see Axel Olrik's classic originally published in German in 1909, "Epic Laws of Folk Narrative," in *The Study of Folklore,* ed. Alan Dundes (Englewood Cliffs, N.J.: Prentice-Hall, 1965), 129–41.

15. John Calvin, *A Harmony of the Gospels Matthew, Mark and Luke,* ed. David W. Torrance and Thomas F. Torrance, vol. 2 (Grand Rapids: Eerdmans, 1972), 71–72.

16. A very balanced and exegetically detailed Calvinist perspective, far more in keeping with Calvin's own views than the "loss of reward" perspective, now appears in Thomas R. Schreiner and Ardel B. Caneday, *The Race Set before Us: A Biblical Theology of Perseverance and Assurance* (Downers Grove, Ill.: InterVarsity Press, 2001).

17. See, e.g., R. T. France, *The Gospel of Mark* (Grand Rapids: Eerdmans, 2002), 199–201.

18. A little known gem of an article from this perspective is T. F. Torrance, "A Study in New Testament Communication," *SJT* 3 (1950): 304–5.

Chapter 8: Seeds, Weeds, and Explosive Growth

1. On another level, v. 36 can be seen as beginning the second major half of vv. 1–52. See esp. David Wenham, "The Structure of Matthew XIII," *NTS* 25 (1979): 517–18. Verses 34–35 form an important hinge in this structure, but they distract from the unity of the parables covered here, so I largely pass them by. If I were preaching a series on Matthew, rather than on parables, I would have to include much more on them.

2. See, e.g., John P. Heil, "Reader-Response and the Narrative Context of the Parables about Growing Seed in Mark 4:1–34," *CBQ* 54 (1992): 271–86.

3. For the book with Robinson, see above, chapter 5, note 13. For a classic, recent exposition of the Latter Day Saints' view, see Kent P. Jackson, *From Apostasy to Restoration* (Salt Lake City: Deseret, 1996). For key examples of Protestant and Catholic interpretation of the Matthew 16 material over two centuries, see J. A. Burgess, *A History of the Exegesis of Matthew 16.17–19 from 1781 to 1965* (Ann Arbor, Mich.: University Microfilms, 1976).

4. Cf., e.g., David Hill, *The Gospel of Matthew* (London: Oliphants, 1972), 235.

5. Or even in more recent times. See D. H. Tripp, "*Zizania* (Matthew 13:25): Realistic If Also Figurative," *JTS* 50 (1999): 628.

6. Cf., e.g., Ruth Etchells, *A Reading of the Parables of Jesus* (London: Darton, Longman & Todd, 1998), 166.

7. See further my *Interpreting the Parables*, 197–99.

8. For several appropriate kinds of cultural engagement, see, e.g., Bob Buford, *Halftime: Changing Your Game Plan from Success to Significance* (Grand Rapids: Zondervan, 1994). For several appropriate kinds of cultural separation, cf. Os Guinness, *Dining with the Devil: The Megachurch Movement Flirts with Modernity* (Grand Rapids: Baker, 1993). I do not agree with every illustration in either book, however.

9. The seed was proverbial for its smallness in Jewish literature. See, e.g., France, *Mark*, 216.

10. See esp. Robert W. Funk, "The Looking-Glass Tree Is for the Birds," *Int* 27 (1973): 3–9.

11. On which, see Elizabeth Waller, "The Parable of the Leaven: A Sectarian Teaching and the Inclusion of Women," *USQR* 35 (1979–80): 99–109; Carson, "Matthew," 319.

12. To find a detailed scholarly defense of this view, with explicit rebuttal of the old-line dispensationalist approach, one has to go back to Oswald T. Allis, "The Parable of the Leaven," *EQ* 19 (1947): 254–73. The one detail that is sometimes inappropriately allegorized is the hiddenness, which in fact is a natural description of yeast in dough.

13. Most recently, see Robert K. McIver, "The Parable of the Weeds among the Wheat (Matt 13:24–30) and the Relationship between the Kingdom and the Church as Portrayed in the Gospel of Matthew," *JBL* 114 (1995): 643–59. McIver surveys both main approaches to the parable and attempts, not very successfully, to combine the two in light of Matthew's overall theology.

14. I. Howard Marshall, "The Hope of a New Age: The Kingdom of God in the New Testament," *Themelios* 11 (1985): 12.

15. Outstanding in its applications and drawing on precisely the imagery of the mustard seed is Tom Sine, *Mustard Seed vs. McWorld* (Grand Rapids: Baker, 1999).

Chapter 9: The Kingdom of Heaven: Priceless

1. For the statistics on belief in an afterlife, heaven, and hell, see Rick Ross, "Most Americans Believe in Ghosts," *World Net Daily* (Feb. 27, 2003), accessible at http://www.rickross.com/reference/general/general533.html as of February 1, 2004.

2. C. S. Lewis, *The Great Divorce*, 66–67.

3. Still helpful with the overall structure of the chapter is Jack D. Kingsbury, *The Parables of Jesus in Matthew 13* (London: SPCK, 1969). More recently, but more briefly, cf. Jan Lambrecht, *Out of the Treasure: The Parables in the Gospel of Matthew* (Grand Rapids: Eerdmans, 1991), 149–79.

4. Cf. Dodd, *Parables*, 112; Eta Linnemann, *Parables of Jesus: Introduction and Exposition* (London: SPCK, 1966), 99.

5. Cf. Hultgren, *Parables*, 421–22.

6. E.g., Jeffrey A. Gibbs, "Parables of Atonement and Assurance: Matthew 13:44–46," *CTQ* 51 (1987): 19–43.

7. And neither illegal nor unethical, given the finer points of rabbinic law, on which see esp. Derrett, *Law*, 1–16. Cf. also John W. Sider ("Interpreting the Hid Treasure," *CSR* 13 [1984]: 371) who believes the re-hiding is significant only in that it reinforces the commitment required to attain the treasure.

8. The parable appears in an early midrash on Exodus. Cf. Frank Stagg ("Matthew," in *Broadman Bible Commentary*, vol. 8, ed. C. J. Allen [Nashville: Broadman, 1969], 159), who nevertheless notes that "paradoxically, salvation is free yet costs everything."

9. Blomberg, *Parables*, 201.

10. See esp. J. D. M. Derrett, "'ΗΣΑΝ ΓΑΡ 'ΑΛΙΕΣ (Mk. i. 16): Jesus's Fishermen and the Parable of the Net," *NovT* 22 (1980): 125–31.

11. See William Crockett, ed., *Four Views on Hell* (Grand Rapids: Zondervan, 1992).

12. See esp. Craig L. Blomberg, "Eschatology and the Church: Some New Testament Perspectives," *Themelios* 23 (3) (1998): 3–26.

13. Cf. further O. Lamar Cope, *Matthew: A Scribe Trained for the Kingdom of Heaven* (Washington, D.C.: CBAA, 1976).

14. Cf. Carson, "Matthew," 330–31.

Chapter 10: The Basement of the Hard Rock Café

1. I first heard Colson use this at a service at Willow Creek Community Church in Barrington Hills, Illinois, in the late 1980s. I have since heard several other preachers quote him (and it), so I presume he has used it widely.

2. See, e.g., Bock, *Luke*, vol. 1, 620–21.

3. See, e.g., Kistemaker, *Parables of Jesus*, 24.

4. For just one of many possible examples, see Joe Garner, "In the Flood's Wake: Memories Kept Afloat 25 Years After Deadly Wall of Water Ravaged Big Thompson Canyon," *Rocky Mountain News*, July 28, 2001.

5. Indeed, a common form of rabbinic parable is precisely such a symmetrically structured "contrast parable." *'Abot* 3.18 in the Mishnah even offers such a similar parable that compares a man whose wisdom is more abundant than his works to a tree with abundant branches but few roots that the wind easily overturns, and a man whose works are more abundant than his wisdom to a tree with few branches but abundant roots that can withstand the ravages of nature.

6. Cf. Michael P. Knowles, "'Everyone Who Hears These Words of Mine': Parables on Discipleship (Matthew 7:24–27//Luke 6:47–49; Luke 14:28–33; Luke 17:7–10; Matthew 20:1–16)," in *The Challenge of Jesus' Parables*, ed. Richard N. Longnecker, esp. p. 291.

7. See R. T. France, *The Gospel according to Matthew* (Grand Rapids: Eerdmans, 1985), 149.

8. Which leads to the much broader question of the role of works in the Christian life in general, on which the recent books of John F. MacArthur Jr. are particularly helpful. See esp. his *Gospel according to Jesus,* rev. ed. (Grand Rapids: Zondervan, 1994).

9. See esp. Dale C. Allison Jr., "The Structure of the Sermon on the Mount," *JBL* 106 (1987): 423–45.

10. See the brief survey of approaches in my *Matthew*, 93–95, and the literature there cited.

11. See, e.g., Robert A. Guelich, *The Sermon on the Mount: A Foundation for Understanding* (Waco: Word, 1982), 39.

12. This concept *is* being understood in an increasingly biblical way among various current Latter Day Saints writers, however. See esp. Robert L. Millet, *Lost and Found: Reflections on the Prodigal Son* (Salt Lake City: Deseret, 2001); and idem, *Grace Works* (Salt Lake City: Deseret, 2003).

13. Again, see Schreiner and Caneday, *The Race Set before Us.*

Chapter 11: The Parable of the Recovering Homosexual

1. Thorwald Lorenzen, "The Radicality of Grace: 'The Pharisee and the Tax Collector': (Luke 18:9–14) as a Parable of Jesus," *Faith and Mission* 3 (2) (1986): 73.

2. See Philip Yancey, *What's So Amazing about Grace?* (Grand Rapids: Zondervan, 1997), 31.

3. The only detailed study of this form is in a work unavailable in English: T. Thorion-Vardi, *Das Kontrastgleichnis in der rabbinischen Literatur* (Frankfurt: P. Lang, 1986).

4. For those unfamiliar with the process, there is a nationwide organization called the Case Teaching Institute, which holds seminars to train people in its use. It also publishes the *Journal for Case Teaching*.

5. See, e.g., Philip Yancey, *Soul Survivor: How My Faith Survived the Church* (New York: Doubleday, 2001), 11–41.

6. See Birger Gerhardsson, "If We Do Not Cut the Parables Out of Their Frames," *NTS* 37 (1991): 321–35.

7. See any recent, detailed Bible dictionary or encyclopedia article on "Pharisees," as, e.g., Stephen Westerholm's entry by that title in *Dictionary of Jesus and the Gospels*, ed. Joel B. Green, Scot McKnight, and I. Howard Marshall (Downers Grove, Ill.: InterVarsity Press, 1992), 609–14.

8. On tax collectors, see John R. Donahue's classic "Tax Collectors and Sinners: An Attempt at Identification," *CBQ* 33 (1971): 39–61.

9. Defending the "extreme caricature" is Luise Schottroff, "Die Erzählung vom Pharisäer und Zöllner als Beispiel für die theologische Kunst des Überredens," in *Neues Testament und christliche Existenz*, ed. Hans-Dieter Betz and Luise Schottroff (Tübingen: Mohr, 1973), 439–61. Defending the picture as entirely normal, see Bernard B. Scott, *Hear Then the Parable* (Minneapolis: Fortress, 1989), 97.

10. Walter L. Liefeld, "Parables on Prayer (Luke 11:5–13; 18:1–14)," in *The Challenge of Jesus' Parables*, ed. Richard N. Longenecker, 260.

11. Bailey, *Through Peasant Eyes*, 153.

12. Cf. esp. E. P. Sanders, *Jesus and Judaism* (Philadelphia: Fortress, 1985), 204–8.

13. For a survey of published reviews, in general much milder even when critical, see Matthew R. Connelly, Stephen E. Robinson, and Craig L. Blomberg, "Sizing Up the Divide: Reviews and Replies," *BYU Studies* 38 (1999): 163–90.

14. One of its most active and successful chapters is the Denver-based organization Where Grace Abounds. For an excellent study of the exegetical and sociological issues involved in a balanced Christian response to homosexuality, see Thomas E. Schmidt, *Straight and Narrow?* (Downers Grove, Ill.: InterVarsity Press, 1995).

Chapter 12: Pray and Persevere

1. David Wells, "Prayer: Rebelling against the Status Quo," *CT* 23 (1979): 1465.

2. The information about one in fifty evangelical marriages dissolving came from a talk by Jimmy DiRaddo, a Campus Life Illinois State Christmas Conference speaker in Champaign, Illinois, in December 1972. Even if the statistics might have represented overly round numbers (though more likely they seem extreme because "evangelical" was not nearly as popular a term for self-identification prior to 1976 and *Time* magazine's "Year of the Evangelical"), the contrast with current trends remains striking.

3. For more recent theological reflection, cf. Dennis L. Okholm, ed., *The Gospel in Black and White: Theological Resources for Racial Reconciliation* (Downers Grove, Ill.: InterVarsity Press, 1997).

4. I.e., it is precisely by the return of the Son of man (v. 8b) that God vindicates his elect (v. 8a). Cf. Gerhard Delling, "Das Gleichnis vom gottlosen Richter," *ZNW* 53 (1962): 22.

5. Bailey, *Through Peasant Eyes,* 135.

6. For representative statistics, cf. George Barna, *Absolute Confusion* (Ventura, Calif.: Regal, 1993), 294.

7. For an excellent anthology of biblical guidance, practical advice, and vital international models, see D. A. Carson, ed., *Teach Us to Pray: Prayer in the Bible and the World* (Grand Rapids: Baker, 1990).

8. On the integral relation of v. 8b to the rest of the passage more generally, despite numerous claims to the contrary, see David R. Catchpole, "The Son of Man's Search for Faith (Lk xviii. 8b)," *NovT* 19 (1977): 81–104.

9. They correspond to what world literature more generally represents as the "picaresque." See esp. Tim Schramm and Kathrin Löwenstein, *Unmoralische Helden: Anstössige Gleichnisse Jesu* (Göttingen: Vandenhoeck & Ruprecht, 1986).

10. J. D. M. Derrett, *Studies in the New Testament,* vol. 1 (Leiden: Brill, 1977), 44. The rendering "give me a headache" comes from Bailey, *Through Peasant Eyes,* 136. Young (*Parables,* 59) thinks the judge fears a literal attack, while acknowledging the more metaphorical usage is also possible.

11. See esp. Colin Chapman, *Whose Promised Land? The Continuing Crisis over Israel and Palestine,* rev. ed. (Grand Rapids: Baker, 2002).

12. Expositors who compare a number of translations of v. 7 will notice no consensus on its exact rendering. Most foundationally, is this a question ("Will he delay long over them?"), with an implied negative answer, or a concessive clause ("even if he delays long over them")? The latter seems more likely. Cf., e.g., Marshall, *Luke,* 675.

13. See esp. Richard Bauckham, "The Delay of the Parousia," *TynB* 31 (1980): 3–36.

Chapter 13: The Cost of Discipleship

1. Sine, *Mustard Seed vs. McWorld,* 160.

2. See, e.g., John Nolland, *Luke 9:21–18:34* (Dallas: Word, 1993), 761–62.

3. Cf., e.g., Stein (*Luke,* 396), who rightly rejects these attempts.

4. Cf., e.g., Michael J. Wilkins, "Disciples," in *Jesus and the Gospels,* ed. Joel B. Green, Scot McKnight, and I. Howard Marshall, 176–82.

5. Cf., e.g., Marshall, *Luke,* 592.

6. See esp. Michael P. Green, "The Meaning of Cross-Bearing," *BSac* 140 (1983): 117–33.

7. See esp. throughout William L. Lane, *Call to Commitment: Responding to the Message of Hebrews* (Nashville: Nelson, 1985).

8. See esp. Michael Horton, ed., *Christ the Lord: The Reformation and Lordship Salvation* (Grand Rapids: Baker, 1992).

9. See esp. Darrell L. Bock, "A Review of *The Gospel according to Jesus,*" *BSac* 146 (1989): 21–40.

10. Cf. A. T. Cadoux, *The Parables of Jesus: Their Art and Use* (New York: Macmillan, 1931), 174, at least on the relationship between the two parables.

11. Cf. esp. Walter E. Pilgrim, *Good News to the Poor: Wealth and Poverty in Luke-Acts* (Minneapolis: Augsburg, 1981), 129–34, defending Zacchaeus's model as reflecting the Lukan paradigm.

12. Cf., e.g., Joel B. Green, *The Gospel of Luke* (Grand Rapids: Eerdmans, 1997), 567.

13. The relevant texts are Matt. 5:13, 13:48, 21:39; Mark 12:8; Luke 4:29, 13:28, 20:15; John 6:37, 9:34–35, 12:31, 15:6; Acts 7:58, 9:40; and 1 John 4:18.

14. Cf., e.g., Craig A. Evans, *Luke* (Peabody, Mass.: Hendrickson, 1990), 128.

15. An exegetical option I entirely omit discussing because I have never heard it introduced at the popular level is that Jesus is the one who counts the cost, not believers. For a detailed defense of this position, see J. Duncan M. Derrett, "Nisi Dominus Aedificaverit Domum: Towers and Wars (Lk. xiv 28–32)," *NovT* 19 (1977): 249–58. For a rebuttal, see Blomberg, *Parables*, 282–83.

Chapter 14: How to Prepare for Christ's Return

1. A statistic I recorded when George Barna spoke at a conference in Denver in the early 1990s. I have not been able to locate it in print or on his current website.

2. For a survey and helpful response, see Robert G. Clouse, Robert N. Hosack, and Richard V. Pierard, *The New Millennium Manual: A Once and Future Guide* (Grand Rapids: Baker, 1999).

3. Cf. Donald A. Hagner, *Matthew 14–28* (Dallas: Word, 1995), 718.

4. Cf. Heinrich Kahlefeld, *Parables and Instructions in the Gospels* (New York: Herder & Herder, 1966), 105.

5. For further unpacking, see Blomberg, *Parables*, 193.

6. For further unpacking, see ibid., 195.

7. For further unpacking, see ibid., 214–15.

8. In my experience, the closest that anyone in print comes to making this assumption is Joe L. Wall, *Going for the Gold: Reward and Loss at the Judgment of Believers* (Chicago: Moody, 1991), 96–99.

9. See Young, *Parables;* and, for comprehensive detail, cf. David Flusser, *Die rabbinische Gleichnisse und der Gleichniserzähler Jesu,* vol. 1 (Frankfurt am Main: Peter Lang, 1981).

10. Cf. further Craig L. Blomberg, "Degrees of Reward in the Kingdom of Heaven?" *JETS* 35 (1992): 159–72.

11. But economics is one important arena of legitimate application. See esp. J. B. Carpenter, "The Parable of the Talents in Missionary Perspective: A Call for an Economic Spirituality," *Missiology* 25 (1997): 165–81.

12. R. T. France (*Matthew*, 349) comments, "In view of such plain statements as [v. 36], it is astonishing that some Christians can still attempt to work out the date of the parousia!"

13. See the intriguing history narrated in Bernard McGinn, *Anti-Christ: Two Thousand Years of the Human Fascination with Evil* (San Francisco: Harper-SanFrancisco, 1994).

Chapter 15: Who Really Are the Sheep and the Goats?

1. The Tertullian reference is from his *Apology,* section 39.

2. Ibid.

3. In addition to the Ronsvalles' annual updates on American Christian giving and expenditures (see chap. 2), many of the statistics on which I draw here are scattered throughout Sider, *Rich Christians*.

4. E.g., Hultgren, *Parables*, 309–30; Kistemaker, *Parables*, 126–34; Jeremias, *Parables*, 206–10.

5. Sherman W. Gray, *The Least of My Brothers: Matthew 25:31–46: A History of Interpretation* (Atlanta: Scholars, 1989).

6. E.g., J. R. Michaels, "Apostolic Hardships and Righteous Gentiles: A Study of Matthew 25:31–46," *JBL* 84 (1965): 27–37; Lamar Cope, "Matthew XXV.31–46: 'The Sheep and the Goats' Reinterpreted," *NovT* 11 (1969): 32–44; George E. Ladd, "The Parable of the Sheep and the Goats in Recent Interpretation," in *New Dimensions in New Testament Study*, ed. Richard N. Longenecker and Merrill C. Tenney (Grand Rapids: Zondervan, 1974), 191–99; J. M. Court, "Right and Left: The Implications for Matthew 25.31–46," *NTS* 31 (1985): 223–33; G. Foster, "Making Sense of Matthew 25:31–46," *SBET* 16 (1998): 128–39. J. P. Heil ("The Double Meaning of the Narrative of Universal Judgment in Matthew 25.31–46," *JSNT* 69 [1998]: 3–14) intriguingly combines both views by reading the parable through the eyes of the different characters.

7. The title he used, with a question mark, for an anthology of classic, contemporary essays on the use of the Old Testament in the New (Grand Rapids: Baker, 1994).

8. On this example, cf. further J. Guhrt, "κόσμος," in *New International Dictionary of New Testament Theology*, ed. Colin Brown, vol. 1 (Grand Rapids: Zondervan, 1975), 521–26.

9. On these and related principles for word studies, see William W. Klein, Craig L. Blomberg, and Robert L. Hubbard, *Introduction to Biblical Interpretation*, 2d ed. (Nashville: Nelson, forthcoming), chap. 7.

10. Cf. further, Craig L. Blomberg, *Contagious Holiness: Jesus, Sinners and Table Fellowship* (Downers Grove, Ill.: InterVarsity Press, forthcoming).

11. For an excellent anthology of biblical and practical emphases, see Bruce J. Nicholls and Beulah R. Wood, eds., *Sharing the Good News with the Poor* (Grand Rapids: Baker, 1996).

12. Obviously a more crucial task when one is analyzing the Latter Day Saints than when one is analyzing most charismatic congregations.

13. For numerous additional creative models that believers in various parts of the world have already adopted, see Sine, *Mustard Seed vs. McWorld*.

14. Cf. Richard T. France, "On Being Ready (Matthew 25:1–46)," in *The Challenge of Jesus' Parables*, ed. Richard N. Longenecker, 193.

Conclusion

1. Frank Tillapaugh, Bear Valley Baptist Church, Sheridan, Colorado, some time in the late 1980s.

Subject Index

Scripture Index

250 Scripture Index

Romans

1   111
1:24   111
1:26   111
1:28   111
9:13   183

1 Corinthians

1:18–2:5   103
5:1–13   228 n. 10
5:6   123
5:9–13   227 n. 1
5:12–13   162
9:19–23   162
12:26   65
14   149

2 Corinthians

8–9   51, 88
8:13–15   51, 230 n. 19

Galatians

3:28   160
4:30   164
5:22–23   149
6:10   207

Ephesians

4:15   163

2 Timothy

3:12   182

Hebrews

8   142
8:8–12   137
8:13   137
10:25   197

James

1:27   207
2:14–17   50, 87
2:14–26   215

1 Peter

3:3   213

2 Peter

3:8–9   176, 180

1 John

2:19   74, 79, 109
3:17   50, 52
3:17–18   87
3:18–19   52
4:18   237 n. 13